James Fable is a children's author, travel writer and novelist from the UK. After moving to Myanmar in 2016, he began work as a freelance travel journalist, writing regularly for Yangon-based magazine *Myanmore* and publishing articles with *Travel360* and *Meditationmag.com*.

James now lives in Heidelberg, Germany, and is currently working on a magical realism novel. To find out more, visit his website, www.jamesfable.com, where you can subscribe to his newsletter and read all about his latest releases.

Chuu Wai Nyein is an artist from Mandalay, Myanmar. Her work challenges traditional views of Myanmar women and she has held several solo exhibitions, including *Fabric of Change* in New York, *Libérées: Reclaim Birmanes Identities* in Paris, and *One-Ten-Hundred* in Yangon, Myanmar.

Chuu currently lives in her hometown of Mandalay. *In Search of Myanmar* is the first book she has illustrated. You can see more of her work on her website, www.chuuwainyein.com.

In Search of Myanmar

Travels through a Changing Land

James Fable

&

Chuu Wai Nyein

Table of Contents

Note from the author on language and names

Timeline of key events in Myanmar since World War Two

Map of Myanmar

Map of Part 1 journey

Chapter 1: Prophecies and Plans
Chapter 2: Off the Banana Pancake Trail
Chapter 3: Legendary Bagan
Chapter 4: Monks and Kings
Chapter 5: Missing Britain
Chapter 6: Myanmar's Ugliest Baby

Map of Part 2 journey

Chapter 7: The Tide Turns
Chapter 8: Killing Karma
Chapter 9: Empty Beaches
Chapter 10: The Golden Land

Map of Part 3 journey

Chapter 11: Into the Naga Hills
Chapter 12: Skullball
Chapter 13: Drink to Death
Chapter 14: Murder and Lies
Chapter 15: Soon Forgotten

Chapter 16: Career Advisors

Map of Part 4 journey

Chapter 17: Water, Water Everywhere
Chapter 18: What Would George Have Said?
Chapter 19: Crocodiles, Flowers and Hornbills: A Natural Metaphor
Chapter 20: The Police State
Chapter 21: Relocation, Relocation, Relocation
Chapter 22: Pulling the Strings
Chapter 23: A Snapshot of Myanmar
Chapter 24: A New Destination?

Epilogue

List of abbreviations

Glossary of Myanmar terms

Acknowledgements

Select bibliography

Note from the author on language and names

Names

Although the name was imposed by the military in 1989, I have opted for "Myanmar" over "Burma" since it is more commonly used by those living inside the country. Accordingly, "Myanmar" can refer to the country's name, its official language (previously called "Burmese"), as well as a Myanmar national or Myanmar nationals (formerly also called "Burmese"). The majority ethnic group, once known as the Burmans, is in this book referred to as the Bamar in both singular and plural.

For the sake of consistency, I have also used the current names of cities, states and ethnicities rather than the colonial ones. Hence Yangon refers to Rangoon, Rakhine State to Arakan State, and Kayin State to Karen State. However, readers should note that the Karen are the majority ethnic group indigenous to Kayin State, and the Karenni the majority ethnic group indigenous to Kayah State. Also, some of the old terms appear in quotes or specialist vocabulary.

The names of many characters in this book have been anonymised either upon request or to protect the individual's identity. Honorifics – Ko, U, Ma and Daw – are dropped after the first mentioning of the person concerned.

Language

To maintain consistency with place names, I have opted for the simplified romanisation system of the Myanmar Language Commission as used on signs in Myanmar.[1] Since the pronunciation is not always clear from the transliteration, here are a few pointers for those wishing to speak the language:

- *ky* is pronounced "ch" or "j": e.g. *kyat* (the name of the local currency) = "chat", while *kyanaw* ('I') = "janaw"
- an initial *h* indicates aspiration, i.e. an audible breath
- a final *t* indicates a glottal stop, which itself sounds like the semi-pronounced "t" in the English slang "innit"
- *oke*, such as in *thoke* ('salad'), is pronounced similarly to the "ough" of English "though"
- *-e*, such as in *ye* ('water'), is usually pronounced like the "ay" of "bay"

Translations have been provided when considered necessary.

---

[1] Those travelling in Myanmar should note that their romanisation system is not entirely consistent. Notably, some place names and common words, such as *paya-gyi*, have been transliterated into more accurately pronounceable transcriptions rather than transcriptions consistent with the romanisation system itself. I use these adjusted transcriptions, for they are now all but standardised.

Timeline of key events in Myanmar since World War Two

1947 February 12th – signing of the Panglong Agreement, which accepted "full autonomy in internal administration for the Frontier Areas"

1947 July 19th – assassination of independence hero Aung San and six of his cabinet members

1948 January 4th – Myanmar gains independence from Britain. U Nu becomes Prime Minister to head a democratically elected government

1958 June 12th – U Nu asks General Ne Win, Commander-in-Chief of the Myanmar military, to take over as head of a "caretaker government"

1960 April 4th – U Nu resumes his prime ministerial role after winning the February elections

1962 March 2nd – General Ne Win assumes leadership of Myanmar in a *coup d'état*. This is the beginning of the 'military junta era' of Myanmar politics

1962 July 4th – Ne Win's military government establishes the Burmese Socialist Programme Party (BSPP) and sets out the "Burmese Way to Socialism", a political and economic ideology conceived in April by Ne Win's revolutionary council, the country's supreme governing body

1964 March 23rd – the revolutionary council issues a decree that abolishes all political parties except for Ne Win's BSPP, transforming Myanmar into a one-party state

1974 – adoption of the new constitution, which formalises the single party system led by the BSPP

1982 – enactment of the Citizenship Law, making the Rohingya stateless

1988 August 8th – start of the 8888 uprising, a series of nationwide, student-led protests and marches against the government

1988 September 18th – another military coup takes place as the State Peace and Development Council (SPDC), led by General Saw Maung, slaughters thousands of the 8888 protestors and usurps power

1989 July 20th – Aung San Suu Kyi, daughter of Aung San and head of the National League for Democracy (NLD), is placed under house arrest

1990 May 27th – first multi-party elections since 1960. Although the NLD wins 392 of the 492 seats, the results are ignored and the SPDC continues to rule

1992 April 23rd – General Than Shwe takes over as Chairman of the SPDC (now officially called the State Law and Order Restoration Council)

2005 November 6th – Than Shwe relocates the administrative capital to Naypidaw

2008 May 10th – constitutional reform that aims to create a "discipline-flourishing democracy" and bans anyone with a foreign spouse or children from becoming president, thereby excluding Aung San Suu Kyi

2010 November 7th – the Union Solidarity and Development Party, a political party mostly comprised of retired military officers and headed by Thein Sein, wins the general elections. The NLD does not partake and Western countries condemn the elections as fraudulent

2010 November 13th – Aung San Suu Kyi is released from house arrest

2011 March 30th – Than Shwe dissolves the SPDC, ending the military junta era. Thein Sein is sworn in as President

2012 April 1st – the NLD wins 43 of 45 seats in a by-election

2012 June 8th – beginning of the 2012 Rakhine State riots, mostly between ethnic Rakhine Buddhists and Rohingya Muslims, which would eventually compel over 125,000 Rohingya to flee to Bangladesh

2015 November 8th – first open elections since 1990. The NLD wins a landslide victory

2016 February 1st – new NLD-led parliament convened, headed by President U Htin Kyaw

2016 April 6th – Aung San Suu Kyi is appointed State Counsellor, a position that makes her de facto leader of the country

2017 January 29th – top NLD lawyer U Ko Ni is assassinated outside of Yangon International Airport

2017 August 25th – Arakan Rohingya Salvation Army attacks army and police outposts. This triggers a brutal response from the Myanmar military, which compels over 700,000 Rohingya to seek refuge in neighbouring Bangladesh

Map of Myanmar

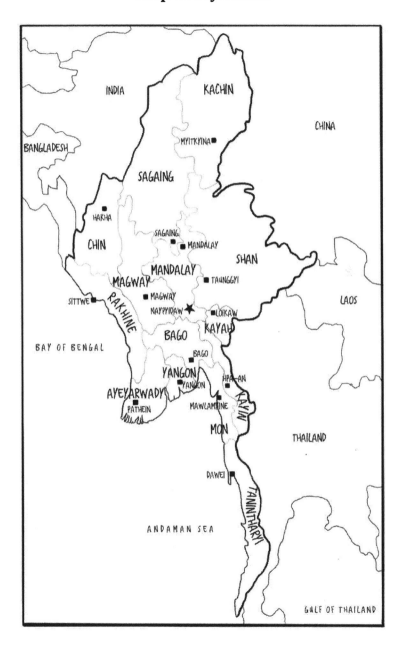

Part 1

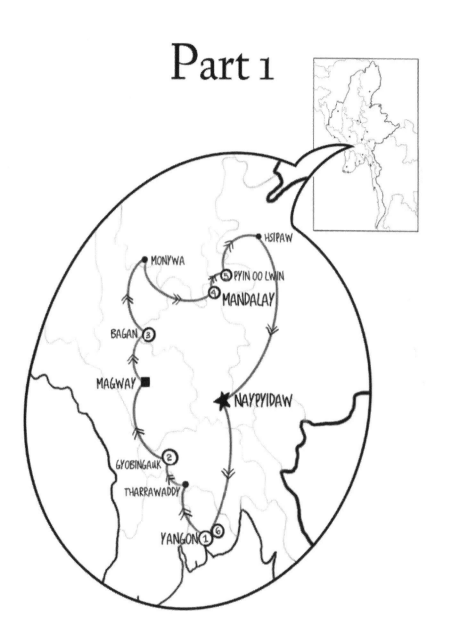

Chapter 1: Prophecies and Plans

The rain was crashing down in sheets as we stood beside the grimy green garage, waiting for our man. Shwe Ei put her hands together in prayer and briefly looked towards the golden pagoda glimmering through the monsoon gloom. Then she turned to me and smiled.

Shwe Ei ('Soft Gold') had dark gold skin, full lips, rich hazel eyes, and flowing black hair that many girls would envy. She wore a silver and purple *ingyi* (a short-sleeved blouse) with a matching *longyi* (a looped sarong). It had been her idea to see the palmist.

A white jalopy pulled into the drive and out jumped a jolly man clutching a laptop case. He gave us each a nod and lifted the garage door, revealing a white-walled office with a floor covered in water. A modest desk sat opposite a dusty bookshelf bent on collapse; framed certificates for astrology, palmistry and fortune-telling littered the walls.

"Sar-pi-pi-la?" asked Shwe Ei. 'Have you already eaten?' is the traditional Myanmar greeting – possibly coined because food used to be scarce, though nobody really knows.

"Sar-pi-pi" ('I have eaten'), said the palmist as he sat down at his desk. He unzipped the black laptop case, extracted a grey brick and turned it on. Windows '98 hummed into action.

Shwe Ei went to see this palmist roughly every six months; her mother sought his advice monthly. I, however, could not decide whether his appearance inspired confidence or warranted despair: his grubby shirt was tucked into an elegant black *longyi* with cream stripes while thick rectangular lenses magnified his brown eyes to popping point. Patchy hair barely concealed a discoloured scalp, and beneath his crooked nose shone an infectious smile.

The computer completed its clunking start-up and the palmist opened Myanmar Traditional Astrology, a programme with a grey interface that produced various graphs based on the date and time of my birth.

"Hmm." He rested his elbow on the desk and his chin in his palm. "Your symbol is a set of scales, which means you're a balanced person: you stick to the straight and narrow and dislike violence." He studied the graphs and diagrams for another minute, occasionally nodding, then looked round at me and beamed.

"Okay, place your hand here." He produced a clean red cushion and rested it on his lap. I lay my right hand down and the palmist began his inspection.

"You don't believe in palmistry at all," he said instantly, still smiling. I muttered something about it being uncommon in England and he returned his attention to my hand.

"You're writing a book."

I nodded. Shwe Ei gave me a nervous smile.

"And you hate imagination."

Well that didn't bode well for my fantasy novel.

"You're Protestant."

"No."

"Catholic."

"No."

"Presbyterian."

"Actually, I'm not religious. But I am interested in Buddhism."

"Hmm." He traced an arcing line in my palm with his index finger. "This is your life line. It's long: you'll lead a prosperous life with no major incidents – but only if you pray. Avoid prostitutes and KTV girls."

Shwe Ei raised one eyebrow.

"You'll be successful in education – maybe you'll publish educational books – and will be loved by... hmm. *Kalar-go Ingaleik-lo be-lo pyaw-le?*" he asked Shwe Ei.

She shifted uncomfortably.

"'*Kalar*' is used for anyone with darker skin than, you know, a Bamar," she said to me. "Normally it means Muslims and Hindus."

"Yes, you will be loved by the *kalar* community," said the palmist with a nod.

Intriguing.

"Do you have any specific questions?" he asked, looking from me to Shwe Ei and back again.

I had so many questions.

"Could you tell me about my next two years, please?"

He beamed and took my palm.

"You'll come into lots of money through fortune – you have a good chance of winning the lottery, though I can't say in which country."

Shwe Ei giggled and clasped my left hand.

"And you'll meet your future wife while travelling. She'll be of a different nationality and religion to you."

Shwe Ei let go of my hand and folded her arms.

"All your relationships until now have meant nothing to you. I'm right, yes?" And he smiled as never before, *hla-de* but haunting.

"Err..." I glanced at Shwe Ei, who was now staring at the wall with her back turned. We had been together six months, but I would start travelling round Myanmar next week – and that would signal the end of our relationship. We had agreed this before officially becoming a couple. For several reasons, including visa complications and personal ambitions, neither of us could see a long-distance relationship working. Our time together had been incredible, but now that we were soon to part, emotions were running high; Shwe Ei in particular was finding things difficult.

"You'll also live in India for two or three years," continued the palmist, his smile once again revealing a set of flawless teeth.

It was time to leave. After a quick selfie – which the palmist later uploaded to his Facebook business page – Shwe Ei and I thanked him and left. The downpour had ended, and the clouds had cleared, allowing the scorching midday sun to take control. We wandered over the puddled *lan* and out the pagoda complex, at which point I assured Shwe Ei that our relationship had not been a mere fling and that she did, in fact, mean a lot to me.

"I went to him before we met," she said, turning soft, unreadable eyes to me, "and he told me that I would 'meet a foreigner.'"

I clasped her hand as my heart sank. Now I knew why she had been finding the imminent split more difficult than me: she believed our coming together had been determined by fate, but she hadn't known I was destined to leave.

Shwe Ei isn't the only Myanmar that believes in astrology, palmistry, numerology and fortune-telling (which I will refer to collectively as "astrology" from now on, since Myanmar astrologers usually employ a combination of these practices). Most Myanmar are superstitious, and astrologers are highly respected. Their main clientele are women aged twenty-thirty seeking counsel in love, but people may ask their advice on almost any topic, including life changes and business deals.

The recently deceased ET – Myanmar's most renowned astrologer, named after her resemblance to the Hollywood alien – charged $1000 per hour and her waiting list was reputedly a year long. Her party tricks included telling the serial number of a bank note in a person's wallet. One of her clients was former leader General Than Shwe, who in 2005 moved the country's capital from Yangon to Naypidaw; many believe he did so on the advice of an astrologer.

Astrology and superstition played an influential role in Myanmar politics for many years. Myanmar signed its declaration of independence from the British on 4th January 1948 at 4:20am – a date and time chosen by Myanmar astrologers because it was deemed auspicious. And in 1987, former dictator Ne Win reformed the Myanmar currency by printing new notes divisible by nine, his lucky number. Some 75% of the old notes became worthless overnight and no compensation was given for them. Millions went bankrupt.

Fortunately, the change to a democratic government means that military generals can no longer make such devastating political decisions on superstitious whims.

*

I had moved to Yangon nine months previously to work as a teaching assistant at an international school. When my friend told me about the job, I had just returned from a disastrous trip round Croatia and Slovenia, so the idea of shooting off abroad didn't initially appeal. Besides, I had never been to Myanmar and frankly knew little about the place.

After just a day of research, however, a burgeoning curiosity emerged for this country, which had undergone such turmoil over the past few decades and which now appeared to be entering a new epoch.

Following a successful Skype interview, I accepted the offer and was ready to leave England a week later. With only one minor hiccup, when the employee at check-in needed convincing that Myanmar was a real country and that Emirates flew there, I was on my way.

My time in Yangon was enjoyable overall but not especially enriching. Everyone had told me that I would have an incredible cultural experience, but I had spent most of my year walking past Insein Road's countless mobile phone shops, staring at adverts reading "perfect selfie", "selfie king" or "selfie master" (a phone's chief selling point being the quality of its front camera), and teaching phonics to elite Myanmar toddlers, one of whom was so famous that he had a Facebook fan page with literally hundreds of thousands of followers. I was trapped in the big city bubble, detached from what was going on elsewhere in "Burma" – as many people still called the country. I knew, however, that Myanmar had to be out there somewhere – be it maiden, monster, or misunderstood – and I was determined to "find" it.

So I began plotting an expedition round the country, hungry for knowledge and experience. To realise my aim of "finding" Myanmar, a nation roughly the size of France and home to over 100 ethnolinguistic groups, I resolved to talk to people from all walks of life and to explore a wide range of landscapes and cultures. This would involve travelling to every official Myanmar state, particularly to regions recently opened to foreigners. Only then, I felt, could I begin to fathom what was really going on in this reputedly fascinating, diverse and turbulent country.

In preparation for my trip, I spent the final few months of my contract devouring books and catapulting myself into learning the language. I had studied Ancient Greek, German and Latin at university, but Myanmar was a whole different ball game. I confused tones, battled with aspiration and spent days trying to decipher the script. After all, was there really any difference between တာ, သာ, ဝါ, and ဟာ? (The answer is yes, a lot). Each of my lunchbreaks was dedicated to grammar; the school nurse gave me writing lessons; and during playground duty – when I should *really* have been paying careful attention to the children – I revised vocabulary from my phone or practised speaking with the cleaners (it's okay, I only ever lost one child).

Once I had exhausted every available language textbook, I switched to reading Myanmar children's stories. Shwe Ei patiently prepared me for conversations with inquisitive monks, probing policemen, and bribeable immigration officers. Gradually, I made headway; and when a travel journalism job for a Yangon-based magazine presented itself, my Myanmar odyssey no longer seemed a fantastical dream but a genuine and alluring prospect.

The thought of leaving Shwe Ei brought me to tears a couple of times over my last few evenings in Yangon, allowing doubts to creep into my mind. But I had already delayed my departure by ten days because of dysentery; it was time to go. So, after an emotional final night with Shwe Ei, we took a taxi to Yangon's central train station, an impressive colonial building coloured grey, green and gold, and passed through the entrance manned by a sleepy police officer sitting beneath a redundant COMPLAINTS sign. With just a few minutes to spare, I bought my ticket for 1950 *kyats* (£1.02) – which included life insurance of K1.61 (£0.001) – hugged my *chit-thu* goodbye and boarded the decrepit wooden train.

The carriage speakers were choking out Buddhist prayers while young female hawkers shouted out the prices of *"pa-ye-thi"* ('watermelon'), *"lepet thoke"* ('tealeaf salad') and *"biyar"* (you guessed it, 'beer'). Their cheeks, cast in soft shadow by the circular food trays balanced on their heads, sparkled with pretty circles of *thanaka* – a golden paste made from ground bark and water, which the Myanmar use as sunscreen.

After a short delay, the train began to move. And as it clicked and clanked its way out of the station at a snail's pace, I waved goodbye to Shwe Ei – who stood still on the platform, wearing an elegant black dress and a sad, loving smile.

A moment later she was gone.

Chapter 2: Off the Banana Pancake Trail

As the train rolled out of Yangon – past dilapidated apartment blocks, stray dogs scouring through piles of litter, and homeless mothers cradling newborns swaddled in filthy blankets – the Myanmar passengers climbed onto the tall plastic seats to stuff their luggage onto the overhead racks. Sometimes this was a two-person job, but all accomplished the task without dropping their bags or losing their balance.

When my turn came, I simply picked up my backpack and placed it overhead – easy as you like. Everyone stared at me, awe-struck, witnessing first-hand that the railways had indeed been designed for tall Brits.

I sat back down and watched Yangon drift by. Once we had emerged from the outskirts and entered the countryside, all the other passengers, as if by unanimous agreement, went to sleep. Some families spread thin bamboo mats out on the floor and curled up snugly, but most stuck to their seats, using the wall or each other as pillows.

That left me alone to enjoy the train's rhythmical clickety-clacketing through verdant rice fields studded with *shwe* pagodas that glowed with religious fervour in the morning rays. Teenage boys dived for freshwater crabs in the irrigation canals while their fathers, uncles and grandfathers scattered seeds in preparation for the next harvest. Not even the scratchy singer-songwriter playing through the carriage speakers could detract from the idyll.

Although my mind was still on Shwe Ei, I was optimistic and excited: I'd finally be able to put all the

Myanmar I had learned into practice, and my first destination, Tharrawaddy, was so off-the-beaten-track that seemingly no travel journalist had ever written about it. Even though I would have to leave Myanmar every 70 days, for business visas cannot be renewed inside the country, I was still hopeful that my travels would grant me intriguing insights into this nation that had only emerged from military rule six years earlier. Living in Yangon had been one thing, but now I was keen to find out how the rest of the country was developing under its new government.

I had first seen Aung San Suu Kyi on TV several years before. She had just been released from house arrest and was walking through the streets of Yangon, surrounded by Myanmar men and women smiling, laughing, and waving little red National League for Democracy flags. Everyone was predicting that she would lead Myanmar into a new era of peace and prosperity. From what I had observed in Yangon, that was largely what she had done.

The train pulled into Tharrawaddy mid-afternoon. I was the only passenger to disembark. Goats were feeding on the overgrown tracks; a baby wearing a ragged Özil shirt was crawling across the platform to join them. The station itself was a mildewed neo-colonial building whose original colour may have been yellow.

I passed through and stepped onto the tarmac *lan* – just in time to watch a couple of children, dressed in their school uniforms of a white *ingyi* and green *longyi*, perform the acrobatics of getting onto their bicycles. Since saddles in rural Myanmar are stubbornly set to adult height, this involves pushing the bicycle along at jogging pace before committing to an all-or-nothing leap. The kids never fail; it's dead impressive.

At the roadside, a couple of wizened guys reclining on rickshaws asked where I was headed. The answer lay just a hundred yards down the *lan*.

Motel Kyal Sin was a medium-sized complex of yellow buildings edged with black and fancier-looking than its name suggested. A spherical, middle-aged Bamar with dark skin was sitting on a navy plastic chair beside the reception.

"*A-hkan shi-lar?*"

"We have room," he said in English. "26,500 *kyats* [£13.14]. You want to see?"

I nodded, deflated by his replying in English, and followed him down the tiled corridor. He opened the first door on the right and revealed a clean but basic double bedroom with aircon and a cramped *en suite*. I leant on the bed, but my hand didn't go down far: the mattress was thin and lumpy. I'm not especially fussy, but as an insomniac the one thing I insist on is a decent bed.

"I think I'll have a look round for another place. Thank you."

"This is the only one," he grumbled.

He turned out to be right. Although an *a-myo-thar* wearing a black London Calling T-shirt drove me to a couple of nearby guesthouses, neither was able to take me as they didn't hold the license required for hosting foreigners.

This regulation is a hangover of the military junta days, when foreigners' whereabouts were meticulously documented. When travel writer Rory Maclean visited Myanmar in 1998, guesthouses had to send thirteen copies of their guest register by 7pm every evening to the following authorities:

External Passenger Control Unit (one copy)
Immigration Office (one copy)
Township Law and Order Restoration Council (four copies)
Ward Law and Restoration Council (one copy)
Police Station (five copies)
Navy Intelligence Unit (one copy)

If a foreign guest arrived after 7pm, thirteen amended lists would have to be prepared and delivered to the authorities before midnight.

Fortunately, this process has been streamlined: today, guesthouses must send just one copy of a foreign guest's passport, visa and arrival stamp to the local immigration officer. Hopefully the next step will be to abolish the licenses required for hosting foreigners altogether. Not only would this enable local communities to benefit from tourist revenue, it would also reduce the money going to foreign-owned hotels or those with crony military connections.

Zaw Min, the 30-year-old punk who had taken me to the other hotels, invited me to dinner that evening. He had short black hair combed over to the left, piercing brown eyes and pointy teeth stained with betel – a mix of the carcinogenic areca nut, tobacco, calcium hydroxide and other substances wrapped in betel leaf and mostly chewed by men. Betel makes your gums look bloody and diseased, tastes of cardboard sprinkled with dust, is highly addictive and great for giving you mouth cancer. The country's addiction has created an epidemic of guys spitting red gunk on the ground, but even worse is the gross gargling sound they make before doing so – like they're gathering a ball of phlegm in the back of their throat.

Zaw Min drove me to an eat-drink-shop with an upstairs, semi-circular stone terrace studded with blinding lights. His 27-year-old brother, who closely resembled him but had a larger nose and cleaner teeth, was already there waiting for us, drinking whisky on the rocks. Whisky is Myanmar's favourite spirit, and bottles of Johnnie Walker are the standard bribe for grumpy immigration officers.

Once seated, we ordered barbecued potatoes, sweetcorn and okra – three of my favourites – along with more whisky and Myanmar, the national lager. Zaw Min put ice in his glass, poured in the whisky and topped it off with beer.

"Bar thauk-ma-le?" ('What will you drink?') he asked.

"Biyar thauk-me" ('I'll drink beer').

He poured me a perfect glass, then Facebooked me and took a selfie. Ritual complete, we returned to normal conversation.

"Myanmar-pyi-hmar ne-dar-lar?" ('Do you live in Myanmar?') asked Zaw Min.

I nodded, and he gave me a beaming betel smile. I let out a deep breath and took a swig, pleased to be speaking Myanmar.

Zaw Min asked for my number and called me, but his phone was out of credit. So he took a K1000 MPT voucher out of his wallet and scratched away the silver foil concealing the top-up code with a toothpick – for no

Myanmar would be so barbarous as to use their fingernail. Before 2013, you could only procure a SIM card with a $1000 bribe, since mobiles were strictly reserved for military personnel. But today there's hardly a slum in Myanmar without a smartphone, and SIM cards cost just $1.

"Do you have a girlfriend?" asked Zaw Min's brother in English.

I hesitated. "Not anymore. We split up the other day. Do you?"

"Yes," he said. "I'll call her now." And he got his phone out, rang his girlfriend and passed me the phone.

"Hello," came a soft voice.

"Err, hi."

"Who are you?"

Zaw Min and his brother giggled.

"I'm James. I've just met your boyfriend and he thought we should chat."

More giggles.

"Or," I continued, "my Myanmar name is Ko Kyaw Thu."

"Kyaw Thu!" chorused Zaw Min and his brother with enormous grins.

Kyaw Thu is a famous actor and humanitarian worker in Myanmar. He's a muscly, tattooed dude, sports a slick ponytail and the beard of a Kung Fu master. In 2001, he founded a free funeral service which is available to anyone, whatever their religion. I was honoured and confused when a friend named me after him.

"Where are you from?" asked the girl at the end of the line.

"England."

Zaw Min splayed both hands on the table and leant forward, his nose almost touching mine.

"Do you know Rooney?"

"Wayne Rooney?"

"Yes," his brother confirmed with a serious nod. "Wayne Rooney."

This was the standard male response to finding out I was English. Or the speaker would tell me he was "Man U crazy."

"I do," I finally answered, sipping my drink and staring Zaw Min down. "He's a good friend of mine."

Zaw Min and his brother exchanged incredulous looks and turned back to me, bursting to ask a thousand questions all at once, apparently not realising I was joking. Fortunately, our food arrived at just that moment and Rooney was forgotten.

"Do you like KTV?" asked Zaw Min as he picked at individual pieces of sweetcorn with his bamboo chopsticks. "We'll go after eating."

"Thank you, but I'm too tired for karaoke," I said. "Long train journey. I'd like to just go back and sleep, if that's okay."

Zaw Min's face fell. His brother crossed his arms. But they eventually agreed to drive me back to the hotel and leave KTV for another night.

By the time we had finished dinner, Zaw Min was wobbling. Fortunately for him, drink driving isn't taboo in Myanmar and is barely regulated; the hotel also wasn't far. He plonked himself onto the red Manchester United seat of his Honda, waved for me to join – and drove in the wrong direction. KTV, it seemed, wasn't optional. I only hoped that the brothel side of it was.

We sped along the main *lan*, passed a *shwe* pagoda illuminated by floodlights and parked in front of an uninspiring building bearing a neon KTV sign. Zaw Min dismounted clumsily and burst through the black double doors, making the two guys perched on the reception desk jump.

"Three beers and three girls!" he roared, clutching his chest.

One of the workers snatched up the phone while the other rushed around the room of empty black couches and glass tables in a haze of cigarette smoke. A cold Myanmar was thrust into my hand. I only had time for a few sips – and to wonder whether waking up at 6am every day for the past year to practise my Myanmar had been worth the effort – before I was ushered into a dim corridor and led to a foreboding black door.

Zaw Min bustled inside and sat down on the end of the right-angled sofa pushed against the far wall. It was a spacious, gloomy room. A glass table stood in front of the sofa, a large TV hung on the wall opposite and a carpeted dance area lay in between.

I sat beside Zaw Min and his brother flumped down on my left.

Then the girls arrived.

They all looked to be in their late teens and wore white T-shirts, skimpy jean shorts and too much whitening cream. Mascara weighed down their eyelashes; thick red lipstick was the finishing touch. Smiling nervously, they wandered over and took their seats, one beside each of us.

"My" girl, Lamin, was the most attractive, with spiralling hazel hair, seductive eyes and a slender, sinuous figure. This was the last situation I wanted to be in after three large beers and as many whiskies.

The girls giggled and asked me the usual tourist questions while the guys got going with karaoke. Zaw Min's brother was the better singer, but Zaw Min was more *mu-de*, making him the superior performer. The girls clapped politely at the end of each song.

After a quarter of an hour, Zaw Min passed the microphone to the girl beside him, who sang a plaintive Myanmar love song – to much applause and wolf-whistling from Zaw Min. He pinched her stomach, laughing, and got a playful punch on the shoulder in return.

"Let's hear James sing!" screamed Zaw Min in English, sloshing Myanmar on the floor.

"Yes! Yes!" piped Lamin with a quick clap and a grin. "I never hear English person sing KTV."

I reluctantly agreed to sing after Zaw Min's brother, then drained my beer. Zaw Min's brother picked another love *thi-chin* and began singing, his hands clasped longingly around the mic.

Suddenly I felt a hand on my right knee. Then somebody got slapped.

Zaw Min giggled drunkenly, his expression like that of a cheeky child who has taken one biscuit too many. He had forced Lamin's hand onto me, only to be slapped by her as she withdrew it.

Not long later, he tried his luck again – snatching my hand and placing it on Lamin's bare upper leg. But she was quick to give him another slap, this time in the face. I was impressed and pleasantly surprised.

At last, the mic was handed to me. Zaw Min searched through the English selection. The anticipation was palpable.

He picked Westlife, whose music differs somewhat from the relentless techno I usually favour. I may have managed *My Love*, but Myanmar KTVs usually only offer the least known songs of Western bands.

I tried my best – I really did – but it became clear immediately that I had no idea what I was doing. Everyone's faces slumped. I was killing the atmosphere. So Zaw Min and his brother took over and performed a duet in strongly accented English, relieving me of the pain.

A couple of songs later and our hour was up. One of the receptionists came in with the bill, prompting the girls to leave. Each girl's company had cost K1500 (£0.78), each beer K2000 (£1.05).

We paid at the reception desk and stumbled back to the bikes. I hopped on with Zaw Min's brother, the less *mude* of the two. He pulled away, waving to the girls standing on a wooden veranda outside a bedroom. Three others were there too, all dressed identically, all watching us leave.

"Such beautiful girls," said Zaw Min's brother, thumping his chest. "Such beautiful girls. We're very lucky."

I guess for some it really is the end, not the means, that matters.

I shut my eyes and exhaled. It had been an eventful and awkward first day. And as we rode back through a night air thick with insects, all I could think about was Shwe Ei and whether I had made a terrible mistake in leaving her.

*

I spent the next morning ambling round the dusty outskirts of Tharrawaddy, stepping over aces, spades, and queens in love – for rural Myanmar towns are always scattered with playing cards – and photographing kids flicking spinning tops. An elderly lady invited me into her home to watch a silent Vin Diesel film with Myanmar subtitles while a group of golden oldies outside drew a crowd with their *chinlone* skills.

Chinlone, the national sport of Myanmar, dates back over 1,500 years and was initially created for the purpose of entertaining royalty. The ball is made from handwoven rattan and makes a distinctive sound when hit – like something being dropped into a wicker basket.

It's played in two main varieties. The less competitive, traditional form resembles hacky-sack as the players walk round in a circle while keeping the ball up. They acquire more points depending on which part of the foot they use; trick shots abound. It's a treat to watch real pros.

The second version, which is played throughout Southeast Asia and is more commonly referred to as *sepak takraw*, is a three-versus-three volleyball game, again without using hands. Each team gets three touches, with the same player allowed to take any number of these at one time. Most players are shorter than the net, but they still manage to smash the ball by performing athletic bicycle kicks.

Feeling Tharrawaddy didn't have much more to offer, I boarded the train north mid-afternoon. It was a similar ride through hypnotic rice paddies, watching aged farmers struggle to yoke their oxen to wooden ploughs – evidence of Myanmar's economic stagnation under the junta, who had prioritised the forging of an ethnoreligiously "pure" nation of Bamar Buddhists. Women young and old carried sacks of root vegetables on their heads, occasionally using their hands to balance the load, while pigs dug in the dirt for food and men fished in litter-strewn streams, though they looked unlikely to catch anything besides cholera.

Many travellers loved Myanmar because it appeared timeless, but scenes such as these also revealed an unpleasant truth: rural Myanmar was still wrapped in a time warp, hardly benefiting from the foreign capital now pouring into the country. In this instance, the foreigner's enjoyment really was the local's suffering.

I was glued to the window for hours until a wrinkled policeman in uniform – navy trousers, grey shirt, black tie – sat down opposite me.

"Where are you going?"

"Gyobingauk."

He pulled out an old Nokia and stabbed a few buttons.

"Foreigner," he barked. *"Gyobingauk."* Then he disappeared down the carriage. We arrived five minutes later.

The entire centre of Gyobingauk was one sprawling fruit and veg *zay* that stank of litter, food on the turn, and general decay. Pariah dogs resembling hellhounds patrolled the dirty streets, ready to turn rabid at the faintest whiff of foreigner. Along the main *lan* stretched a small strip of restaurants and beer stations, the Myanmar equivalent of a pub: dominated by men and furnished with shiny metal chairs and tables, they're as to-the-point as their name suggests. On the outskirts, a mud path led into the surrounding rice fields, where elderly women harvested their crops with experienced hands, the recycled foil pinnacles of their handwoven bamboo hats glinting in the sunshine.

I had called up Paradise Hotel from Tharrawaddy to check the price and ask if they could host foreigners. But by the time I had arrived in their tasteful garden compound of paving slabs and shrubberies, the financial agreement had changed.

"Locals pay 5000," explained the owner, "but we thought 15,000 would be fairer. After all, you are a foreigner."

It was a formidable argument, plus his smile was irresistible, so I consented and took the keys.

If the garden was paradise, my bedroom was purgatory and the *en suite* hell. Although the yellow double bed was comfy and the mosquito net comprehensive, the aircon was temperamental and the floor revolting. Ants infested every corner of the bathroom; the toilet stank of dysentery and thin black leeches slithered up between cracks in the tile floor whenever I showered. 5000 would have been fairer.

To my amazement, there was another Westerner staying at the hotel – a determined middle-aged *Frau* who had been pedalling round East Asia for eighteen months on a tricycle specially designed to offer shade and comfort (the Germans take travel seriously: say you're going travelling for six months to a Brit and they're dumbfounded; say you're heading off for a year to a German and they don't bat an eyelid – they've probably just returned from two years abroad themselves). She complained relentlessly about the poor quality and high prices of Myanmar hotels, which I could understand, then began slating Myanmar itself.

"I've done twenty countries while travelling and Myanmar has been the worst by far," she said in strongly accented but fluent English. She raised her hands in an appeal for agreement. "Myanmar just isn't a special country. Bagan and Inle Lake are nice, but otherwise it has little to offer. I'm going back to Thailand."

I felt like asking her what she meant by having "done" twenty countries and whether she knew anything about Myanmar's turbulent history and political situation. But I proved too much of a coward and just stared at her blankly, neither agreeing nor disagreeing with her calumny.

After an arduous haggle with an eat-drink-shop owner, I managed to hire a faulty motorbike for the next morning. I first drove to the Bago Yoma, the mysterious, misty hill range that ran parallel to the train tracks on their eastern side.

For driving 62 miles over stony, potholed roads, I was rewarded with mediocre views of deforested green hills. There were wild elephants in these *yoma*, but all I saw was an obstinacy of domesticated buffaloes. They emerged from the scrub on my left and began bumbling across the *lan* a few metres in front of me.

In sheer, unnecessary panic I beeped my horn repeatedly. They took fright and raced away into the thickets. Then a boy bearing a wooden staff came out and stared at me, mouth agape.

It seems I had sent his livestock the wrong way.

I grinned guiltily and sped off, only now noticing my blazing, mauve forearms. Alas, my sunscreen was at the hotel. I cursed and drove *myan-myan* to Minhla. It soon began pouring with rain, so I stopped by the roadside to dig out my cagoule – only I had forgotten that too. How could I have been so hopeless?

I finally arrived in Minhla sodden, sunburnt and shivering. Minhla's Mosque of 100 Pillars must have been impressive years ago, as must the stone Hindu temple on the same *lan*, but both had become dilapidated relics. The town of Zigon could do little better: apart from a smattering of rotting colonial houses and a *lan* lined with incongruous London streetlamps, it was as grey and grotty as Gyobingauk. Suddenly I felt incredibly naive and foolish for having believed that heading off the beaten track would be as rewarding as the notion is romantic. Perhaps being somewhere where every eat-drink-shop offered banana pancakes would have been more worth my time after all.

Defeated, I rode back to Gyobingauk and returned my motorbike. I had just begun walking down the *lan* in search of an eat-drink-shop when a man on a moped, carrying a bunch of bright red roses, ploughed into a cow.

Metal screeched and scraped as the driver went skidding to the roadside. The distressed cow mooed and hobbled away. For a moment the driver lay motionless. Then he got *pyay-pyay* to his feet, picked up the red roses and inspected their heads, brushing off any dirt they had collected in the crash. A minute later, he was back on his moped and all was forgotten.

I turned around and started wandering through town, only to be intercepted by a couple of immigration officers wearing dark green uniforms and sturdy black boots.

They did not look pleased to see me.

"Where are you going?" asked the tallest, whose breast pocket was well decorated with medals.

"To a restaurant."

"Passport."

I rummaged through my bag and the officer asked what I was going to eat for dinner. I told him my favourite dish was pennywort salad – a mix of tomatoes, red onion, fried garlic, bean powder and pennywort, a bitter green herb that's good for the eyes.

They led me to a daunting wooden and metal shack encaged in wire meshing. It looked foreboding, like a torture chamber.

Was this the end of my Myanmar travels already? And more importantly, how would they end?

We stepped inside, and I was commanded to sit down on a dusty bench. Five straight-faced officers sat round me; the room was bare and lit by a cruel single light.

"What are you doing here?" asked the senior officer as he began smoking a cheroot, a thin green Myanmar cigar. He had neatly combed hair, an uncompromising expression and a strong build. His partner in crime was stern and silent.

"I'm just visiting."

He took a drag of his cheroot and gazed listlessly through the smoke.

"Where have you come from?"

"Tharrawaddy."

"And what were you doing in Tharrawaddy?"

I shrugged. "Visiting."

The officers sat to my left also lit cheroots and began talking in Myanmar. Although I couldn't follow the conversation, I heard *"myin-kwar-ywet-thoke"* ('pennywort salad') said several times.

My interrogator stubbed his cheroot out and leant heavily on the table, arms crossed. "Give me your visa and passport once more."

I fumbled through my bag and passed them over, hands trembling. He checked them meticulously for five minutes, during which I distinctly heard *"myin-kwar-ywet-thoke"* repeated by the policemen beside us.

"You're a teacher?"

I nodded. He pulled his phone out and punched some buttons. I heard someone pick up at the other end and the immigration officer began communicating all he knew about me, nodding coolly as he did.

"Where is your school?"

I gave him the address, which he repeated loudly. The police officers briefly fell silent, then started talking once more about *myin-kwar-ywet-thoke*.

A few tense minutes later, the immigration officer hung up and slid my travel documents back across the table.

"Okay," he said, clearing his throat, "you're not a problem. You can go."

I thanked him and jumped up.

"But first one of my men is going to take you to the best restaurant for a pennywort salad."

Oh yeah?

He nodded at one of the adjacent officers, who led me out of the interrogation shack and ushered me onto his motorbike. He drove no more than 30 seconds down the *lan* – and stopped outside the eat-drink-shop that I had eaten at the night before.

I thanked him for the lift and hopped off, but he followed me inside with purposeful strides. The bright, lime green room fell silent. Everyone gaped at us. The owner looked up, bemused.

"Is everything okay?"

Silence.

"He would like a pennywort salad," said the policeman.

It was the worst pennywort salad I have ever eaten.

Chapter 3: Legendary Bagan

BAGAN / ပုဂံ

When I was eighteen, I visited Madrid for a few days with a friend. It was the first time I had been out of England without parents or guardians and that was pretty exciting.

We turned out to have quite different ideas of what sort of holiday it was to be, so for one day we followed our own agendas. I woke up early and began striding around the city. Since we only had a few days, I wanted to pack everything in: experience every sight, smell and sound. I must have walked nearly twenty miles that day, and, fuelled by adrenaline and freedom, only ate breakfast at 9pm.

It was wonderful – I had never done anything like it – and while strolling through Plaza del Sol, I sent my dad a clichéd text he would never forget:

`I've had an epiphany. I'm a solo traveller.`

This remains the case today, though I could often have done with sharing my troubles with a friend during my travels off the beaten track in Myanmar. For one, the accommodation was usually disgusting and overpriced – "Burma standard", as it's known. The place I stayed in after Gyobingauk was unbearably hot and had a floor so filthy I could trace my name in the dirt covering it; a pair of dirty boxers hung from the towel rack and cockroaches infested the bathroom.

These awful guesthouses were typically accompanied by absurd encounters with the local authorities. It became a regular routine for immigration officers to find me at night, question me about my intentions, then drive off to take copies of my passport and visa. The elderly officials were always incompetent and terrified – hallmarks of authoritarian rule (the old ways die hard) – and usually mistook my Indian visa from 2010 for my Myanmar visa. Most took photos of my travel documents using their phones, but on several occasions, I was left standing by the roadside for almost an hour, hoping my passport would find its way back to me.

This constant hassle and discomfort soon got to me, so after quick stops in Pyay, a characterful riverside city whose every resident seemed to be the friendliest person in Myanmar, and Magway, a web of dirty roads and ugly buildings that appeared to be decaying at the same rate they were being renovated, I arrived in Bagan, a breathtaking myriad of brick temples and pagodas rising above sparse trees. At sunset, a profound haze of ambers, ochres and jades melted into the Ayeyarwady River backdrop, lending the ancient city an indistinct, numinous air. When viewed from above, the pagodas transformed into pawns and bishops scattered over picturesque plains – chess played on a divine scale, its magnitude outstretching human comprehension.

Unfortunately, the story behind Bagan is less pretty. Strapped for cash, and with their reputation in tatters after butchering thousands of civilians during the 1988 student protests, the military government began transforming Bagan into an international tourist destination in the early 1990s. They hoped to secure the ancient city UNESCO World Heritage status by renovating its spectacular stupas, but their own cruelty and uselessness proved their downfall. To make room for hotels, over 5,000 Bagan locals were forced from their homes. The army simply turned up and announced that everyone was to move out. Compensation then equivalent to £1.50 was paid for each property; the houses were demolished a couple of weeks later. The inhabitants began rebuilding their lives three miles south of the destruction, and so was born New Bagan.

The junta followed this display of heartlessness by proving their incompetence. Their subsequent restoration of Bagan's temples and pagodas paid such little attention to original designs that it came under criticism from archaeologists, conservationists and art historians all over the globe. You see these pagodas dotted here and there, rebuilt from top to bottom by unskilled masons using modern materials – artificial copies that stick out like sore thumbs.

Even when I visited in August 2017, it was evident that the conservation efforts had some way to go. Most noticeably, climbing the ancient monuments was still permitted. I clambered up a small stupa one evening, hoping it would provide the perfect sunset spot, but as I pulled myself up a ledge my foot slipped – and over 1000 years of history crumbled away beneath me.

In a bid to gain UNSECO World Heritage status once and for all, the new government finally banned climbing on the Bagan stupas at the beginning of 2018.[2]

With its stunning colours and sweeping views, Bagan is understandably the most popular tourist destination in Myanmar. Yet it certainly wasn't my favourite. I travel for the quirks – that four-year-old in a mountain village who gives you a handful of tiny seashells and wants a pencil in return; the tuk-tuk driver who slurps

---

[2] Surprisingly, the move was successful: Bagan gained UNESCO World Heritage status on 6th July 2019.

his tea off the saucer because it cools more quickly; the elderly farmers stuffing you with rice wine at 9am – but Bagan was not quirky at all. There were no giggly girls keen to smother me in *thanaka*, no guys playing *chinlone* with *longyis* tied up into tight thongs, and no beaming residents eager to offer immaculate hospitality; only slaves to mass tourism. Perhaps I am guilty of "traveller's snobbery", but in Bagan I was unable to engage in any meaningful interaction with locals – usually the most enriching part of travel. Having become used to benevolent and honest treatment while living in Yangon, I was dismayed in Bagan to be perceived merely as another potential source of easy money.

Nevertheless, I enjoyed exploring the ancient pagodas, transported back to the days of the Bagan empire – the period from which several of the greatest Myanmar legends stem, including my personal favourite: the love triangle of King Anawrahta, Princess Manisanda and General Kyansinttha. Renowned throughout central Myanmar, it is as rich and didactic as the best European folktales and has been compared to the legend of King Arthur, Lancelot and Guinevere. Early Myanmar history was rarely separated from myth, meaning it often contains fantastical elements, but this tale of forbidden love, treachery and deception has firm historical roots.

It retells the story of Kyansittha, a general in the 11th century who was banished from the Kingdom of Bagan for falling in love with his king's fiancée, the princess Manisanda. His exile was rescinded following a conspiracy against the crown, led by the one-eyed Yamankan, but Kyansittha cared more for love than freedom and swiftly resumed his affair with Manisanda, forcing the new king to banish him once more.

Like any true romantic, Kyansittha struggled on. After hiring a wizard to raise the morale of his troops, he marched into battle against Yamankan and sent the usurper fleeing down the Ayeyarwady River. Initially, Yamankan looked set to escape; but he was eventually struck in his only good eye by one of Kyansittha's archers, whose mimicry of a rare bird had lured Yamankan into poking his head out the barge window.

The rebellion quelled at last, Kyansittha was crowned King of Bagan and finally married his beloved Manisanda, for whom he had twice endured exile.

Many Myanmar folktales follow a similar pattern: a trusted military general or royal advisor elopes with his king's fiancée, since breaking a king's trust was the greatest betrayal possible and therefore indicated the intensity of the illicit love. In Hollywood movies, the love triangle motif often takes the form of husband-wife-partner's best friend, for today that's the greatest betrayal Westerners can make in love.

Chapter 4: Monks and Kings

From Bagan I took a minibus to Monywa, a city of 370,000 inhabitants situated roughly between Bagan and Mandalay. Such journeys are hit and miss: sometimes you end up crammed in the back with five people sharing three seats; other times you can stretch your legs while watching the money collector lean out the minibus door, reeling off destinations so quickly they merge into a single, incomprehensible spell.

The money collector for this trip was a skinny young Bamar with a flawless betel smile and eyes that made me feel like a princess. His shoes were in disrepair, his Barcelona shirt rancid, and a grubby orange Shan bag was slung over his shoulder. As we raced along, he swung out the vehicle with careless ease. The wad of *kyats* he clutched in his free hand seemed destined to be blown away, yet never was. And though he hung onto the metal door frame for hours on end, which must have been both dangerous and exhausting, he always seemed relaxed. Like many whose life is the *lan*, he oozed freedom and contentment.

I can only romanticise this lifestyle: the chilly morning air and exhilarating ride must be the perfect way to wake up after a heavy evening of whisky and Black Shield, a tasty strong stout sold on tap in Myanmar, and seeing the world slide by is surely mesmerising. I watched our money collector for the entire journey, transfixed by his enlightened aura, imagining him cruising into nirvana.

Monywa was the city of alcoholics. Wherever I walked, there were beer stations; and whenever I peeked inside them, guys were getting ratted. I wouldn't be surprised if Monywa has the country's highest concentration of beer stations.

I went down to my guesthouse's small garden – several sets of wooden tables and chairs beneath a vined pergola – for coffee at 7am. Already a group of five young Myanmar were knocking back beers. By 8am they were onto the whisky; by 9am they were breaking bottles and speaking in slurs; by 10am they had all passed out. When I returned for dinner twelve hours later, they had just finished repeating the cycle. They were not popular with the waitresses.

Having dallied too long, I headed to a teahouse for brunch. Always loaded with testosterone, usually squalid and never disappointing, teahouses are the home of Myanmar culture. You go there to gossip over a breakfast of greasy deep-fried bread and 3-in-1 coffee mix. The air, hazy with cheroot smoke and the steam from cups of *ye-nway-kyan* (a gratis weak green tea), the low tables and the tiny plastic stools create an intimate atmosphere. Cooks pound and slap dough balls on metal tables before dropping them into sizzling plans, meaning neither eyes nor ears are ever bored.

Satisfied, you shout *"shi-me!"* – which prompts a waiter to come and do some furious arithmetic on the spot before declaring a price. If you've pigged out, your shout of *"shi-me"* is echoed by one waiter then another until a guy sitting behind a desk at the back hears. He looks up to find the source, checks his notes and commences another chain reaction of shouts – and that's how you get the bill.

After a plate of *parata*, deep-fried pancake eaten with egg or sugar, I rented a motorbike and followed the signs to A Myint, an ancient city allegedly founded by Kyansittha. The *Lonely Planet* described the "unusually well asphalted" road there as a "lovely 15-mile ride through agricultural villages".

It must have meant a different *lan*, for the one I took was an arse-shattering, unasphalted nightmare: unending potholes tortured my semi-automatic Kenbo into confessing its mediocrity with ominous clunks, trees cast the deepest pits in devious shadow and cruel dust clouds choked me. I couldn't even enjoy the charming bucolic scenes playing all around, for the *lan* demanded my full attention.

I finally reached A Myint after almost an hour, my bum sore and my body broken. I dropped into second and cruised along, watching flimsy branches of emerald leaves flapping in the breeze, as well as children traipsing around in filthy pyjamas. As I parked up, a *thanaka'd* harridan clutching a metal food tray marched over.

"Lepet thoke! Lepet thoke!" she barked, shoving tealeaf salad down my throat. Then she dragged me by the arm to a nearby alms collection ceremony.

"Lepet thoke! Lepet thoke!"

She rammed another dose down my gullet. Around us milled dozens of karma-hungry locals laden with flowers, fruit and vegetables, waiting for the monks and laymen to begin begging. Over the *lan* stood a series of elegant brick stupas connected by a tiled walkwa–

"Lepet thoke! Lepet thoke!"

"Ugh."

Seeing my discomfort, she began preparing a curative fourth spoonful – when suddenly a bell sounded: her cue to dash off and earn karma, my chance to escape.

I slipped away and started strolling through the village centre, along dusty, intertwining paths cast in cool shade by magnificent acacias, occasionally stumbling into people's gardens. Kids played high jump or the rural favourite, Hit-the-Pile-of-Stones-with-a-Flip-Flop, while guys clustered round small tables to play *twe*, a gambling game that involves casting shells into a bowl and seeing which way up they land. Cows, infamous philistines, shat in overgrown pagoda complexes, showing their contempt for 13th century Inwa architecture. Ominous bangs shattered the somnolent air at irregular intervals, begging investigation.

I followed the explosions and discovered their source to be two novice monks and two young boys playing with firecrackers in a new crimson and white pagoda complex. None of them was older than eight.

"Money! Money!" begged one of the monks, rushing up to me with cupped hands.

Then one of his friends casually chucked a firecracker at us.

BANG! BANG!

But why two bangs? He had only thrown one firecracker.

I looked round – and the mystery was solved: the second explosion had come from the fleeing monk smashing his shaven head against a pole.

The boys began laughing as blood gushed from his forehead and onto his bare feet. I dropped everything and handed him some tissues. His friends continued to light explosives while the other monk began brushing the dust off my bag – for in Myanmar the floor is considered dirty and belongings should not be placed on it.

I ignored him and replaced the blood-drenched tissues. The injured novice tried to hide his embarrassment and concern by grinning, but he wasn't fooling anyone. When I finally applied the plaster, he exhaled ashamed relief.

"*Let-hsaun! Let-hsaun!*" cried his monk friend, and he gave me a firecracker the size of my index finger as a thank-you 'present.'

I offered the patched-up monk some water and suggested he sit down. But he didn't want water, and he certainly wasn't going to sit down: he wanted to light more firecrackers.

Such incidents are common in Myanmar. For Myanmar Buddhist monks – particularly novices, who traditionally join the *Sangha* for a minimum of three months at the age of seven – monkhood is a lifestyle that adheres to the *exact* precepts and laws of Theravada Buddhism. Westerners, conversely, imagine monkhood as a lifestyle centred around being as "spiritual" as possible, perhaps because most monks in the West are so by choice.

This is why Westerners see "hypocrisy" where the Myanmar don't: monks can chew betel, but not drink alcohol; they go barefoot in pagoda complexes, yet litter in them too; they can't have sex, but may have girlfriends. For Westerners, these are compromises of spirituality and therefore acts of hypocrisy; for Buddhist Myanmar monks, they are simply the rules (or at least a permitted, very literal interpretation of them).

My most curious monk encounter came in Dala, a township of Yangon situated on the other side of the Yangon river. Shwe Ei and I had just returned from the local *mwe-paya*, a snake pagoda, when I spied a grand red arch with "VEGETARIAN MEDITATION CENTRE" imprinted in gold font.

Intrigued, I convinced Shwe Ei to come with me. We drove up the dirt *lan* flanked by betel trees and modest white houses but saw no sign of a monastery. A skinny old monk came by, so Shwe Ei asked him if the meditation centre was nearby. He pointed to a wooden shack twenty metres away.

"Shack" is too flattering. It was half a shack: the front and right walls were missing and there was no proper floor, bar a thin bamboo mat laden with metal food bowls. On the right stood a bare wooden bed topped with a rickety table holding half a bottle of whisky, and slumped against the head of the bed lay a ginormous monk with a triple chin and scabby scalp. Flies were ubiquitous, the stench of feet overwhelming.

Shwe Ei performed a *kadaw* before the monk, who roused himself as he realised he had visitors. It took half a minute for him to sit upright.

"How much do you weigh?" he asked me.

I glanced at Shwe Ei, whose expression confirmed that this was not a normal monk question.

"Err, 70kg."

The monk shuffled about on his bed.

"How much do you think I weigh?"

"Around 90kg?" I squeaked.

He sat up straight and inhaled deeply.

"I weigh 142kg," he boomed. "Can you believe it?" He sighed, making his triple chin ripple. "Where are you from?"

"England."

"And are there many fat bastards like me in England?" he asked, looking glum but hopeful.

"We do have an obesity problem," I mumbled, unable to take my eyes off his stained saffron robes.

"James wants to learn about meditation," said Shwe Ei.

"Yeah... I'm hoping to stay in Pa-Auk Tawya Forest Monastery for a bit."

The monk nodded, causing each of his chins to slap against the other.

"You don't have to do that," he said. "You can learn here. I can show you how to reach enlightenment. It's easy actually." He paused and swatted away some flies. "So easy. It doesn't take long at all. In fact, this world would be at peace if everyone were enlightened: Buddhists, Christians, Muslims – everyone would be happy and there would be no fighting."

I exchanged glances with Shwe Ei while the monk fished a large white Samsung out of his robes.

"Look! This is me with my Hindu friend. You see? Yes, Hindu." He showed me a picture of him standing beside a lady wearing a purple sari and looking uncomfortable. "And me with my Muslim friend. Look! Look!" It was a similar photo: the monk looked the same, but his partner was smiling awkwardly. "Yes, Muslim," he echoed. The monk then pulled up a photo of him with a Christian nun. "Are you Christian?" he asked.

"I'm not religious," I replied, "but three of my aunts are Buddhist."

He gave me a penetrating stare, eyes narrowed.

"Impossible!" he spat.

I escaped to the loo, a slippery squat toilet in a dark wooden cubicle stuffed with mosquitos and cobwebs. Meanwhile, the conversation ran as follows:

Monk: Is he your boyfriend?
Shwe Ei: No, my friend.
Monk: Are you a virgin?
Shwe Ei: Yes.
Monk: Where do you live?
Shwe Ei: San Chaung
Monk: Which road?
Shwe Ei: San Chaung Road
Monk: Which number?
Shwe Ei: I'm not sure I should say...
Monk: What's your phone number?

(Shwe Ei reluctantly gives him her phone number. Monk sighs heavily.)

Monk: Have you ever seen a monk as fat as me?
Shwe Ei: Yes! Yes! I've seen a way fatter monk!
Monk: (excited) Who?! Where?! Which monastery?!

At this point I returned, and we swiftly bade goodbye.

*

Continuing my journey through Myanmar's heartland, I travelled east to Mandalay, a city whose name promises romance, exoticism and everything in between. In Rudyard Kipling's poem *Mandalay* – origin of the phrase "on the road to Mandalay" – a former British soldier yearns to be back among the beautiful Myanmar women. Boris Johnson, then British Foreign Secretary, was caught reciting the pro-colonial poem in 2017 at Shwedagon Pagoda, Myanmar's most important Buddhist pilgrimage site. It was fittingly distasteful that he chose to recite the poem at Shwedagon, for the British dug up the pagoda in the hope of finding treasure. Boris was politely told to shut up by the British Ambassador.

It's always easier to romanticise what you don't know. Neither Kipling nor Boris ever visited Mandalay, which is a putrid gridlock of grimy streets infested with enormous rats and maniacal drivers. The mingling of dust and fetid gutter stench is asphyxiating, the heat oppressive, the night sky starless. Mosquitos are everywhere; and no matter whether it's the elderly rickshaw drivers trying to support their families, the importune motorbike taxis taking their jobs, or the middle-class Myanmar displaying their wealth by ordering too much food at restaurants, everyone seems discontent, desperate to escape.

The worst thing about Mandalay, however, is its central location, which makes it a major transport hub and consequently near unavoidable. The city's one redeeming factor is Mandalay Hill, from the top of which you can turn your back on downtown, look out over the verdant rice fields, the Shan foothills, the winding Ayeyarwady River – and pretend you're somewhere else entirely.

Mandalay was founded in 1857 by King Mindon and designed on the advice of Brahmin astrologers. Since it was believed that humans who suffered hideous deaths became *nats*, spirit beings violently protective of their abodes, 52 men, women and children were brutally sacrificed and buried beneath points of the city considered important or vulnerable; most of them went the traditional way, crushed beneath massive teak posts. The preferred victims were pregnant women, presumably because this killed two birds with one stone: i.e. one human sacrifice produced two protective *nats*.

It's possible that Mindon carried out these sacrifices unwillingly, for otherwise during his reign he broke free of traditional trammels, demonstrated good political insight and avoided conducting pogroms. Following the murder of his Heir-Apparent during the 1866 rebellion, he became reluctant to name a successor for fear of violent repercussions. Keen to retain influence in court, Hsinbyumashin, one of Mindon's queens, plotted to crown young Thibaw king since he was in love with her daughter Supayalat. Gradually, Hsinbyumashin lured other princes into the palace – saying the dying Mindon wished to bid them farewell – then arrested or murdered them.

Thibaw, having thus succeeded to the throne through massacre, then had to cement his kingship by performing the age-old court ritual of slaughtering the last ruler's relatives. To circumvent the taboo of spilling royal blood, Thibaw had the princesses strangled and the princes bludgeoned to death inside of red velvet sacks. The 80 odd victims were cast into a mass grave in the palace courtyard, sometimes still alive, but the gases produced by the corpses caused the earth to erupt. Although elephants subsequently stamped it down, the stench returned to haunt Mandalay as the bodies decomposed.

Things didn't get any better for Thibaw. Following an ill-omened inspection of the sacred oil jars that had been buried along with Mindon's human sacrifices, court astrologers advised abandoning Mandalay in 1883. Thibaw refused and pursued the alternative of sacrificing 500 people, including 100 foreigners, for the good fortune of the city.

His plan did not sit so well with the Europeans, who fled down the Ayeyarwady, and the British governor soon put a stop to it. A year later, Thibaw – fearing intrigue from the Myingun Prince, who had escaped the succession "purging" – staged a jailbreak to eliminate remaining royal family members and political prisoners. The jailer received secret orders to release some of the inmates; and while they ran away, the palace troops rushed in and raised the alarm. Some 200-300 were shot or hacked to death by *das*, among them women and children, then the jail was set alight.

Thibaw was the subject of an incredibly successful British propaganda campaign, which famously framed him as a "gin-soaked tyrant", and the death counts were likely exaggerated.[3] Nonetheless, these massacres provided the British with the perfect pretext for waging the Third Anglo-Burmese War in 1885 and annexing Upper Myanmar, which was at risk of falling into French hands.

---

[3] This may account for the great variety in numbers between sources.

Within just 24 hours of their arrival in Mandalay, the British demanded the unconditional surrender of Thibaw and his kingdom. The next morning, the royal family were forced onto a bullock cart and loaded onto a steamer on the Ayeyarwady. They were exiled to Ratnagiri, a port city on the Arabian Sea in India. King Thibaw died in 1916 and was buried there along with one of his consorts.

British imperialists made sure that Thibaw was the last king of Myanmar. Decades later, the junta similarly prevented royal descendants from rising to power, fearing they could rally a rebellion. Members of the *Tatmadaw*, the Myanmar military, actually assumed symbols of royalty and the former dictator Ne Win "even went so far as to marry a member of the royal family in an attempt to exploit domestic affection for the monarchy. But she left him after five months."[4] No surprises there.

Since Aung San Suu Kyi's National League for Democracy (NLD) took power in 2015, however, interest in Myanmar's royal history has been rekindled. British national Alex Bescoby, a former student of Myanmar history, has been working with Soe Win, one of King Thibaw's descendants and once manager of Myanmar's under-19s football team, on a campaign to return Thibaw's body to the Royal Mandalay Palace.

Supayalat, Thibaw's widowed queen, first requested Thibaw's body be returned to Mandalay shortly after he died. The British refused. Three years later, when Supayalat and the couple's four daughters were granted permission

---

[4] https://www.theguardian.com/world/2016/dec/30/myanmar-Myanmar-royal-family-monarchy-king-thibaw-comeback <Accessed: 22.01.2018>

to return to Myanmar, she asked again. Again, the British refused.

In 2016, a century after Thibaw's death, Alex Bescoby and Soe Win visited his grave in Ratnagiri. It was a promising development, but for the campaign to be successful permission from both the Myanmar and Indian authorities will be required. The last king of Myanmar may have to remain in exile for a while longer.

Chapter 5: Missing Britain

Although now almost 400 miles from Yangon, my starting point, I was still connected to my friends by that invention which has revolutionised travel: the mobile phone. And over the past fortnight, I had been messaging Shwe Ei about the possibility of meeting in Pyin Oo Lwin, 40 miles east of Mandalay.

I was optimistic about our chances of meeting, since Pyin Oo Lwin was Shwe Ei's hometown and she still had family there. Otherwise, organising short excursions from Yangon had proven tricky for reasons I had never imagined. The crux of this had come just a few months earlier, when I suggested we spend a weekend in Bangkok – a short holiday before I left Yangon to travel.

Shwe Ei jumped at the idea, but her family was less certain. None of them had ever been abroad, so I was unsurprised when the entire family applied for passports. Eventually, her mother decided we could visit Bangkok – if Shwe Ei's two brothers accompanied us.

It wasn't quite the romantic sojourn we had imagined, and I did not want to spend my weekend acting as a tour guide, so I suggested we all go for a meal together in Yangon, hoping to prove that Shwe Ei wouldn't need chaperones. My aim was to try and give off the impression that I would not sell my girlfriend into prostitution, for there is a long history of Myanmar girls being trafficked into Bangkok's brothels and I didn't doubt this had occurred to her mother. I just hoped she would be more open-minded than some of Shwe Ei's friends, who had been warning

Shwe Ei that I would sell her as a sex slave before flying home, even though they had never met me.

For the dinner, I dressed smartly and spoke the best Myanmar I could manage. Shwe Ei's mother was friendly and forgave my poor pronunciation; her brother was oddly complimentary of my beard, perhaps because he couldn't grow one himself.

To our great relief, Shwe Ei's mother concluded that I was "not like other Westerners" and that we could visit Bangkok alone. It seems I had come across as genuine (or whatever the opposite of a human trafficker is), though her mother was still hugely relieved when we touched back down in Yangon.

Visiting Bangkok was the only overnight trip we managed together. Nor would we be lucky with Pyin Oo Lwin, though on this occasion our meeting was only made impossible by timing issues. Nonetheless, the disappointment made me realise just how much I missed Shwe Ei; and so it was with futile longing that I boarded a standard Myanmar pickup – white body, silver railings, black canvas roof – for her hometown.

The pickup gained a couple more passengers in downtown, bringing our numbers up to five. As we drove through Mandalay's outskirts, escaping the dust, the misery and the heat, the Shan foothills shed their silhouette skins and became undulating ridges scattered with straggly trees. A single road snaked through them, leading us into the cool refuge of the hills, and *shwe* sunbeams were filtering through the departing clouds.

On the road from Mandalay.

After 45 minutes, we passed a pickup that had broken down halfway up the hill, stacked with the ubiquitous blue pipes endemic to Myanmar plumbing. Our driver got out and, following a quick chat with the obese driver of the stranded vehicle, tied a piece of rope to its front grill. We pulled away and started ascending the hill, but the rope snapped after a couple of minutes.

Attempt Two. This time everybody helped. Our driver produced a thinner but less frayed piece of rope, which the team tied to the broken pickup's chassis. We pulled away, everyone on tenterhooks. The rope strained and twisted – but held, enabling us to tow the pickup to a petrol station. Our journey time increased by at least an hour, but we arrived on time – as you always do in rural Myanmar, even if that turns out to be later than expected.

Pyin Oo Lwin revealed itself as the greenest town I had visited thus far, literally and metaphorically, and I immediately understood why it was popular among domestic tourists. Towering evergreens, collected into cool copses that made ideal picnic spots, stretched for the sky; colonial mansions with flawless lawns and colourful front gardens diffused grandeur, and squalor was less apparent. Hyacinths blossomed around tranquil ponds, spindly saplings promised the sustenance of natural beauty. A cleansing breeze trickled through the treetops and swept over fields of pineapple, ginger and other cultivated crops while a neighbourhood group picked litter off the roads. Only the miserable-looking horse-drawn carts – still a veritable form of public transport in Myanmar – tainted the idyll.

Pyin Oo Lwin was founded as a British hilltop station in 1896 by Colonel James May, who narcissistically named it Maymyo ('May's Town'). The British presumably chose the spot for its climate, for in the rainy season it's plagued by distinctly British drizzle, which must have made the homesick colonials feel like they were back in Blighty. They built the country's first golf course, as well as botanical gardens modelled after those at Kew. Inside the Kandawgyi National Gardens, as General Than Shwe renamed them in 2000, stood a proud wooden sign reading, "Our Culture, Our Tradition, Our Heritage". It was a lie: the gardens were all British. I felt as though I were back in London.

The best part of this incongruousness was the butterfly museum, where the specimens had been arranged into curious patterns, including love hearts and helipads. Perhaps a Myanmar employee had been asked to organise the exhibition cases but couldn't understand why on earth anybody would want to stare at a bunch of dead butterflies, so arranged them into pretty patterns instead. Whoever made the decision, and for whatever reason, was a genius: they breathed new life into those dead insects.

Under the military government, Maymyo was renamed Pyin Oo Lwin, its precolonial name. However, locals young and old still call the town Maymyo.

"Some general just changed the name to Pyin Oo Lwin on the advice of some astrologer," a beefy Bamar told me. "That's why we still use Maymyo." He paused, and a broad smile spread across his flabby cheeks. "We love the British. We want them back."

Like Boris Johnson, many Myanmar romanticise colonialism – even though the national hero is Aung San (father of Aung San Suu Kyi), who was instrumental in obtaining independence from the British. In *From the Land of Green Ghosts*, author Pascal Khoo Thwe, a member of the Padaung tribe from Shan State, recalls how his grandmother referred to the days of British rule as a prosperous golden age.

Overall, the colonial period was nothing of the sort: many British regarded the Myanmar as savages and provoked widespread rebellions by refusing to remove their shoes in pagodas. The British waged brutal wars, plundered the country of its natural resources, particularly its teak and rubies, and overthrew the monarchy. Almost all of modern Myanmar's major issues, including the civil wars and the Rohingya expulsion, have their roots in colonialism.

For numerous ethnic minorities in Myanmar, however, British rule was an era of empowerment. The states of some hilltribe peoples, including the Shans, became self-administered British protectorates; and as part of the colonists' divide-and-rule tactic, the Kachin and Karen in particular were granted prestigious positions in the army, ranking more highly than the Bamar, Myanmar's majority ethnic group. With the influx of immigrants, Yangon transformed into a lucrative *entrepôt* studded with magnificent buildings. One elderly taxi driver of Indian descent told me that Yangon used to be "the most beautiful city in Southeast Asia."

The Pyin Oo Lwin Anglophile, however, was Bamar – so why did he romanticise colonialism?

The answer, surely, is that the colonials were simply not as bad as the generals who followed. While the British did commit unspeakable horrors, they also transformed

Myanmar into a prosperous, interconnected nation by turning the delta marshes into arable, irrigated land and by laying the railways. Under colonial rule, trade boomed, education flourished, and many Myanmar came into wealth.

The junta, in contrast, were both cruel and incompetent. After usurping power in 1962, Ne Win and his military accomplices established the Burmese Socialist Programme Party (BSPP) and commenced "The Burmese Way to Socialism", which was essentially a botched Marxism-Leninism riddled with Bamar-Buddhist nationalism. In their attempt to create an economy run by and for the Bamar, the BSPP deported foreigners and introduced the Enterprise Nationalisation Law, allowing them to assume ownership of large businesses, including foreign-owned companies.

Their actions were short-sighted: with the expulsion of immigrants and foreign businesses went Myanmar's skills and trading connections. Commerce dried up, and damage not inflicted by economic isolation was done so by successive demonetisations. In a matter of decades, Myanmar fell from being Asia's "rice bowl" to one of the world's ten poorest countries.

Ne Win was finally ousted in 1988 during another military coup. The BSPP were replaced by the State Peace and Development Council (SPDC), who ruled until 2011 under the names of various military proxy parties. From the mid-1990s, the generals abandoned their socialist economic policy in favour of crony capitalism. Because of Western sanctions for human rights abuses, the SPDC turned to China, the "natural ally of repressive regimes,"[5] selling them teak, gems, and implementing enormous extractive industry projects, such as the infamous Myitsone dam. Money finally flowed into Myanmar, but only cronies benefited: the rest of the country remained poverty-stricken and oppressed.

For some Myanmar, British rule was thus the best in living memory. As for the younger generations, they see only the majestic colonial buildings, the railways and the cultivated Ayeyarwady delta – a far grander visible legacy than the junta's, which consists solely of Naypidaw, Myanmar's artificial capital. The Myanmar's fondness for the colonial era even gets passed onto modern-day Brits: telling people I was English almost always received a "very good" with a thumbs-up – a reaction far more favourable than most Europeans got – though the Premiership, David Beckham and Wayne Rooney must also have played a major role in cultivating this Anglophilia.

It was while strolling around Pyin Oo Lwin's grand colonial mansions that I met Ya'ara, a five-foot Israeli girl with curly, mousy brown hair, gently tanned skin and trekkers' legs. She was wearing a short sleeve white Shan shirt and a friendly smile.

We quickly established that we both wanted to visit a nearby waterfall, so the next morning I rented a motorbike from Grace Guesthouse. Few people in Myanmar

---

[5] As described by Paul Theroux while travelling through Myanmar in the mid-2000s. P. Theroux (2012), *Ghost Train to the Eastern Star: On the Tracks of* The Great Railway Bazaar (Kindle Edition), Penguin, pos. 5082.

ride mopeds. They prefer semi-automatic Hondas or Kenbos, which they free of their repressive wing mirrors. Occasionally you get a bike with a decent clutch; sometimes one with a working speedometer; hardly ever one with a petrol gauge pin that doesn't just swing with the corners.

This time, however, the bike worked well and even had wing mirrors almost able to be twisted into a useful position. Ya'ara arrived after breakfast, then, helmets on and tank full, we departed. We soon emerged from the congested town centre and began cruising along a straight stretch flanked by trees, the breeze whistling coolly by.

"This road is surprisingly good," said Ya'ara, clinging on behind.

"Yeah, I was about to say the same."

Our timing was immaculate. At that moment my concentration slipped and we sped into a series of dirt moguls hidden in shadow. I slammed on the brakes, but lost control as we bounced around. Suddenly the bike was over and my left calf searing. Blood was spreading through my green and black *longyi*, skin was peeling off my left elbow.

"Sod's Law," I mumbled as I unwrapped my left leg from around the exhaust and struggled to my feet. A couple of guys from an adjacent teahouse ran out to help us hobble off the road and slump into tiny plastic seats.

"You should drink something sweet," said Ya'ara, who had suffered a few minor grazes and bruises but nothing worth worrying about. I, on the other hand, had a burn on my calf and a deep gash in my knee.

Two teahouse employees rushed out with water and another drove off to buy bandages.

"There is hospital not far," said one of them. "You should go."

I washed my wounds with water, then began applying antiseptic.

"What do you think?"

Ya'ara gave my knee a scrutinising stare. "Hmm, you may need stitches, but it's hard to tell."

"Could you take a photo?" I asked. "I'll ask my friend who's a medical student."

"Always handy to know a doctor."

Ya'ara took a few close-ups, which I immediately sent on. Although I was too proud to show it, I was panicking.

My phone buzzed almost instantly:

`No idea. I haven't done first aid yet. Sorry.`

I had another look. The gash was deeper than I had first thought, but by my judgement not fatal – so I decided to postpone the question of "hospital or not?" until later. I'm one of those hypochondriacs who thinks they have something when they don't and denies they have something when they do. The worst type, in other words.

The third teahouse employee, my knight in a PTT lubricants T-shirt and dirty *longyi*, returned with bandages and betadine solution, which he began glugging over my elbow.

"*Ya-bi. Ya-bi*" ('That's good. That's good'), I said.

He poured the antiseptic with extra vigour.

"I need to put the bandage on."

This did not deter him either. I moved his hand away. He moved it back again.

"Honestly, I think that's enough."

"But you need this or you get infection," he barked, and he pinched the sides of the bottle so that the betadine solution streamed out. My whole upper arm was bronze by the time I managed to force his hand away.

"You need more," he told me.

"No, I need a bandage... Ya'ara could you?"

Ya'ara laughed and wrapped a bandage *pyay-pyay* round my elbow, then another round my knee.

"How do you feel?" she asked.

"Shaken, but not in too much pain. You?"

"Same, though you've certainly got it worse." She paused. "Do you think you can still drive?"

"I'll be fine."

We paid up and wandered down to the bike, which Mr Betadine was inspecting.

"It's broken," he said as he tried unsuccessfully to switch gears. He looked the bike over again and gave the gear pedal another tap. Nothing. He grunted and whacked it with his machete.

"Ya-bi," he grinned.

We thanked him and got shakily back on the bike, my confidence shattered and Ya'ara's trust waning. Through fortune or foolishness, we made the journey to the waterfall – where a bashful young *a-myo-thami* wearing a jade bracelet and a thin black blouse bade me follow her to a nearby wooden building. She disappeared inside for a moment, then returned with a black toolbox stuffed with medical supplies.

"I'm with the Red Cross," she said.

What a lucky sod I was.

She produced an alcoholic wipe of excruciating potency – though I didn't let the pain show, desperate to retain at least a sliver of pride. She blew a thin stream of air onto my cut, then patched me up with sterile bandages.

"You will be okay," she said.

"Do I have to go to hospital?"

She shook her head.

"You will be okay."

Sadly, she was not able to cure me of feeling like a knob for the next month.

*

The Shan hills are popular among trekkers, and Ya'ara had heard rumours that Pyin Oo Lwin was "the upcoming place", so the next morning we commenced a three-day trek round the local countryside. You don't go on "walks" in Southeast Asia – they are always called "treks", even if it's just a two-hour stroll along the beaten track. In Myanmar, these are invariably advertised as opportunities to learn about the cultures of local tribespeople, but really they are chances for you to find out how the Myanmar perceive your own culture. Our five guides, who had recently completed their training, would turn out to be quite enlightening.

"Do you see the pineapple plantation," asked Zay Yar, a healthy, loyal Shan in his early thirties, as we strolled along the mud track.

"Which one?" I asked. "They're all pineapple plantations."

"Yes," he said. "All. And they are all organic."

"Organic" and "community-based tourism" were to become Zay Yar's two favourite buzzwords, and he never once failed to point out a local plantation – even if we had just passed several producing the same crop. I soon had a pretty good idea of what his trekking guide training had consisted of.

"Here," said Zay Yar, indicating a modest home with white concrete walls and a thatched roof. "This family is Nepali."

Kyaw Kyaw, our youngest Shan guide, went to fetch the elderly Nepali couple from their home. They trotted out and posed awkwardly, evidently having been assured they were interesting to foreigners but not understanding why.

"That's thirty minutes of walking done," said Zay Yar. "Now we'll pause for two minutes."

Ya'ara and I remained standing while Zay Yar slumped onto a grassy bank and took a swig of water. He leant over and showed us his silver watch.

"See, thirty minutes walking, two minutes break. That's what we'll do. All day, every day. Thirty minutes on, two minutes off."

His trekking timetable sounded suspect. It's no myth that most Myanmar loathe walking and consider it an unpleasant necessity; the concept of "going for a walk" is quite literally foreign to them. (I once had to convince a travel agent in Bagan that climbing Taung Ma-gyi, Mt Popa's true summit, would not take two days, but three hours, and that we would not get lost on the way. She took some persuading, but finally agreed to arrange a cab for us.)

Zay Yar and our other guides insisted they enjoyed walking – and perhaps they genuinely did – though they constantly talked among themselves about what food might be awaiting them at the next stop. They had also had difficulty understanding why two Dutch guys, who had paid for a two-day trek, did not want to do the same walk each day.

After precisely two minutes, we continued down the rocky track and arrived at plush rice paddies shrouded in mist. We weaved through them, sidling along their narrow banks, and reached the foot of the hill. Here, the weather turned British: fog slunk across the Shan countryside, obscuring all but a couple of protruding hilltops – giving the impression that we were standing upon Mother Earth's naked belly while she bathed in steam. Rain pattered our faces, refreshing but relentless, and a foreboding wind rippled through the trees.

We duly began the ascent, occasionally turning off the path and into thick foliage, which our guides hacked away at with their Shan knives, only to rejoin the beaten track ten minutes later. When we reached the brow of the hill, Zay Yar raised his hands to the sky, as if about to invoke divine aid, and cried:

"Such beautiful nature! Such wonderful views!"

What a profound proclamation!

I turned around, gazed at the miserable clouds, thick fog and dreary drizzle that had turned the sky colourless – and theorised that showing enthusiasm must have been a component of his training.

"But we can only see about 200 metres ahead of us," I said. "There is no view."

Zay Yar's smile melted. My comment, I quickly realised, had been rash: by publicly contradicting Zay Yar, who was older than me, I had caused him to lose face – a source of great shame in Myanmar culture and socially unacceptable. Fortunately, losing face seldom leads to suicide, as it can in other cultures. In theory, I, having precipitated the loss of face, would face a penalty. I wondered what it would be.

"Here we go," said Zay Yar, once we had climbed the hill and reached another opaque viewpoint. "That's another thirty minutes of walking done. We'll pause for two minutes." He motioned for us to sit down beside him on a wooden bench and eat some fat "organic" bananas.

"You can't see anything today – too gloomy – but this is what the viewpoint normally looks like," said Zay Yar, showing us a photo of cascading hillsides basking in soft sunbeams and glowing with ethereal splendour before falling into an eternity of blue skies.

"Wow, that's... that's nice," said Ya'ara.

Break over, we descended into the jungle, which tried its best to offer the excitement almost all jungles promise but fail to deliver. Thickets of baby bamboo clustered around the treacherous mud steps carved into the hillside while snatches of sunshine struggled through the mist, desperate to prove our K90,000 had been a worthwhile investment.

"Tha-di! Tha-di!" I called as one of our guides slipped on the jungle staircase for a third time.

"Why do you keep saying that?" said Zay Yar, looking confused and frustrated.

"Does that not mean 'careful'?" I asked.

No, it didn't. Although 'careful' was written *tha-di*, it was pronounced *da-di*, and my pitiful pronunciation had made the guides think I was saying *"theik-di."* I hadn't been warning my fellow trekkers to be careful whenever they slipped, I had been shouting, 'heroism!'

Myanmar uses four contrastive tones to distinguish meaning: neutral, high, checked and creaky. The tonal contrasts are subtle (at least to a native English speaker's ear) and involve pitch, phonation, duration, intensity, and vowel quality. Confuse *hsi* (neutral tone) with *hsi* (high tone), and you'll get confused stares: the former means 'petrol', the latter 'urine'.

The tones, however, are arguably not the most difficult aspects of the language. Myanmar also has aspirated consonants – misleadingly transliterated in Myanmar with an initial *h*: *hsa, hka, hta* – which English lacks. When distinguishing, for example, between *hsa* ('salt') and *sa* ('eat'), a technique I've found useful is to pronounce unaspirated sounds using the back of my mouth and the aspirated using the front.

The other main linguistic element of Myanmar that causes confusion is the glottal stops. We use them in English slang: imagine a London teenager saying "innit"; that missing "t" is a glottal stop. The difficulty regarding glottal stops does not come with speaking Myanmar, but with understanding locals speaking English. Where English uses a final consonant, Myanmar often has glottal stops. Hence many Myanmar don't fully pronounce, for example, the "t" of "sit", the "k" of "book", or the "ll" of "ball."

But the main challenge of learning Myanmar is an unexpected one. About half the locals speak while chewing betel ferociously, occasionally pausing to spew bloody liquid on the ground. Not only is it hard to understand what they are saying because their mouths are so stuffed, it's almost impossible to focus: there's something mesmerising about their repulsive red teeth, discoloured gums and stained chins. I am yet to discover a technique for getting around this.

When we finally reached the village that we would be overnighting in, Ya'ara and I were alarmed to find that the guides were ousting one of their friends from his comfortable home to accommodate us. The modern kitchen had a polished wooden floor and was furnished in a Western style; both bedrooms were cosy and warm. One of them was graced with two supremely ugly posters of naked babies superimposed onto trippy backgrounds of blue and pink swathes twinkling with artificial stars. In one, a boy wore a red baseball cap and clutched a red apple while his stubby cocktail sausage pointed accusingly at the viewer. In the other, a boy held a red apple to his mouth and stared out the frame with a look of *I'm-going-to-be-that-baby* on his face while a girl, clothed in a pink frilly hat and pink dress, posed on the floor in a position that, were she a sinuous lady, might have been erotic.

"They're from China," said Kyaw Kyaw, confirming my suspicions. "So you will share a room?"

"I think we'll take separate rooms," said Ya'ara.

"What about you?" I asked. "Where will you sleep?"

"I will go back home. I live nearby."

"To your wife?"

"No, to my family."

"Do you have a girlfriend?"

"Yes. I have three."

He left to commence the cooking. Ya'ara rolled her eyes.

"All these guys who have three girlfriends or a wife and three girlfriends," she moaned. "What do they do with them?"

"Well, I asked the driver of one of the kids I used to tutor. He had a wife and two girlfriends. I think he was around fifty." I took a sip of *ye-nway-kyan*. "He told me they held hands, went to the cinema, had dinner together–"

"And sex?"

"'Sometimes they let you,' he told me. 'If you pay them.'"

"That sort of girlfriend," laughed Ya'ara.

She sat down on the bed. I remained standing, marvelling at the Chinese baby posters.

"You know," I said, "you could probably convince them that in Israel roles are reversed and that girls have multiple boyfriends. I don't think I could get away with it – they know too much about England – but Israel may be just far enough off the Myanmar radar."

"Maybe I'll try later," she said, thumping the bed in several places. "This mattress is lumpy and cramped against the wall. Also, I'm not sure I can handle the babies."

"I love the babies."

"I think I'll sleep in your room."

"That'll confuse them: saying we will stay in separate rooms, then sharing a double bed."

After we had each showered, we went and sat outside with Zay Yar and our other remaining guide, a muscular, handsome Bamar with a cyclist's body and a chess master's eyes.

"Here, take this," said Zay Yar, thrusting a furry black puppy into Ya'ara's arms.

"Oh! Okay. Is he yours?"

"Yes, I bought him."

"How much?"

"5000 *kyats*." £2.62.

The puppy wriggled around, unsure about the change of situation, then snuggled against Ya'ara's chest and began making little whimpering noises.

"You're popular."

Ya'ara giggled. I went inside to find the hat I had spied earlier, which was made of straw weaved into concentric circles and spanned almost four feet. Beside it on the wall hung decorated Shan swords, whose sharp blades shone a royal silver. I donned both and stepped back outside, where everyone was now drinking rice wine.

"Where did you get those?" asked Ya'ara. "I need one."

She plonked the puppy on the floor and disappeared inside, returning a moment later wearing a conical farmer's hat and brandishing an engraved Shan sword.

A lengthy photo shoot followed, after which it was time for dinner – fried vegetables and rice, plus a delicious Shan dish: fried bean balls. As the rice wine flowed, the conversation steered towards sex.

"So how many girlfriends do you have?" Ya'ara asked our sturdy Bamar guide.

"Two."

"Two? Why two? Why not one?"

He shrugged and offered no answer.

"And what about you Zay Yar? You're married, aren't you?"

"Yes, I am." Then, with a proud smile: "I have a baby boy. Here, I show you."

Zay Yar found a picture of himself smiling at the camera and dominating the frame; his baby lay on a chair behind him, swaddled in clothes and attended by his wife.

"Very cute," said Ya'ara.

"And I have no girlfriends," added Zay Yar. "Just me and my wife."

"What about you two? You aren't together?"

A brief pause followed.

"He's my sixth boyfriend!" said Ya'ara.

Our guides exploded.

"Six," repeated Kyaw Kyaw, falling towards Zay Yar in hysterics. *"Chauk."*

Still they roared, tears welling in their eyes.

"Six?" whispered Zay Yar, pink-faced.

"Six," grinned Ya'ara.

Zay Yar held six fingers up. Ya'ara nodded, then winked at me.

Pff, she could have at least placed me in her top five.

The next morning, after a breakfast of Shan noodles, one of Myanmar's favourite dishes, we set off to visit a waterfall. The weather was on our side, and everyone was in high spirits, albeit a little hungover.

We started along a rust-red track that soon wound into floral meadows. Terraced rice paddies climbed the hills and rows of sprouting crops rooted in rufous soil acted as leading lines, directing the eye towards quaint thatched huts. I was just reaching for my camera when the sky clouded over, apparently having sensed that the trek's first true photo opportunity was presenting itself.

We stopped for lunch at a Shan village, whose primary income came through selling flowers at a nearby *zay*. Here we acquired a sixth guide, a wizened local, who would lead us to the waterfall.

This turned out to be a proper trek: along tiny tracks and over fallen logs, through foliage that pinged back into our faces with rugged insistence, enjoying sublime views of serrated ridges. As we began descending, the path disappeared and the hillside turned perilously steep. We scrabbled from one bamboo thicket to another, slipping and sliding down the soggy slope, our man up ahead hacking out a route. Three times I lost my footing and slid down several metres; three times I was saved by a clump of fallen branches.

We reached the waterfall in a filthy, sweaty mess, feeling like bona fide explorers. It was an impressive sight: craggy and cascading, absorbing the fading light of day.

"Now we go up it," said Zay Yar.

We didn't question him. Already our chief guide and Kyaw Kyaw were improvising a route up the edge using rotten logs.

Ya'ara and I began climbing – and that's really what it was: full-on rock climbing. Ya'ara, being a regular climber, excelled; I, having given up the sport years ago to become the next David Beckham, was not of the same calibre and had to rely on hand- and foot-ups from Zay Yar.

Progress was arduous: not only was there the water to contend with, but the rocks were covered in slippery algae. Some parts were narrow, and the steep rock face had been designed so as to provide only a smattering of half-arsed handholds.

"Give me your hand," said Zay Yar as I struggled up a particularly nasty ledge, which one of our group had propped a branch against.

I'm not one for heroics, so I gave him my hand. But even then, it was difficult to scale the Y-shaped branch and heave myself onto the ledge.

Once up, I offered assistance to Ya'ara, who was also struggling.

"Let me use my legs," she said to someone beneath.

She got up, more gracefully than I had, then we navigated our way over a shelf of fast-flowing water and onto a series of smooth rocks. We looked out through the clearing, towards the distant hills – and finally noticed one of our guides standing before the most treacherous ledge, lagging behind the rest. He stood there for a good two minutes, trying out different handholds.

Then he turned around and began traipsing back up the hill.

"Hey! Hey!" shouted Kyay Kyaw. He spun around and scrambled back down the waterfall to join his friend, who was walking away with his head down.

Ya'ara and I exchanged glances, then peered down at the razor rocks that would slice us to smithereens if we fell upon them. We looked at each other again, silently acknowledging that clambering up the waterfall had been a moronic idea. At least one of our group had sense.

Nevertheless, fuelled by adrenaline and completionist desires, we continued. The village elder had already crossed the waterfall and was skirting a cliff edge overlooking the jungle. We soon reached him and began navigating the slippery ledge – falling would almost certainly have meant death. It started off maybe four feet wide, but after ducking under a couple of branches it narrowed, finally becoming little more than a leafy strip along the hillside.

Then, at long last, the path! Maybe twenty metres ahead: small mud steps carved into the hillside, begging the question of why we had not taken them in the first place.

"Arghhh!"

I turned around – to see dirt and leaves falling through the air. Ya'ara's legs were flapping over the edge, but Zay Yar had his arm around her waist, having materialised at just the right moment. He had probably saved her life.

Ya'ara took a short breather, perched on the edge with Zay Yar watching her, then scrambled over to the steps and began climbing. The jungle canopy gradually thinned, thin shafts of sunlight fell to the floor, the steps became firmer. Ya'ara and I upped our pace. Soon we were jogging – running – eyes never leaving the path, desperate to escape.

"Look!" cried Zay Yar as we emerged into the light, sweaty and trembling.

"What is it?"

"A pineapple plantation!" He charged forward and pushed his way through some towering elephant grass. "Yes! We've done it!" he boomed, standing amid a clearing, oozing triumph. "We've found the path! Now, when trekkers want a little adventure, I shall take them to this waterfall!"

"Zay Yar."

"Look! A ginger plantation!"

"Zay Yar."

"Yes?"

"Never take people there again," said Ya'ara.

Zay Yar stared at her.

"No?"

"It's too dangerous," I said.

"Even for a little adventure?"

"Yes," we said simultaneously.

Zay Yar fell silent and plodded on. I could tell from his body language that he would not take our advice and would continue to bring unsuspecting trekkers there in the future.

After ten minutes, we rejoined the other two, who were sitting on a bank, smoking.

"I couldn't see," mumbled the guide who had wisely given up climbing the waterfall. He waved his hand in front of his eyes to suggest he had suddenly lost his vision upon reaching the most dangerous and challenging part of the ascent. Well, he had to save face.

We paused for a drink, then began making our way back to the flower village.

"You know," said our Bamar guide to Ya'ara as we strolled along, "I can understand Israel's policy on Palestine. I have some Muslim friends, but I don't like how they think." He pointed to his temple and twizzled his finger. "They all think like terrorists."

Ya'ara did not point out the contradictory essence of his statement, nor was it the first Islamophobic generalisation I had heard in Myanmar.

"You must be happy about Brexit," a couple of Buddhist Bamar had said when I first arrived in Yangon.

"Why would I be happy about Brexit?"

"Because it means not so many Muslims will come to your country."

This was perhaps *the* misinformation that swayed the referendum, but I hadn't expected to hear it regurgitated in Myanmar. However, through further conversations like this, I gradually learnt that the information which reached Myanmar regarding Islamic terrorism had been grossly exaggerated. Many Myanmar seemed to believe attacks in Europe were constant and that Europeans lived in a state of fear. Toxic generalisations – such as "all Muslims are terrorists" – were voiced regularly; one person I met was even convinced that every Muslim was part of a world-wide conspiracy to exterminate non-Muslims. Their news invariably came from Facebook, which for many Myanmar *is* the internet. Most worryingly of all, it tended to be the university-educated youth who were the most Islamophobic.

Chapter 6: Myanmar's Ugliest Baby

After a day of rest and treating wounds, Ya'ara and I travelled to hilly Hsipaw, the easternmost town of northern Shan State not to be plagued by civil skirmishes waged in the name of federalism between local ethnic insurgent armies and the central government. The train took us over the Gokteik Viaduct, an impressive colonial railway bridge spanning a 689m gorge, in what proved to be a vicious countryside ride. The open windows spewed severed twigs and leaf trimmings into the carriage, occasionally permitting a thicker branch to sneak in and whack my injured elbow. Luckily, sweeping views of the craggy gorge, hypnotic meadows, and birds' nests shaped like cocoons dulled the pain.

We had been fortunate to find empty seats in the cushioned first-class carriage, but after a couple of hours I wandered into ordinary class to stretch my legs. Numerous elderly Myanmar women were squatting on their hard seats, still uncomfortable with sitting. Squatting is good posture – particularly when excreting, for it straightens the Puborectalis muscle and makes everything flow better. Some Myanmar even squat on Western toilets, though the toilet doors of Yangon restaurants are plastered with anti-squatting posters.

Many of the Myanmar families in ordinary class were clutching traditional lunchboxes, a handful of cylindrical pots collected into a stack and connected at the top by a handle. These used to be made of beautifully engraved black and red lacquer, but shiny metal ones are now preferred. They are one of the loveliest Myanmar contraptions – perfect for storing rice, curry and salads – and I am optimistic that their practicality will ensure they survive modernisation. I shall be greatly disheartened if in ten years they have been replaced by tacky Tupperware.

Our arrival into Hsipaw was disconcerting: local guesthouses had shipped teenagers to the train station to collect potential customers and there was a worrying number of other backpackers. But things quickly improved: Hsipaw boasted blue skies, tremendous waterfalls and serene hillsides. The elegant Duthawadi River wound its way through town, and blankets bearing shredded sweetcorn lay spread on the roads to dry. It was roasting by day, thunderous by night.

Most pleasing of all, however, were Hsipaw's residents, who smiled constantly, even though their town had become touristy. Suffice it to say, whoever called Thailand "The Land of Smiles" had clearly never been to Myanmar. Though not their first language, the Shan locals beamed whenever I spoke Myanmar. And if making people happy isn't a good reason for learning a language, what is?

Hsipaw is renowned as a trekking hub, but Ya'ara and I were not interested in another "little adventure." We had come to see the Shan Palace, previously home to Sao Kya Seng, the last Hsipaw *sawbwa*, or 'sky prince'.

For years, Shan State, Myanmar's largest state by square mile, was a feudal system of 34 separate kingdoms each ruled by a *sawbwa*. This hereditary tradition of moral and administrative control dated back in legend to the second century BC and even survived the colonial era, for

British sovereignty ruled through the *sawbwas* with minimal interference.

As romantic as being a 'sky prince' sounds, Sao despised the system's medievalism. The revenue from gambling festivals always belonged to the *sawbwa*, as did all the crops grown within "his" principality – which, in Sao's case, was an area roughly the size of Northern Ireland. He had also been disgusted by his father, who had abused his feudal privilege by discarding wives to make room for new ones. Sao sought to reform this system by promoting federalism and democracy, but instead it was crushed out of existence in 1962 by Ne Win ('Brilliant as the Sun').

The full story begins with the assassination of Aung San and six of his cabinet ministers on 19th July 1947, just six months before Myanmar gained its independence from the British. Following the murder of its independence hero, Myanmar suffered a decade of parliamentary democracy fractured by dacoits and armed ethnic insurgent groups distrustful of the new Bamar government.

In an attempt to combat the Kuomintang, Chinese anti-communist forces who had been forced out of China and were wreaking havoc in the northern Shan hills, the central Union of Burma stationed *Tatmadaw* forces in southern Shan. For many Shan peasants, this was their first direct contact with any Bamar, "and their encounters were, in most instances, frightening and deadly." The Shans, who call themselves "Tai" ('free') and are related to the Thais, saw their autonomy undermined, compelling some to move into the jungle and form guerrilla units.

While they fought for federalism, Sao sought it through the pen. To strengthen the Union, he and the other

33 *sawbwas* relinquished their feudal powers to become a single Shan State administered by an elected government. "They reasoned that by restructuring the federal system, the Union would survive, and the fledgling insurgency would be undermined."[6]

But Commander-in-Chief of the *Tatmadaw*, General Ne Win, had other ideas. Fearing Shan State might secede from the Union – as the 1947 Panglong Agreement had made their constitutional right – he staged a *coup d'état* on 2nd March 1962. The military claimed intervention was necessary "to prevent the disintegration of the Union," but it achieved the opposite: rebellions flared anew all over the country, particularly in the Kachin and Shan states, where fighting with the *Tatmadaw* continues to this day.

Sao, whom Ne Win had loathed, vanished. The *Tatmadaw* denied detaining him, but a Kachin military Captain, who was more loyal to the hilltribe people than the Bamar, smuggled a signed letter from Sao to Inge Sargent, his Austrian wife. The letter revealed that Sao was imprisoned in Ba Htoo Myo military camp near the Shan capital of Taunggyi.

For the next two years, Inge entertained hopes that Sao would be released. As Myanmar turned into an Orwellian state and important political persons disappeared, various messengers exploited Inge's sorrow for money, fabricating news of Sao's wellbeing or claiming to have seen him personally.

---

[6] The above two quotes come from B. Lintner (1994), 'Foreword' to *Twilight over Burma: My Life as a Shan Princess* (Kindle Edition), University of Hawaii Press, pos. 230-59.

Inge was blinded by love. She remained optimistic that Sao might still be alive, even though she was the only Shan princess prohibited from visiting her "detained" husband. After receiving contradictory information from separate military sources regarding Sao's whereabouts, Inge finally fled Myanmar with her two daughters, Mayari and Kennari. Everyone on the flight cheered when the plane left Myanmar airspace. Nobody heard from Sao again.

The Shan palace, known as the East Haw, turned out to be a stately two-storey manor in the colonial style. Elegant French windows and tasteful terraces looked out over a lawn that, in its heyday, was no doubt immaculate; flowers edged a small front garden. Inside, monochrome pictures of Shan royalty stood on the mantlepiece and sunlight flooded through thin pink curtains, casting the living room in an amber glow. Above the windows hung a proud Shan flag – identical to its Myanmar counterpart, except for a moon, not a star, in its centre.

Several other backpackers had made it to the East Haw, where Sao Sarm Hpong, the niece of Sao Kya Seng, recounts the story of the military takeover to tourists almost daily.

"Should we call the country Myanmar or Burma?" asked one German in the Q&A.

"Well, the military changed the name of the country, without consulting the will of the people," said Sao Sarm Hpong, almost quoting Aung San Suu Kyi from 2012. "That's why I say Burma."

She moved on to another question, frustrating the German desperate to quote the 2014 *Lonely Planet* he was clutching back at her: but isn't Myanmar more inclusive of the ethnic minorities?

No, it wasn't. "Myanmar" ('fast and strong') was the literary name of the country and etymologically only referred to the Bamar, as did "Burma". The topic of what to call the country is no longer so polarised nor discussed. Most people today use "Myanmar", and in 2016 Aung San Suu Kyi told foreign diplomats they could use either name and even vowed to use "Myanmar" herself on occasion.

"Are the *sawbwas* still powerful?" asked his girlfriend.

"They hold no power anymore – the military does – but people still respect their families and recognise us in town."

"Why is the Shan flag so similar to the Myanmar flag?"

Sao Sarm Hpong waggled her finger, a sure sign that she possessed esoteric knowledge, then sat down and straightened her ponytail. Soft light was falling gently on her face, giving her an air of wisdom.

"No one is sure why the Myanmar military changed the flag in 2010. But according to one story, a military general was told by an astrologer that the Shans would one day rule the country. To trick the fates, the *Tatmadaw* adopted the Shan flag, but swapped the moon in the middle for a star."

This was probably just a patriotic Shan conspiracy, but I decided to research it nonetheless. After all, the similarity was curious, especially considering the junta had been at war with Shan insurgent groups for decades, and the military government made many strange decisions based on astrology.

The Myanmar flag consists of a five-pointed white star set on a horizontal triband of yellow, green and red (from the top down). The yellow represents solidarity; the green evokes lushness and serenity; the red symbolises courage and determination; and the star stands for the importance of union to the country. This colour scheme was used in the 1943 State of Burma flag, which may have been the inspiration for readopting it.

In the Shan flag, the yellow represents Buddhism, the dominant religion of Shan State; otherwise, the colours and the white moon symbolise the same or similar ideals/aesthetics as in the Myanmar flag, only they apply to Shan State alone. In this regard, adopting this colour scheme would also incorporate Buddhism into the Myanmar flag.

Then there's the star. The move from moon to star seems obvious, for it continues the astrological theme, but another flag in Myanmar is stamped with a five-pointed white star: the *Tatmadaw* flag. The modern Myanmar flag thus evokes the military, Buddhism and nationhood by intertwining the three in a manner the *Tatmadaw* itself envisioned. If a general really was told that the Shans would one day rule the country, the modern Myanmar flag would, in this regard, have been a suitable choice, since its design both "tricked" the fates and propounded the military government's aims.

So what's the verdict: rumour or reason?

I'm no conspiracist, so would put the similarity down to coincidence. However, there is certainly reason to believe otherwise. After all, many rumours based on astrology in Myanmar have a basis in truth; and considering the military government watched American political drama *The West Wing* to see how democracy was "supposed to work",[7] does changing the country's flag in the hope of tricking fate really seem so far-fetched?

Hsipaw signalled the end of the road for me and Ya'ara: she went to Inle Lake, a popular tourist destination, and I headed for Myanmar's capital, Naypidaw, about which I had heard many things – none of them good, but all of them intriguing.

I jumped on a battered, grimy bus that promised a slow journey. Fortunately, I was granted the front seat, which offered superb views of the Shan hills as we passed through Kalaw. After a short climb, we started down a squiggly road, tracing the trickling river below. Soon a shallow, picturesque valley appeared, awe-inspiring, like an image from a lost world.

I got my camera out and took a few snaps. Five minutes later, we reached a checkpoint and two armed police officers boarded the bus.

"No photos!" the commanding officer barked at me, clutching an AK47.

I nodded obsequiously and looked out the window, where another policeman spotted me.

"Mingalabar!" he shouted with a grin, warranting an icy stare from his superior.

---

[7] See R. Cockett (2015), *Blood, Dreams and Gold: The Changing Face of Burma* (Kindle Edition), Yale University Press, pos. 3593.

They searched the larger cardboard boxes on board, checked the boots of other vehicles and questioned their owners. Everyone was calm, suggesting it was normal procedure, but my large Nikon bag made me feel like a target. Finally, the policemen taped the searched boxes back up and waved us on.

No drugs this time.

Myanmar's history of opiates is complex and fascinating. By March 1953, Myanmar had collected enough evidence on the Kuomintang (KMT) to make a formal complaint to the United Nations. The issue had also become an embarrassment to the USA, whose CIA had been delivering weapons to these anti-communist forces for two years in an attempt to repel the threat of communism.

The KMT were subsequently ordered to withdraw from Shan territory, but they did so half-heartedly and continued to engage the Chinese forces in guerrilla warfare. No longer backed by the US, they were forced to fund their own army. General Tuan reached the following conclusion:

"We have to continue to fight the evil of communism, and to fight you must have an army, and an army must have guns, and to buy guns you must have money. In these mountains, the only money is opium."[8]

The production of opium, for which the British had already laid the groundwork, subsequently soared. China's ban on opium production in the 1950s gave the KMT a monopoly in Shan State, enabling them to expand their territory into the Kachin hills. When Myanmar gained its

---

[8] General Tuan Shi-wen (1967), *Weekend Telegraph*.

independence in 1948, annual opium production stood at 30 tons. By the mid-1950s, it had increased twentyfold.

The KMT were finally ousted from Myanmar in 1961, but they had already paved the way for private narcotics armies in the Golden Triangle. One of these was led by Olive Yang (AKA "Miss Hairy Legs"), the lesbian opium princess of Kokang. Although born into an ethnic Chinese family of *sawbwas*, Yang spurned royalty as well as traditional expectations. She flouted the regional custom of feet-binding and, according to relatives, frequently fell for her brothers' romantic interests. Concerned by her cross-dressing, homosexuality and rebelliousness, her parents arranged for her to marry a younger cousin. But Yang abandoned him shortly after becoming pregnant, leaving her child to be raised by other family members.

By her early twenties, Yang already commanded her own army, which would later come to be known as "Olive's Boys." She was renowned for her sharpshooting, carried a Belgian pistol on each hip and became the first person to send opium to Thailand by the truckload. Armed with weapons supplied by the CIA, her militia dominated Kokang's opium trade from the end of WWII until 1963, when Ne Win cast her for six years into Yangon's notorious Insein Prison, where she allegedly endured torture. Olive Yang finally died in July 2017, at the age of 91, and is regarded as a heroine in Kokang.

Following her came Khun Sa, an illiterate Chinese Shan who had received military training under Yang, and Lo Hsing Han, who had studied at a school in Kokang established by Yang. In return for fighting ethnic insurgents and communists, the junta permitted their respective militia units to use government land and roads for growing opium, hoping they could become self-sustaining. Myanmar thereby became the world's first Narco State.

Between the 1960s and 1990s, Khun Sa and Lo Hsing Han each dominated the Golden Triangle, depending on which of them was in jail at the time. It wasn't until the surrender of Khun Sa's Mong Tai Army in 1996 that this reign of terror ended.

Supported by the UN, America's Drugs Enforcement Administration and other sundry agencies, the Myanmar military government commenced an eradication campaign, resulting in the decrease of national poppy cultivation by over 80% between 1998 and 2006. However, Myanmar has only seen regression since then: in 2013, poppy cultivation "rose by 13 per cent on the previous year, to 57,800 hectares (143,000 acres)."[9] Most of the opium poppies are grown by farmers in the Shan hills, where poor transportation infrastructure makes growing legal crops, which require exportation, less profitable.

Myanmar remains the world's second largest producer of opiates after Afghanistan. About 100 narcotics militias are still active in Shan State today, permitted to operate by the *Tatmadaw*, providing they share the profits. The arrangement has created a unique dynamic in Myanmar politics as the military proxy party, the Union Solidarity and Development Party, has a commanding grip on Shan State, having won more seats there in the 2015 elections than any other party.

---

[9] United Nations Office on Drugs and Crime (2013), *Southeast Asia Opium Survey, Lao PDR, Myanmar*.

For an alternative history of opiate cultivation and trafficking in Myanmar, visit Yangon's Drugs Elimination Museum!

Occupying ludicrously large grounds that could be put to better use, the museum building is dilapidated, rarely visited, and sure to get you wondering why on earth it hasn't been demolished yet.

On the ground floor you can read all about how drugs were never part of Myanmar culture but were introduced by the British. Be sure not to miss the dark, creepy room containing a series of statues vividly depicting the deterioration and death of a stereotypical hippy addict. "And what are those chilling, distant voices?" you ask. The sounds of babies crying and women screaming, of course!

Ascend the stairs and you'll reach our spacious second floor. Still believe the military government was involved in trafficking drugs? Let these pathetic photos of small-scale drug burnings prove otherwise! And now you can be part of the solution too. See that model scene of a drugs seizure? Press the big red button TO SAVE LIVES. You did? Excellent! Enjoy watching those crappy fake flames burn bottles of narcotics. You earned it!

On the third and final floor you'll find even more photos of small-scale drug burnings. Believe now that we weren't involved? Please?

Open Tuesdays-Sundays, 09:00-16:00. Entrance for foreigners K4000; for Myanmar nationals K100 (because they already know the truth).

*

Naypidaw, which etymologically means 'Seat of the King',[10] is a perfect microcosm of the military government's appallingly administered rule. The total land area of Naypidaw Union Territory is 4.5 times that of Greater London, yet its population density is 42.7 times lower. I assumed we were nearing the city centre when the *lan* broadened to several lanes, a dramatic shift from the usual single-lane Myanmar highways. I guess we technically had been getting nearer, but it was still almost an hour before we arrived there. And where even was "there"? I passed no hub of business or social activity, so I took the centre to be the "p" of "Naypidaw" on Google Maps.

The city itself was a lifeless contrast of concrete square blocks set between sprawling rice fields. Its absurdly large highways – allegedly designed to serve as aircraft runways – were the smoothest in Myanmar and the emptiest. Its pedestrian crossings were the best functioning in the country, but hardly a soul was around to use them. The hotel zone was silent, situated miles away from the nearest residential districts; and since there was no public transport and the *Tatmadaw* owned the only taxi company, I was forced to hitchhike my way around.

There wasn't much to see in Naypidaw. As is compulsory for tourists, I rolled around on the ghostly 20-lane highway and visited Naypidaw's *paya-gyi*, a hideous imitation of the Shwedagon Pagoda in Yangon. Several elephants were chained up opposite the entrance in celebration of World Elephant Day, looking chronically

---

[10] See D. Preecharushh (2010), 'Naypidaw: The New Capital of Burma', *Engineering Earth*, p. 1021.

depressed. Tourist stalls surrounded the pagoda, but I was the only tourist.

Just as people adore pugs for being so ugly and inbred, I loved Naypidaw for being such an enormous waste of time, space and money. It appealed to that distinctly British part of me drawn to uselessness, and for the first time in my life I bought a tourist T-shirt: I LOVE NAYPIDAW.

There are various theories on why then-dictator Than Shwe quietly relocated the country's administrative capital from Yangon in 2005. Perhaps the most popular belief is that an astrologer warned Than Shwe of the West's supposed plan to attack Yangon by sea, prompting the paranoid general to move the government offices inland, though the official explanation for the move was that Yangon had become too congested and lacked room for future expansion. Whatever the reason, the new capital gained its name on 27th March 2006: Armed Forces Day, a national holiday.

There are some good logistical reasons for making Naypidaw the country's capital. Situated exactly between Yangon and Mandalay, Myanmar's two largest cities, it is well connected and located adjacent to the conflict-ravaged Shan and Kayin states. As the newly democratic Myanmar develops and international businesses flood in, Naypidaw's magnitude may eventually prove useful.

But the most convincing arguments for the relocation are the sinister ones (and, yes, I regretted buying the I LOVE NAYPIDAW T-shirt once I had learned about them). Inspired Indian journalist Siddharth Varadarajan declared Naypidaw "a masterpiece of urban planning designed to defeat any putative 'colour revolution,'" noting that the absence of a city centre or confined public space would prevent political protests while its distance from Yangon meant the government offices could remain operational if Yangon was brought to a standstill.[11]

Another theory is that Than Shwe wished to recreate a precolonial, entirely Bamar Myanmar. As observed by Richard Cockett, author of *Blood, Dreams and Gold: The Changing Face of Burma*, "almost everything in Naypidaw attempts to evoke the traditions and glories of Burma's royal past." Three of Myanmar's most renowned kings, Anawrahta, Bayinnaung and Alaungpaya, all of whom "extended Burman power well into the territory that is now Thailand and India", tower over Naypidaw's military parade ground. In Uppatasanti Paya, the imitation of Shwedagon Pagoda, murals depicting episodes from the life of the Buddha hang beside those glorifying scenes from the lives of Bamar kings. The intertwining of religion, royalty and military rulers are thus enshrined in the city's most important temple. The Naypidaw presidential palace is modelled on the Mandalay Royal Palace and its reception room, draped in red and gold and lavished with a high-backed chair, is a "barely disguised" throne room.[12] Perhaps most revealingly of all, since 11 is considered the 'master number' in Myanmar, its doubled one numerals supposedly representing the combination of male and female energy, Naypidaw's first 11 ministries were opened at 11am on 11/11 – a move in keeping with the ancient

---

[11] http://svaradarajan.blogspot.com/2007/02/dictatorship-by-cartography-geometry.html <Accessed: 03.01.2019>

[12] The above three quotes, as well as most of this information, come from R. Cockett (2015), *Blood, Dreams and Gold: The Changing Face of Burma* (Kindle Edition), Yale University Press, pos. 1284-1466.

tradition of evolving royal capitals based on astrological factors. So far as I know, Than Shwe did not conduct any human sacrifices, though he did forcibly relocate people living in the area.

But alas, Naypidaw possesses no royal prowess. The city is vacuous and the buildings are shoddily constructed, just as Than Shwe's cabinet was. Despite pleas from the Myanmar government, none of the foreign embassies will relocate to the capital, for they don't wish to inflict such misery on their employees and their families. Naypidaw may symbolise "a significant attempt to turn back to traditional roots" and recover the Bamar national pride lost during colonial rule,[13] but every Myanmar national hates it. Anyone who must visit – must, for no one would go there willingly – groans, then mumbles, "I have to go to Naypidaw."

Rather fittingly, Than Shwe lost power just one year before Naypidaw was completed in 2012. The transition to democracy was initiated by Than Shwe in the early 1990s – possibly because he knew how unpopular he was and did not want to end up like his predecessor, Ne Win, who lived under virtual house arrest after relinquishing power, though the prospect of converting illicit earnings into veritable revenue must also have appealed to Than Shwe and his crony cabinet. The greatest benefit of initiating the reform process themselves – as opposed to waiting for their authoritarian regime to be toppled by public protest, as happened in East Germany – was that it enabled the generals to retain predominance: of the 664 seats in today's parliament, the *Hluttaw*, 25% are reserved for the military,

---

[13] As argued convincingly by D. Preecharushh (2010), p. 1025-6.

who also control the Ministry of Defence, the Ministry of Border Affairs and the Ministry of Home Affairs – all the firepower.

It was a devious handover of power, and the *Tatmadaw* don't look as though they will be ousted from the *Hluttaw* anytime soon. On 29th January 2017, top NLD lawyer U Ko Ni – who created the position of State Counsellor for Aung San Suu Kyi after the military government ratified a law prohibiting anyone with a foreign spouse or children from becoming president – was assassinated at Yangon International Airport. He had just returned from Indonesia, having been part of a delegation studying conflict resolution and democracy.

Theories as to why he was murdered range from government destabilisation to hate crime (Ko Ni was Muslim), though four of the five men suspected of coordinating and carrying out the attack were ex-military. No one directly accused the *Tatmadaw* of involvement – who would dare? – but the timing was uncanny.

One day was enough for Naypidaw, and before I knew it I was on the coach and heading back to Yangon. Almost two months had flown by, during which I had become increasingly attached to Myanmar. My first of four extended trips round the country had made me even keener to experience more of Myanmar and to learn all I could about it.

I reclined my comfy seat, thinking about everything I had seen and heard, and had just shut my eyes when my phone vibrated.

`When are you coming back? Shwe Ei`

`This evening!` I wrote with fumbling fingers, my palms sweating and my heart clattering against my ribcage. I immediately started obsessing over how I should greet her, how I should start the conversation and which story I would tell her first. And as I did, my insides began to churn and my heart went all wonky.

And then it hit me.

"Oh fuck," I said aloud, startling the passengers sitting adjacent.

How could I have been so stupid? But the worst bit about my realisation was that it had come long after Shwe Ei had said she loved me. In fact, the Myanmar fall in love really *myan-myan*: it's not uncommon for someone to tell their date *"chit-deh"* ('I love you') on just their second or third meeting. The cleaner at my school in Yangon once met a guy on a Thursday and told me she loved him the following Tuesday. They broke up a week later.

I arrived in Yangon that evening in a huff and hurry. Shwe Ei and I fell into each other's arms in a flurry of smiles and sobs.

"It was really hard when you left," she said, mascara tears spilling onto the white duvet. "You never said you loved me, but I knew you did."

I hugged her more tightly.

"I'm sorry," I mumbled. "There was so much going on... You knew how much I wanted to leave Yangon. I... I'm sorry."

I was guilty and we both knew it. Towards the end of our relationship I had hardly spared a thought for my feelings or hers – the only thing that had mattered was my pending trip – and now we were both suffering the consequences of my selfishness.

It was an emotional night. I wanted to stay with Shwe Ei – promise her we could work something out, apologise as only the English can – but my Myanmar visa was about to expire, and I had to catch a flight for Laos the next day.

So once again I left her, only this time the wiser; and for the next month her fragrant hair, soft eyes and lulling voice were mere memories, and my heart was a hollow burden.

Part 2

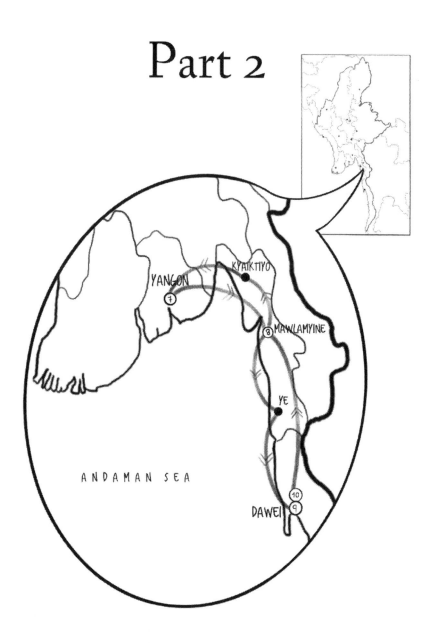

Chapter 7: The Tide Turns

On 25th August 2017, the Arakan Rohingya Salvation Army attacked around 30 police and army outposts in northern Rakhine State, killing twelve security personnel. In response, the *Tatmadaw* launched a brutal clearance campaign, compelling over 700,000 Rohingya, a stateless ethnic minority of roughly one million Muslims and Hindus, to seek refuge in neighbouring Bangladesh. The Myanmar military were accused of arson, rape and murder, and a later UN report labelled their retaliation "genocide."

Aung San Suu Kyi, who denied the severity of the situation by claiming there had been "violence on both sides", promptly fell from madonna to whore. Previously praised as only a woman can be, she was then vilified as only a woman can be. The State Counsellor was stripped of various awards – including her Freedom of Oxford award and her Freedom of Dublin award – and there were even calls for her Nobel Peace Prize to be revoked.

In Myanmar, however, Aung San Suu Kyi was lauded. She had already gained respect for denying visas to a UN fact-finding team established to investigate allegations of crimes against humanity in Rakhine; and as she fell from grace in the eyes of the international community, many Myanmar rallied together in Yangon to show their support for her.

Most Myanmar call the Rohingya "Bengalis", a derogatory term which implies they are not native to Myanmar but originate from Bangladesh. The issue has its roots in colonialism: when Myanmar was part of British India, the British encouraged Indians to emigrate, considering them loyal workers. On average, 250,000 came each year; and by 1931, 212,000 Indians lived in Yangon alone, outnumbering the Bamar almost 2:1. The Indians not only shifted the demographic, "but their economic muscle and favouring by the British meant they were seen by the local population to have displaced Buddhists from their work in their tens of thousands."

Gradually, as rising anti-colonial sentiment conflated with xenophobia, Myanmar Muslim communities who could trace their lineage back generations were "lumped together with the more recent arrivals."[14] Muslims were perceived as diluting the bloodline, threats to the Buddhist order crafted by early Myanmar kings, for Buddhist women who married Muslim men often converted and raised their children as Muslims.

After Myanmar gained independence, Ne Win attempted to reforge a Buddhist-Bamar national identity by banishing groups who would not conform to the "one voice, one blood, one nation" ideology. The Rohingya were among many ethnic minorities to be persecuted, but their case is particularly severe, for they have been never granted citizenship.

The junta initially depicted the Rohingya as Bengali interlopers seeking to Islamise Myanmar and later branded them "terrorists" – a characterisation that especially gained credence in 2016, when hundreds of Rohingya in Maungdaw, Rakhine State, attacked three police outposts, leaving nine policemen dead. One video showed a group of

---

[14] The above two quotes, as well as most of this information, come from F. Wade (2017), *Myanmar's Enemy Within: Buddhist Violence and the Creating of a Muslim Other* (Kindle Edition), Zed Books, pos. 492-495.

armed men calling on Rohingya to "get ready for the jihad" and justifying martyrdom using the same religious reasoning that Islamist militants elsewhere have done. The group went by the name Harakah al-Yaqin ('Faith Movement'), but later changed to the Arakan Rohingya Salvation Army (ARSA). Many Myanmar today lump all Rohingya with the acts of this single group.

I returned to Myanmar two weeks after the ARSA attacks, with the world finally realising there was more to this fairy tale of democracy than the Lady and her struggles against the generals. The Myanmar knew international eyes were on them – you could sense it in the way they interacted with foreigners – yet they remained fiercely outspoken in their beliefs. Volunteers lined the streets to collect "counterterrorism" donations, sporting large banners that condemned the Rohingya as "illegal immigrants", while my Facebook feed became a catalogue of Islamophobic rhetoric.

Learning that your friends hold opposite views to yourself can be a strange experience. When an Austrian friend revealed herself to be pro fox-hunting, I was a little shocked; but when Myanmar friends openly supported the Rohingya genocide, I didn't know how to react – for how do you approach such a controversial issue, especially when your friendship is cross-cultural?

Out of an unspoken mutual understanding, Shwe Ei and I had always avoided discussing the Rohingya – and that wasn't about to change now. Huddled over a cup of coffee in an overly air-conditioned Yangon café, we intentionally ignored the subject and instead spoke about personal concerns. I told her that I wanted to try and make a long-distance relationship work and that we could find a way to navigate the difficulties presented by visas, careers and personal ambitions. After all, we loved each other – and that's what mattered most.

But I was wrong.

"The day you left for Laos," she said in a quiet, almost embarrassed tone, "I went back to my astrologist and he said that I would meet someone in September."

My insides shrunk.

"I met a guy from Shan State last week and... Well, I'm not that optimistic, because I still love you, but I'd like to see how it goes."

She tried to smile apologetically; I tried to smile back understandingly; we both failed. I was really beginning to hate this astrologer.

"Do you see him much?" The thought made me queasy.

"We've met a couple of times," she said, visibly uncomfortable. "He has to work a lot in a black area of Shan State – you know, where there is no phone connection."

"And how often does he come back to Yangon?"

She shrugged. "Every few months."

"That's all? "You've met him twice, can't contact him and only see him once every few months?"

Shwe Ei squirmed and didn't answer. It was also wrong of me to ask: I was angry, jealous, and disappointed with myself. Besides, I could hardly offer her a more stable relationship. The only consolation was that my next destination was Pa-Auk Tawya Forest Monastery, where I could practise meditation for a week and try to forget about poor life choices.

I arrived early afternoon and was dropped outside the monastery's green and gold archway. At the Foreigners Registration Office, U Kumuda, the monk responsible for looking after foreigners, taught me the Eight Precepts of Buddhism, by which I would have to abide:

1) To refrain from killing living creatures
2) To refrain from stealing
3) To refrain from sexual activity
4) To refrain from incorrect speech (such as lying)
5) To refrain from taking intoxicating drugs
6) To refrain from eating after noon
7) To refrain from dancing, singing, music, using perfumes, and beautifying the body with cosmetics
8) To refrain from sleeping on cushioned beds

Then he gave me a crash cause in Pa-Auk meditation.

"Concentrate on the area between your upper lip and the bottom of your nose," said Kumuda, thereby introducing me to the concept of the Focus Point. "Let's practise for twenty minutes now." And he furled up into the full lotus position, hands in his lap, palms facing upwards.

I have the suppleness of an ox, so did not even attempt the full, half nor quarter lotus. Instead, I crossed my legs as best I could, shut my eyes and rested my hands on my shins. How these elderly monks managed to remain so flex-

Focus Point! I checked myself. Focus Point! My thoughts had drifted after no more than five seconds. It was going to be a long twenty minutes.

I took a deep breath and refocused. Was I supposed to follow my breathing, as in most forms of meditation I had practised, or just be aware of it?

Maybe ten seconds that time.

After the first two minutes, I had lost focus a dozen times. Gradually, however, I improved, and after ten minutes I managed a 30-second stint of concentration. By this time my body was shaking, especially my legs. I thought of the Saigon burning monk image and how peaceful he had remained while his skin melted, wondering how many reincarnations it would take me to reach that level of composure.

Eventually, I could take the pain no longer and opened my eyes – to find Kumuda still sitting there, unmoved. Someone came into the room a couple of minutes later, awaking the monk from his trance.

"Buddha did this every day for six months," he told me. "You can manage six days."

At least someone had faith in me.

I left the registration office and was led by a smiley senior monk to my kuti, a kind of hermitage hut. A broad, middle-aged Westerner was sat in a chair outside.

"Well, I can tell you're British from your silhouette," he said in an American accent.

Was that a compliment?

"How long are you here for?"

"Just one week," I answered. "And you?"

"I've been here almost a month, though I've been practising meditation for ten years now."

He was shaven, and a large lump the size of a golf ball protruded from the centre of his scalp. I wondered whether this might be symptomatic of a terminal illness and had compelled him to seek enlightenment in his final days.

"And how have you found Pa-Auk meditation?" I asked.

"Honestly, it's the only method that's really worked for me," he said.

We wished each other good night, then I went to my room, where the monk was waiting for me.

"This is your bed," he barked, pointing towards a plain wooden rack. "And your bathroom. And your umbrella." He handed me an ochre monk umbrella. "And here is the net for catching mosquitoes. Ooh! Ooh!"

He snatched the white fishing net and caught a juicy mosquito buzzing by his ear. Then he pushed the door open and released it back into the wild.

"No killing! First Precept." He gave me another grin and departed, leaving me to wonder what the empty Pringles tin in the corner was for.

It turned out to be for removing scorpions and was surprisingly effective.

I've tried numerous forms of meditation over the past few years but have never got along with any of them. I'm neither spiritual nor religious, but I do believe in the healthiness of a calm mind and believe this can be achieved through meditation.

In many ways, I'm your archetypal writer – frantic, always complaining about their editor, never able to relax – but I'm also a lifelong insomniac, suffered for years from depression and more recently from stress-induced psychosomatic pain. Therapy sessions had helped relieve me of psychological pain temporarily, but now I was seeking long-term treatment. One week at Pa-Auk would not be long enough to tackle the various mental illnesses I had accumulated, but perhaps it would provide me with the tools for self-practice.

The Pa-Auk meditation method is based on the *Visuddhimagga*, a treatise on Theravada Buddhist doctrine written by 5th-century Indian scholar Buddhaghosa. It focuses on achieving *samatha* ('tranquillity'), primarily through *ānāpānassati* ('mindfulness of breathing').

As I had already discovered, concentrating on the Focus Point was bloody difficult. Even though I managed to sit through my entire first session – 90 draining minutes – I only retained focus for a maximum of one-two minutes at a time. My average was probably fifteen seconds. By the end of the sitting, my whole body was quivering, painful and numb.

I had missed the morning alms collection by going for a walk, so when lunch came I was ravenous. I would have to pig out, for eating after midday was forbidden. Although monks must "beg" for alms, they eat well, since greatest merit is believed to be achieved when directed towards the wise and morally righteous. As for beggars, orphans and other unfortunates, the general attitude is that they are suffering for the sins of their last life and are thus less deserving of charity.

I normally feel sorry for monks and nuns collecting alms in town, for almost everyone gives them rice – meaning they end up with a horribly imbalanced rice-curry ratio, one of the greatest culinary sins. Fortunately, Pa-Auk was organised and the cooks fantastic. First, I collected the tray holding my cup, bowl and cutlery from downstairs. Then I returned to the wooden walkway and lined up. The queue took the order of foreign monks, local monks, foreign laymen, and finally local laymen. After reciting prayers, everyone began treading with gentle footsteps through the carpeted corridor and towards the kitchen. Before it stood a whiteboard that listed the electricity financers and those who had donated special foods, such as dragon fruit. Sometimes these were individuals, but usually they were Buddhist organisations – often foreign, along these lines:

The whole week's electricity donated by:
The Vietnam Association of Theravada Buddhism

There were also signs requesting you only to accept as much food as you expected to eat. But this proved to be nigh on impossible, for everyone wanted to give you grub and thereby boost their karma – particularly the Chinese, Myanmar and Thai tourists, who came loaded with all sorts of goods sure to hasten our passage to enlightenment, among them, razors, paracetamol, handkerchiefs and diarrhoea treatment. I eventually discovered that the trick to accepting a manageable amount of food was to cover my bowl with a plate and put my head down when passing by a cook whose food did not tempt me. However, in doing so I felt as if I were personally insulting the cook.

An elderly nun ended the line of donators, always with something curious to offer.

"Take! Take!" she insisted, piling my tray with pills.

"What is it?"

"Vitamin pill."

On another occasion, I let her spoil my food by accidentally accepting a tablespoon of fish sauce. Although Buddhist monks and nuns were not allowed to eat meat at Pa-Auk, the consumption of fish was permitted – perhaps because the Myanmar conception of vegetarianism includes fish. According to travel writer Norman Lewis, who visited the country in 1951, the Myanmar deem fish okay to be eaten if the animal died after being taken <u>out of water</u>.[15] If he is correct (for I was unable to verify this), then humanity has another supreme example of twisting common sense for its own culinary benefit. The epitome of this must be *Maultaschen*, a German dish consisting of meat enclosed within pasta dough, which Cistercian monks allegedly created so that God would not see they were eating meat during Lent. Throughout my travels in Myanmar, I repeatedly caused great confusion by asking for food that was *"thet-that-lut"* ('vegetarian'), but which included egg (traditionally considered meat) and excluded fish sauce.

---

[15] See N. Lewis (2011), *Golden Earth: Travels in Burma* (Kindle Edition), Eland Publishing, pos. 3287. In volume four of *The Book of Disciples*, Buddha said that monks could consume meat or fish, providing the animal was not killed for them specifically and that they neither saw nor heard the animal that was slaughtered. The idea that fish is vegetarian is therefore not a Buddhist one *per se* but may be specific to Myanmar.

Lunch collected, I returned to eat in the room designated for foreigners, which came with the luxury of tables and chairs. There was a sign on the wall requesting noble silence, though this did not seem to apply to the Chinese monks.

Both laypeople and monks washed up their own bowls. Untouched leftovers were piled on special plates beside the taps. On one occasion, I saw a chronically obese senior monk instructing a layman to hand him fried bread from the plates of uneaten food before stuffing them into his robes, since his stomach prevented him from reaching over the bins and taking them himself. The clock had been about to strike twelve.

After lunch came personal time, during which I usually went for a walk among the rubber trees planted in hypnotic lines, enjoying the chirrups of birds and tracking long trails of ants. One time I almost trod on a slender green snake, then proceeded to play a potentially perilous game of Hide and Seek. It eventually won, though not until I had taken a few fabulous photos. I also saw large red ants chasing an earthworm through the undergrowth. Spurred on by the terror of being eaten alive, it moved with a speed I would never have thought it capable of, and before I knew it the ants had reached me and were devouring my bare feet.

I ended every day by walking to a nearby hilltop and watching the sun diffuse rufous *shwe* rays as it set over the Thanlwin River. I was consoled by the knowledge that, even if all my ambitions in life fell through, I could return to Pa-Auk Tawya to live in tranquillity, eat delicious food, and enjoy sublime sunsets for the rest of my days.

My meditation improved considerably on Day Two as I managed to sit through three whole sessions and keep concentration for perhaps five minutes on more than two occasions. The *sīma* ('meditation hall') was ideal for inducing a state of calm: there were cushions for yogis to arrange beneath their hanging green mosquito nets and the breeze wafted in through the open doors, providing essential relief from the humidity. Beeping digital watches were prohibited, but in Myanmar rules are there to be broken.

The primary natural distraction in the *sīma* was flatulence, though even this was dealt with in a manner to reduce disturbance. The room would be silent for long periods at a time – until somebody eventually let one rip, setting off a chain reaction of farts as everyone used the moment to rid themselves of pent-up intestinal gas. It seems that no yogi, whatever their level of enlightenment, is ever liberated from the embarrassment of breaking wind.

On Day Three, my meditation took a turn for the worse. So, after a hopeless sitting session – during which I could not, for the life of me, think of anything other than sex – I visited the library in pursuit of guidance. It was well stocked with books in German, English, Chinese, Myanmar, Pali (the language of Buddhist scripture) and other languages. I picked up *Four Elements Meditation and Mindfulness of Breathing* by the Venerable Pa-Auk Sayadaw, one of the monastery's head monks. It didn't recommend a technique for pacifying horny travellers, but it did detail one for refocusing a busy mind: inhale, exhale, "one"; inhale, exhale, "two" – up to eight, thereby reminding the meditator of the Noble Eightfold Path.

Eager to put this into practice, I closed the book – and gasped.

Stamped on the back cover in bold capitals was the message: **FOR NON-MUSLIM ONLY**.

I dropped the book in disgust. Was this for real? Pa-Auk was the last place I had expected to find hatred and discrimination. I felt physically sick, repulsed, disillusioned. Where was the compassionate Buddhism my aunts swore by and had centred their spiritual lives around? Had the West been wrong about Buddhism being a peaceful and accepting religion?

I reread the message to check my eyes weren't deceiving me, then flicked to the foreword:

> This is to ensure that the sponsors' intention –
> the promulgation of the Dhamma
> for the benefit of all living beings –
> is achieved without hindrance.
>
> Printed in Kuala Lumpur

*

Initially, it's hard to believe that Buddhist monks, whose religion is centred around compassion, can become disseminators of hatred. But when nationalism enters the fray, the two emotions can easily merge. In this sense, Islamophobic Myanmar monks are hardly different to populist right-wing politicians across the globe, though the reasons for their outspokenness lies in the evolution of their roles over time.

Under non-Buddhist British rule, monks lost their importance as state advisors and became marginalised by society. It wasn't until Ne Win made them an essential part of his "Burmanisation project" and sent many to the frontier states as missionaries that they regained public status.

The renewed authority encouraged some to become vocal on the "threat" of Islam; and as the number of global Islamic terrorist attacks rose around the turn of the millennium, so did the popularity of anti-Muslim monks. This in turn prompted the emergence of ultranationalist monk organisations – the most notorious of which was Ma Ba Tha, an abbreviation of the anti-colonial rallying cry of the 1920s and 1930s: *"Amyo, Batha, Thanatha"* ('Race, Religion, Teachings of the Buddha'). Ma Ba Tha received favourable treatment from the military government, who shared similar nationalistic visions, and successfully backed the "Protection of Race and Religion Laws". Among other discriminatory clauses, this bill regulated the marriage between Buddhist women and non-Buddhist men.

Ma Ba Tha's large following made political parties reluctant to condemn them; and as the 2015 elections approached, they encouraged voters to ask six questions of each candidate, including whether they were Buddhist and whether they might try to alter the law that had made the Rohingya stateless. They portrayed the NLD as Muslim sympathisers, a characterisation reinforced by the online circulation of fabricated photos of Aung San Suu Kyi in a hijab. Fearing repercussions from Ma Ba Tha and its legion of supporters, the NLD "rejected the candidacy of more than a dozen of its Muslim members, as did other parties."[16] In a twist that Westerners would consider ironic, but which many Myanmar wouldn't (for who said democracy should empower everyone and not just the ethnic majority?), Ma Ba Tha had made religious exclusion a necessary step towards democracy.

Ashin Wirathu, the head of Ma Ba Tha (who were declared an unlawful organisation in 2017 but remain popular), has been described as the "Burmese bin Laden" and once said that Buddhist women are better off marrying dogs than Muslims. Under mounting international pressure, the junta sentenced him to 25 years imprisonment in 2003 for distributing Islamophobic pamphlets, but he was released nine years later during an amnesty for political prisoners.

His anti-Muslim campaign has thrown Myanmar Buddhism into disrepute. Ashin Issariya, a prominent monk and fierce critic of Ma Ba Tha, accused Wirathu of "misleading the people" after he likened the suspected assassins of Muslim lawyer Ko Ni to "Buddhas-to-be."[17] Issariya has the support of the Minister for Religious Affairs and the State Sangha Maha Nayaka Committee, who regulate Myanmar's Buddhist clergy, but the ultranationalist monks have powerful allies.

---

[16] F. Wade (2017), *Myanmar's Enemy Within: Buddhist Violence and the Creating of a Muslim Other* (Kindle Edition), Zed Books, pos. 2429-2432.
[17] https://frontiermyanmar.net/en/as-preaching-ban-on-u-wirathu-ends-split-in-the-sangha-widens <Accessed: 13.09.2018>

Just a week after Issariya criticised Wirathu for misrepresenting Buddhism, Commander-in-Chief of the *Tatmadaw*, Senior General Min Aung Hlaing, said in an address at the Coastal Command Headquarters in Myeik that the duty of the *Tatmadaw* was not merely to defend the nation but to protect state sovereignty, religion, culture, traditions, and the lives and property of the people. He did not elaborate, but there's little doubt where his allegiances lie.

Chapter 8: Killing Karma

The intolerant meditation book put a slight downer on the rest of my week at Pa-Auk, though I did enjoy my remaining meditation sessions and to this day find time to practise; I also learnt how to meditate away hiccups. I expect Pa-Auk had worked better for me than techniques I had tried previously, for it had not centred on following every inhalation and exhalation. Instead of leading me to obsess about each breath – Is it hot or cold? How far up my nose can I feel it? How much do my nostrils flare? – practising mere mindfulness of breathing opened a secondary level of meditative clarity that worked in tandem with concentration on the Focus Point. At least, that's what I theorised.

Leaving Pa-Auk was difficult – I knew I would never find such tranquillity again – but I was eager to continue my southward travels, tracing the sliver of land that skirts the Andaman Sea and resembles a piece of string trailing down from central Myanmar, giving the country its kite shape.

To break up the slow minibus journeys, I first travelled to Ye, which I had been warned was a firm "nay". I stepped into the riverside guesthouse surrounded by litter and dusty teahouses and was immediately handed a scrap of paper titled "Presidency Note" by the owner.

> Ye is not safe. Foreigners are only permitted to stay one night.

"Why?" I asked. Neither of us had smiled nor said "hello" yet.

She twisted round and waddled towards a dusty map of Myanmar on the wall. I knew instantly what she was going to say. She traced an arcing line from northern Rakhine State, through the Indian Ocean and down to Ye. Rohingya fleeing by boat for Malaysia had been washing up on the nearby coast; dead or alive, she didn't say.

Besides the undertones of ethnic persecution, Ye turned out to be a charming small town. The narrow roads were lined with stalls all selling the same items, begging the question of how much they actually sold, mothers encouraged their *thanaka'd* toddlers to wave at the whitey and every resident was infected with the giggles. Kids used plastic bottles to mark out their football pitches; guys were keen to invite me for cups of *ye-nway-kyan*.

When I reached the suburbs, someone sat beneath a wooden balcony began clapping desperately and waving his arms at me. Clapping or pursing the lips and making a high-pitched smooching sound are the preferred ways of attracting attention in Myanmar, even in restaurants. The British piss around by tentatively putting their paws up and hoping someone sees, afraid of addressing them directly lest they cause offense. Once you're used to the overt techniques used in Myanmar, you realise how much more logical they are.

The guy was in his late twenties, had spikey hair and an enchanting grin. He had been jamming with his buddies, who wielded guitars, keyboards and bongo drums and were drinking Myanmar.

"There's a concert tomorrow at the KTV. Could you sing an English song?" he asked.

"I'm sorry, but I have to leave for Dawei tomorrow."

His shoulders slumped and his grin vanished, making me feel horribly guilty. The others looked over listlessly, embroiled in beer and cigarettes, hardly aware of the catastrophe that had unfolded.

My friend flumped into his chair and twiddled his thumbs while I stood round awkwardly. After an uncomfortable silence, he picked up his acoustic guitar and began half-heartedly strumming a familiar tune. A second guitarist joined in with a modest solo, followed by the bongos.

And suddenly the sounds fused.

Everyone grinned at each other. They were jamming: their heads were bobbing in mutual musical understanding and their faces were glowing. Enthusiasm filled the air.

The moment was coming.

Any second.

Any second now…

"On a dark desert highway, cool wind in my hair
Warm smell of colitas, rising up through the air
Up ahead in the distance, I saw a shimmering light
My head grew heavy and my sight grew dim
I had to stop for the night."

Everyone's eyes lit up. The atmosphere was relaxed yet uplifting; vibrant, joyful and true. The music was full and free and the real world was far away…

"Welcome to the Hotel California
Such a lovely place (such a lovely place)

Such a lovely face.
Plenty of room at the Hotel California
Any time of year (any time of year) you can find it here."

For the next few minutes all barriers were broken, blended and subsumed by music, the universal language of mankind (luckily for me, the medium of that universal language happened to be English). Then, after smiles and handshakes, I continued on my way: a quirky episode of connection – exactly why I travel.

My feet took me to Ye's central pagoda, which sat on a lake. At sunset, children came to feed red-eyed rabbits and guinea pigs housed in cages on the pagoda platform while adults scattered breadcrumbs into the lurid water for greedy carp – benevolence sure to earn them favourable karma.

I hung around, watching couples, families, the elderly, and the lonely flock to the lakeside. They sat on benches or on the grass, drinking, eating, and chucking their rubbish into the water. As the carp gobbled up the bread, they also swallowed bits of plastic. Then they floated to the surface, dead, having tackled one indigestible morsel too many. It was visible proof of the harm of plastic – hardly a social concern yet in Myanmar – and an opportunity to observe complete apathy at play. The worshippers gave life with one hand and took it with the other. They cannot have missed the hypocrisy: it was sheer negligence. I hope for their sakes that they don't become Ye carp in their next lives.

As the sun set a deep scarlet and the pagoda switched on its furious LEDs, I retreated to a park bench. A pretty girl my age, endowed with inquisitive eyes and cherry lips, kept catching my glance as she tore up tissues and let the pieces drift down into the water.

The bond was instant, and after a few giggly minutes she asked to sit beside me. She wore a red lace *ingyi* and an elegant black *longyi*; her skin was honey gold.

"Your name?"

"James. Yours?"

"Htet."

From there our conversation blossomed into an adorable flirt of broken English and suspect Myanmar. We talked about the future, our friends and past loves, and established that she found the flashing pagoda lights *hla-de* whereas I found them repulsive. We took each other's hands and let the warmth flow through, knowing we would never meet again and that nothing could happen between us anyway – our lives were simply too different. It was cute and transient, directionless and authentic, all staged beneath a sunset sky of Myanmar fairy tales.

She texted me the next day to say she loved me.

*

Though disappointed to have stayed only one day in the surprisingly pleasant Ye, I was eager to reach Dawei. The stories of its pristine empty beaches had the romantic, secretive air of rumours and had enticed me from afar. They seemed too good to be true (if the beaches were so beautiful, why were they empty?), but I had been assured that Dawei's coastline was every bit as breath-taking as the stories were fantastical.

Unsure where to buy my ticket at Ye train station, a slim *a-myo-thar* pointed me towards an office of patchy walls and cobwebs, headed by an obese chap.

"Hello," he stated. "Dawei?"

"Yes please."

He wrote out my ticket with care, his chubby cheeks wobbling in concentration.

"Dawei is very nice. You should go to Po Po Kyauk beach. It is the best."

"Thank you. I'll remember that."

"Beach is good place to be," he continued. "Lots of trouble in Myanmar at the moment. You know?"

I said I did in Myanmar.

"Aww, Myanmar sagar pyaw-dat-da-lar?" ('Aww, you can speak Myanmar?') he said with an enormous smile. *"Kalar-twe-ga pya-tha-nar loke-ne-de."* ('The *kalars* are creating problems.')

"Rohingya-lar?"

"Ma-hoke-bu. Rohingya ma-shi-bu. Bengali ma-shi-bu. There are no Rohingya," he repeated in English. "There are no Bengalis."

"Oh."

"There are only Muslims. No differences between."

Try telling that to Shias and Sunnis.

"They are illegal immigrants," he continued. "And they cause terrorist attacks."

Despite ample evidence to prove their indigenousness, including the logs of historians and colonial scholars, the Rohingya were made stateless by the 1982 Citizenship Law. Although a census conducted in 1973 by Ne Win's government counted 144 native ethnicities, the number used for the Citizenship Law was 135 – the count of the 1931 census. Among the removed labels were "Chittagonian Muslim" and "Rakhine Muslim", names under which the Rohingya had likely been categorised by the British in 1931.

Why the number of recognised ethnic minorities was dropped is unclear. It was likely because 135 was the first recorded number and therefore deemed to represent a "pure", pre-colonial Myanmar. It may also have been because the individual digits of 135 add up to nine, Ne Win's lucky number.

"Only a few Muslims are terrorists," I said.

He shifted his plastic chair. "Not all Muslims are terrorists, but all of Al-Qaeda are terrorists."

Silence followed. The tautology had stumped me.

"I like your *longyi*."

"I'm sorry?"

"Your *longyi*," he repeated with a broad smile. "I like that you are wearing a *longyi*."

"Oh right. Thanks."

I took my ticket and left.

The train arrived 30 minutes later. The upper-class seat was cushioned and comfortable, but little did I know that dense vegetation would obscure nice views for the entire journey. I later discovered that the Ye-Dawei train was the slowest in Myanmar. It was also the dullest. I should have taken the bus.

A quarter of an hour into the journey, a Mon local boarded and perched on the arm rest of the seat beside mine. He was about 30-years-old, had betel teeth and kept slipping onto the floor in a slapstick manner. I smelt whisky on him. He pulled out a notebook containing handwritten English phrases and began asking me the usual, leaning over the well-to-do man sat between us.

"How are you? Where are you from?"

"The UK," I said. "The United Kingdom."

He flicked through his book for a good minute, visibly confused.

"Where are you from?" he asked again.

"Myanmar-lo dat-de" ('He speaks Myanmar'), breathed the man between us.

"Hoke-lar?" spluttered Mr Betel. He produced a small book in Pali from his left jeans pocket and began reciting what I immediately recognised from Pa-Auk Tawya as Buddhist prayers.

I laughed and asked to read them. He was over the moon that I could.

"Anyone who speak Pali is good," he declared in laboured English. "Muslim no speak Pali. That why they bad."

Did that mean most of the world was made up of bad people? Would his opinion of me change if I revealed that I had no idea what the Pali actually meant? I decided not to find out.

"They're all alright," I mumbled.

"You like Muslims?"

His stare was intense, fed by disbelief. All eyes in the carriage were on me. The atmosphere turned sour and weighty. Suddenly I felt very foreign, an outsider.

I didn't answer, and the topic was dropped. Mr Betel displayed his best smile and handed me the book of Pali prayers as a gift, along with two oranges – once again reminding me of how lucky I was to have white skin. He alighted at the next station.

I arrived in Dawei on the full moon of Tazaungmon, the Festival of Lights. Nearly every building was draped in colourful fairy lights, residents lit elegant paper lanterns and released them into the evening sky, and a float of dancing women and transvestites paraded through town, accompanied by ear-splitting music and Bacchic followers.

In Taunggyi, the Festival of Lights is celebrated with a hot-air balloon competition, a tradition begun by the British in 1894. The balloons are filled with fireworks and launched into the sky, where they implode almost immediately. Fireworks then rain down on the crowd in a display closely resembling an artillery strike; those in the firing line flee for safety, barging fellow celebrators out the way in their desperate scrabble for shelter. Injuries are common, but the festival draws large crowds every year.

Festivals and their dramatic entertainments, collectively known as *pwes*, are integral to Myanmar culture; you can hardly claim to have "experienced" Myanmar until you've attended one. They were especially treasured during the decades of military rule, when there was little else to celebrate.

Most *pwes* are held on the full moon and honour the infamous *nats*, tutelary spirits that play meaningful roles in both the private and public lives of many Myanmar. *Nats* occupy an ontological plain above that of humans, making them both happier and freer, yet their distance from the incorporeal felicity of nirvana means they are still subject to carnal desires – many even have human wives (*nat-ka-*

daws). These *nat-ka-daws* serve as spirit mediums at *nat pwes* and are often male transvestites or homosexuals – presumably since *nats* have morals and desires contrary to mainstream Buddhism, though some Myanmar say it is because transvestites and homosexuals are "weaker" and therefore easier to possess. When possessed by a *nat*, a *nat-ka-daw* may have to dance and binge drink to satisfy their depraved husband.

Although *nat* worship predates Buddhism in Myanmar, the *nats* were syncretised with the Buddhist devas – sentient beings that live longer, fuller lives than humans – in the 11th century as part of King Anawratha's campaign to make Theravada Buddhism the national faith. He also destroyed *nat* shrines, formalised the number of Great *Nats* to 37 and restricted the indigenous worship to the village of Taungbyone. This he did by fatally castrating the Shwe Hpyin brothers, celebrated generals, on the pretext that each had neglected to contribute a brick to a pagoda under construction there. [18] Their status as decorated heroes, combined with their particularly gruesome deaths, qualified them for the *nat* pantheon and led to the foundation of the annual *nat pwe* in Taungbyone, which remains the country's most important animistic festival.

The *nats* are notoriously devious and the best that worshippers can expect from them is indifference. Typically, people pray for good luck in exams, wish for riches or a peaceful life, though specific requests may also

---

[18] Travel writer Norman Lewis also offers a historical explanation for this execution. See N. Lewis (2011), pos. 1400-1414.

be directed towards certain *nats*. Curiously, the ball-less Shwe Hypin brothers are thought to patronise lovers.

A *nat-sin* ('spirit house') often occupies a space beside Buddha in temples, houses and even corporate offices. The custom of honouring a residence's guardian *nat* by hanging an unhusked coconut wrapped in a *gaung baung*, a traditional headdress, on the building's main southeast post continues today. Nearly every Myanmar village has a *nat* shrine, and beside the traditional offering of a green coconut placed between three bunches of green bananas you may see cans of Red Bull or Shark.

Before heading to the acclaimed Dawei peninsula beaches, I signed on for a snorkelling trip to the Moscos Islands, an exquisite island chain in the Andaman Sea, with the hope of freelancing an article. Our guide, Win Tun, was a tall and charismatic Bamar who had worked on the Thai island of Koh Tao for five years, first in an Australian bar and then in a British bar. He had not been impressed by the Brits abroad.

We were a group of ten – the French dominated, as always in Myanmar – but I managed to befriend a Korean-Myanmar couple. The sea was sparkling, the sun blistering and the sticky rice breakfast delicious. Enormous eagles circled above the jungled interior of Auk Bok island, seducing us into forming conspiracies about what creatures lived there; its *shwe* shore glistened with polystyrene and plastic jellyfish slipped beneath the vessel's hull.

Fortunately, the pollution did not encroach on the shallows where we were snorkelling, though the coral was dead anyway. There was one Myanmar couple on the trip:

a timid, attractive *a-myo-thami* with her vain, rich *chit-thu*. He came equipped with two DSLR cameras, four lenses, a drone and a specialised full-face snorkel. He attached the 200mm lens and handed over the camera to his girlfriend, who was to take pictures of him relaxing on the beach.

Keen to snap article photos, I undertook the hazardous task of wrapping my camera in a plastic bag and swimming to shore, three-limbed. But it was worth the effort: the image of the red wooden boat bobbing on the sapphire waves was idyllic. A tree of otherworldly contortions sprawled into the sea like a giant squid snatching at a ship, entrancing and impossible to capture, while a static stream of litter and broken calamari nets stretched across the shore, proving that human activity could even taint the uninhabited. The Myanmar boyfriend swaggered across the sand, occasionally posing or splaying himself on the ground in positions that he presumably considered erotic.

"Apparently the next beach is the really nice one," said an Australian UN lady to me, watching the wannabe model don his lifejacket.

"I was wondering."

I took a few more photos, strolled to the end of the beach, then began swimming back to the boat. As I drew near, someone started shouting. I reached the ladder and heard a loud slap followed by a splash. Climbing up, I found just the *a-myo-thami* on board, her right cheek pink. She noticed me, and we silently locked gazes for a few seconds.

"Asin-pyi-lar?" ('Are you okay?')

"Asin-pyi-par-de," she answered, though her red and bleary eyes suggested otherwise.

A tragic moment of understanding followed, in which she acknowledged my empathy and recognised my powerlessness. Once again, I wished I were not a foreigner but a local, so that I could intervene without merely intruding; her despair willed the same. Unfortunately, it would probably have made little difference, for in Myanmar perceptions are largely shaped by emotions rather than reason, which makes it extremely difficult for objective analysis to enter personal situations: her boyfriend would likely have taken any comments I made on domestic abuse as personal insults.

We cast our eyes around for about 30 seconds – examining the suddenly fascinating breakfast leftovers, the nails holding the wooden panels in place, and our own toes – until the rising drone of a motor distracted us. A wooden boat steered by a fisherman and headed by a navy officer was speeding towards us.

They pulled up beside the boat and talked to Win Tun in concerned whispers. He shook his head and the boat moved on, skirting the coastline.

"What was that about?" I asked.

"They lost one of their crewmembers last night and wanted to know if we had seen him."

"Oh no."

"Yeah."

Win Tun and I nodded in silence for a few moments.

"Alright then, governor. Ready for some nosh?"

"Err, sure."

"You're a good geeza," he said, his accent jarringly perfect.

The snorkelers returned and we left for the next beach, where the coral was allegedly flourishing. An ominous metallic ship loomed in the distance, having seemingly appeared from nowhere. Everyone stared at it, as though it were the Black Pearl, and asked each other why it was following us. Soon it was close enough for us to identify military personnel in navy uniforms stood at the railings, spying us out. They caught up and cast a rope onto our boat, which our guide used to secure our vessel to theirs. Then he was pulled onto deck and led out of sight.

"What is the officer doing?"

"Looking for bribes."

"There's a naval base on the Moscos Islands."

The Frenchies fell silent. Everyone looked round, confused. Only the arrogant boyfriend appeared unperturbed.

Suddenly there was a clanking of boots, followed by rushed Myanmar mutterings. Then a beefy Bamar clad in a white PTT Lubricants T-Shirt and a navy *longyi* jumped onto our deck.

"I am the commanding officer of this military ship," he declared. "This is a restricted area. You are not allowed to be here. Do you understand?"

No one answered.

"Do not post about this on social media and do not upload photos. Do you understand?"

Again, silence.

"Give us your cameras."

A handsome young officer appeared and began collecting people's cameras, dangling them precariously from their straps. As I watched the Nikons and Canons bump against each other, I remembered that the photo of the meditation book **FOR NON-MUSLIM ONLY** was still on my SD card. Somehow, I doubted the navy would be sympathetic to my intentions of sending it to a newspaper.

I wondered whether to go back through my pictures and delete it, but eventually decided that if the officer confiscated my camera while doing so I would be doomed. So I prayed to Lady Luck instead and watched as other people's cameras were collected.

Gradually, the deleting began. But it was comical – apparently the navy had not been instructed on the operation of cameras – and soon the officers were asking each other for help, comparing camera screens and pressing buttons randomly.

"Actually," said the commanding officer, seeing the farce unfold, "delete photos of the islands yourselves and we'll check after."

The cameras were returned – but my camera still hadn't been seen, even though my huge Nikon bag was sat beside me.

Should I delete the photos? I wondered. Without them I wouldn't be able to write my article. I stroked my camera bag... then stroked it again.

And contrary to my usual self, I made the sensible decision.

"Deleted?" asked the young officer. I nodded and showed him. He slid away, as did the commanding officer, then we were permitted to leave. Win Tun went into the cockpit. The engine spluttered – and died. He tried again, and again, but without success. The cook went to join him as our boat drifted back towards the forbidden island. The navy officers gathered on the rear ship balcony and pulled out their phones to take pictures. How humiliating.

About ten minutes later, the engine choked to life and we were underway.

"He asked for your passports," said Win Tun, handing out cans of beer, "but I said you left them at the hotel."

"Good thinking," said the French solar engineer amid laughs and compliments. "Did he ask for money?"

"No, but it might have changed things." He shook his head. "I'm sorry, we've been doing this trip for two years and have never had any problems. I think because of the fighting in Rakhine State they are on extra security."

"Did anyone keep their photos?" drawled the boyfriend. "I switched the SD cards when I saw the boat."

"Good thinking," said the engineer again.

"I know how things in this country work," he boasted, pulling a patronising grin.

I glanced at his girlfriend. She was staring at the floor, tears in her eyes.

Chapter 9: Empty Beaches

For my trip down the Dawei peninsula, I was joined by two friends living in Yangon: Ben, a dreadlocked illustrator who feared looking like a stereotypical artist, and Thea, his more composed girlfriend and a budding photographer.

We hired Hondas from Dawei and left our heavy belongings at the guesthouse. It was the first time I had driven since my crash, and I knew there were tricky beach roads ahead, so I took it easy. Fortunately, it was a pleasing ride past blankets of brain-like chopped areca nut spread on the roadside, rubber trees trickling milky white sap into coconut cups, and jagged hill lines sprouting pagodas. Soon I had regained my confidence and was enjoying the drive.

"This is it," said Thea, when we finally reached the turn-off for the beach.

"Apparently the road's dodgy," I said.

"Alright, you go first then," said Ben.

I grumbled and set off, switching between third and fourth as I weaved round bends flanked by towering grass. A Thai guy and a topless European whizzed by, oozing the confidence that comes with experience and making me feel small.

I steered round some potholes and scaled a couple of steep hills no problem. But then the *lan* degenerated into treacherous downhill tracks of loose sediment and jagged rocks; even at a slow speed my wheels slipped. The *lan* was wide, but for our bikes there was only ever a narrow strip of hardened dirt amid clusters of razor rocks.

It was grim going, compounded by the dust and heat, and after the dirt hills came jungle. This section was steeper, but parts of the path were paved. Soon we came to a long, opaque puddle.

Knowing hesitation would only make me more nervous, I hit the throttle. Water flew up all around, the bike bounced and my bones rattled. But then I was through – as were Ben and Thea a moment later, shaken and soaked.

It turned out we had done the hard part, and within ten minutes we were gliding along a smooth red mud track, through a hamlet of wooden houses and kids goading on rubber tyres with sticks – the rural Myanmar equivalent of Hoop Rolling. At the end was a steep concrete path that led down into the mangroves.

"I'm not taking my bike down there," said Ben.

"Na, I think we walk here."

I had been hoping to roar "We've made it!" as soon as I stepped onto the sand. But there was no sand: the mangroves were flooded. A daunting, watery maze beckoned.

"Is this really the way?" asked Thea.

"There's an arrow over there," said Ben, pointing to a nearby sign directing us through a narrow channel of mangrove trees.

We put on our swimming stuff, tightened the straps of our small rucksacks and put our backpacks on our heads. Then the wade began – initially only reaching up to our knees, but gradually making its way up to our midriffs.

It was arduous, and I regretted not leaving more clothes in Dawei. At first, we were excited – "it's all part of the adventure" – but after fifteen minutes tiredness took hold. And as the little ribbons indicating the way became harder and harder to spot, conversation steadily fizzled out.

"I hope there aren't any saltwater crocodiles."

We froze and stared at each other. Then Ben began lifting his legs right out of the water in an absurd march and stormed ahead. My eyes darted around for any signs of large, ravenous reptiles. Thea splashed along behind me.

We struggled forwards, rounded the next corner, then another – and were finally blessed with the wonderful sight of a sandy outback of straggly shrubs and clumpy grass. Five minutes later, we arrived at Sinhtauk Beach, a sublime one-mile shoreline enclosed within a cosy cove of verdant hills. Crashing waves interrupted the reigning silence, imbuing the scene with a powerful, raw beauty. White sand recorded our every step with a joyous squeak and a pair of empty wooden swings looked out over the Andaman sea, watching the tired ruby sun dip below the horizon and set exactly in the centre of the cove.

All the effort, pain and fear of the past hour was instantly forgotten. Then, exhausted beyond words, we sat down in the beachfront eat-drink-shop – where we learnt that there were no saltwater crocodiles in the region and that we could have taken a boat across the mangrove swamp. Famished, we each ordered a Thai dish and revelled in the coconutty goodness.

It took me a year to confess that the Yangon expats were right and that Myanmar cuisine was, for the most part, disappointing. Some of the minority ethnic food – particularly Kachin, Kayah and Shan – is tasty, but in Myanmar oily dishes predominate. These include *hsi chet, hsi tamin* and *hsi hkaut-hswe* ('oil chicken', 'oil rice' and 'oil noodles'). You get what you order.

Nevertheless, food is a favourite conversation topic, presumably for reasons similar to why *sar-pi-pi-lar* is the traditional greeting. There are dishes I love – such as marlar curry, ginger salad and banana leaf dumplings – but the only major plus of Myanmar food culture is that the eating of raw garlic is socially acceptable.

After a day of relaxation, we drove south to Grandfather Beach. It was a serene ride down the peninsula, gliding along smooth roads that skirted hillsides overlooking the sapphire sea, seeing snapshots of local lives: fishermen pushing their boats out; three smiling teenagers squeezing onto a single motorbike; a mother feeding rice to her baby.

We eventually arrived at Nyau Pyin, the fishing village located before Grandfather Beach. School children smothered in *thanaka* ran out and shouted *"Mingalabar!"* as we passed, rolled their rubber tyres along the dusty, stony streets, or giggled and pointed delighted fingers. Beyond the wooden homes, women spread mats of anchovies and shrimps on the golden beach to dry while wooden fishing boats flying colourful flags bobbed with the waves.

Grandfather Beach was just a short drive away. We began the ascent, prepared for enormous stones, tiny tracks and terror. But it wasn't so bad, and soon we were descending the final slope that led to the beach's southern side.

"Fuck me," said Ben.

He couldn't have put it better. Before us stretched a sweeping, *shwe* shore enclosed at the far end by a dazzling blue lagoon. The sea sparkled on the left and the right was flanked by low, jungled hills. Not a soul was in sight.

It was a similar story at Paradise Beach, which I relocated to after Ben and Thea returned to Yangon. In addition to its picturesque cove and palm trees, Paradise was strewn with fabulous seashells of all shapes and sizes, including spirals, conches and cowries. I resolved to bring the prettiest back for Shwe Ei, who had been hoping to join us, but Murphy's Law had determined that every single beautiful shell should be inhabited by a hermit crab – and I thought that forcing a creature from its home would not be very Buddhist – so I was forced to settle for an inferior, empty one.

The most seductive story I had heard about Paradise was of phosphorescent plankton that appeared at night. So that evening I waded in past the waves and gazed down into the water. At first, I saw nothing. So I started moving on to try somewhere else – when there: a faint flash.

I swished my hand beneath the surface and a series of yellow sparkles followed it. I swished again, this time seeing the shapes of small crustaceans glowing underwater. They looked too large to be plankton: perhaps they were shrimps.

I thrashed my limbs and the water around me lit up like stars beneath the sea. I felt, as one German had described it, like a "magician", and it was some time before I finally dragged myself out the water and into bed.

Eager to make the most of my final day, I awoke early the next morning and headed for Myat Shin Maw, the pagoda at the peninsula's southern tip. Again, it was a hillside cruise there, graced by spectacular views of the vast Andaman Sea. Before the entrance stood a handful of women and children holding silver bowls containing money and stones – donation bowls, only Myanmar currency doesn't include coins, so they use rocks to make the rattling sound. A desk stood by the roadside, Buddhist flags flapped in the breeze and loudspeakers pumped out the tune of a woman whining as chimpanzees blew shrill pipes and elephants beat kittens with cymbals. Suffice it to say, it's understandable that Myanmar's younger generations are not particularly fond of their country's traditional music.

"Hello," said a leathery-faced local with a broken nose and friendly aura. "You're from?"

"England."

"You like our country?"

"Yes, very lovely. Especially this part."

He gave me a betel grin.

"You have been to Po Po Kyauk?"

"Grandfather Beach? Yes, I have."

"Aww, good, good," he said, nodding. He took a pack of betel from his shirt pocket, stuffed a leaf in his mouth and offered me one.

"No, thank you."

"You don't like?"

"No, and I'm not sure it's good for the teeth."

"It is good!" he exclaimed, spewing a river of red. "Without tobacco, it leaves mouth fresh and makes teeth not hurt."

I could believe the drug functioned as a pain killer, and betel was somewhat redolent of menthol, but I did not believe this made it "good" for your teeth.

"If you say so," I replied, listing it as another example of how the Myanmar sometimes did the opposite of Europeans but for the same reasons. The epitome of this was using water instead of toilet paper. Certainly, water cleaned your anus more thoroughly, I had confessed to a friend earlier that year, but it came with the compromise of using your fingers to do the wiping.

After a gentle stroll round the pagoda, I stopped by Myin Kwa Aw beach, also *hla-de* and empty, before coming to another fishing village. Here, a couple of cute kids played Hide and Seek behind stacked calamari nets, giggling every time I caught their eye. Shapely blue and black wooden boats edged with red graced a peaceful, azure lagoon – a stark contrast to the opposing mess of litter-strewn sand paths that connected rows of untidy stilted huts.

"Myauk! Myauk!" barked a lady, pointing to a hut on my left.

I glanced underneath – and a macaque perched on a blue wooden plank bared its teeth at me.

I jumped back, and the lady laughed. Then I asked her about reaching a nearby beach accessed via a jungle path. I was in luck: three women were heading that way shortly.

I waited for them by the areca palms, between which a narrow trail led into the jungle. After several incomprehensible exchanges with other villagers, they waved for me to join, evidently embarrassed to be accompanied by somebody so sunburnt. I turned out be a quicker walker than them and soon succeeded in getting lost. But GPS came to the rescue, allowing me to navigate myself onto a picturesque micro-beach. I later learnt its name was Dream Beach – appropriate, I thought. Again, it was empty.

And why was it empty? Why were these pristine beaches not flooded with tourists? No other travellers seemed to be asking this question, but I refused to believe it was simply because the area was off the beaten track.

Part of the reason, I later learnt, was that the region had been closed to tourists until 2013, at which time it was only reachable by plane; but mostly it was due to outdated legislation, complicated bureaucracy and corruption. Over the past few years, the building of several resorts had been aborted because of petty permit problems. This included an eco-resort at Myin Kwa Aw beach and the luxury Mandolis Resort at Tizit beach, which was set to open in October 2016 but has been delayed by over two years because the owners are still waiting on the essential recommendation letter from the Chief Minister of Tanintharyi. When I visited in 2017, only Sinhtauk Beach Bungalows and Paradise Beach Bungalows were licensed to accommodate foreigners; and just a week after I left, Sinhtauk was temporarily shut down by the authorities.

The procedure for gaining planning permission involves upgrading the beaches from "garden land" to "commercial land", which can sell at $44,000 per acre. A local tour operator told me this had led to widespread corruption, especially since the local government spurned foreign involvement (most of the interested investors were European).

The beaches of the Dawei peninsula harbour millions of dollars of untapped tourist potential, yet a survey conducted by the UN in 2015 found the coastal regions to be the poorest in Myanmar. Learning this put a bitter edge on my travels in Dawei, which were otherwise the most blissful of my entire journey. Once again, I was reminded that a traveller's paradise can be a local's suffering: the empty beaches were great for me, but they came at the economic expense of the peninsula residents. Although it isn't what a traveller would typically say, I hope the area will become more touristy.

I ended my final day in Dawei with a sunset visit to Nyau Pyin fishing village, which had become a hive of activity and euphoria abounding with opportunities for cultural insight. When I arrived, children were flocking around a beached boat while its crew handed out bags of coconut sticky rice and sticks of sugar cane.

The fishermen invited me on deck and helped me clamber up. The crew numbered about a dozen; all were men and several wore football shirts. They were hauling up the net, which took up most of the floor space. We were roughly fifteen feet up. Behind us, colourful fishing vessels danced on the waves and distant promontories faded with the setting sun, shrinking into the dusk.

"Eat! Eat!" said a chubby-cheeked teenager, thrusting a bowl of coconut sticky rice into my hands.

I did eat. It was delicious. Then a young Messi fan handed me a stick of sugar cane.

"I just bite it?"

He nodded. It was tough – I thought I might crack my teeth – but eventually I broke into it and sweet juice seeped into my mouth. I saw no elderly people eating sugar cane: presumably their teeth had been eroded by the excessive consumption of it as a child.

"Why are you handing this out?"

"It is for good luck," said Messi.

"For the next fishing trip?"

"For the boat spirit. It is traditional." He smiled. "We sometimes give out cigars or betel, because the boat spirit also likes them."

I did not doubt it.

"Photo," said Messi, making a camera with his hands.

I nodded and photographed them hauling up the net. But they wanted a picture of me working with them. I feared I would look ridiculous. My fears were not unfounded.

I thanked them and took the camera back. Then, just as the first stars were appearing, I gazed once more over the twilit beach. The low tide had turned the wet sand into a shimmering astral mirror, upon which children played football, shrieking and shouting happily. Women were traipsing back to their homes, the day's business over, and gentle music was emanating from the village centre.

Sated, I returned to Paradise Beach and crawled into my tent, where I slept like a baby.

Chapter 10: The Golden Land

KYAIKTIYO / ကျိုက်ထီးရိုး

Having visited the area of Myanmar that most attracted me, I set off for a destination which receives mixed reviews from travellers: Kyaiktiyo (AKA "Golden Rock"), an important Buddhist pilgrimage site. Although my most trusted friends had warned me that Kyaiktiyo had been "Disneyfied", I had decided to go anyway, having reasoned that I wouldn't get a proper understanding of Myanmar if I only visited the destinations that most appealed to me.

The first leg of my journey there, a northbound bus from Dawei to the colonial port city of Mawlamyine, proved eventful. Dirty and uncomfortable, it broke down after ten minutes, which led to a protracted repair process that involved the driver and conductor jumping up and down on an enormous metal bar attached to the left rear wheel. To keep us entertained for the next two hours, they turned on a TV at the front and played a melodramatic Myanmar film whose crude plotline could have been understood without any knowledge of Myanmar language or culture.

A lady had fallen in love with a guy whose best friend was gay. (He wore tight pink clothes and one scene was a montage of him rubbing up against large mossy rocks: front and back, then shake it all around!) The lady assumed her beloved was straight but kept walking in on scenes which suggested otherwise – like him lying on top of his friend, clothed in just a towel. What a catastrophe: was he straight or not?!

Fortunately, these seemingly compromising scenes were merely the results of slapstick clumsiness, such as tripping over door frames. It turned out he wasn't gay. Crisis averted.

The bus passengers loved the film, particularly the mossy montage. Myanmar holds conservative views concerning LGBT rights and same-sex sexual activity is even punishable with life imprisonment, though Section 377 of the penal code has not been enforced in years. Although LGBT residents still face discrimination, attitudes are slowly changing: Yangon nightclubs run FAB events regularly, which are popular among LGBT and non-LGBT clubbers alike; the Yangon LGBT Choir was established recently; and 2018 saw the fourth instalment of the &PROUD film festival.

Following a brief night's sleep in a cheap Mawlamyine guesthouse on the riverside, I departed for Kyaiktiyo. Boarding the same bus was an elderly Australian Buddhist monk. He forewent the front seat reserved for Buddhist clergy and sat beside me to envelop me in his putrid breath.

"Are you going to Yangon?" he rasped.

"No, to Golden Rock."

"I'm going to Yangon. I need to catch a flight tonight."

"You should be fine," I said, sensing he wanted reassurance. "This bus will take around six hours."

He nodded, and for the next couple of minutes we said nothing, listening to the regular hooting of horns, the screeching of wheels and the crunching of sunflower seeds, Myanmar's favourite snack.

"Were you at Pa-Auk?" I asked.

"No," he croaked, "but I have been there before."

"I liked it," I said, "though I'm not sure how I feel about living there and having everything paid for you."

"Yes, but the monks give something back spiritually," he said. "They are supposed to be focused and always working towards enlightenment."

"Even when they aren't meditating?"

"Yes," he said. "In fact, if someone comes to the monastery in need of help – say a girl that has just been raped – the monks should technically call a layperson to help her, so that they do not shift their concentration."

"Is that not... selfish?"

The monk gave a knowing nod. Presumably he had been asked this question many times.

"From a Western perspective, it's selfish. From a Buddhist perspective, it isn't: the monk will return his spiritual enlightenment to the community later in life."

"I see."

Again, we paused. I turned to the window and watched forested hills slide by, motorbikes piled with boxes of sweets overtake us, and families sitting outside their shops, suffocating in the dust kicked up by the wheels of trucks.

"So what were you doing in Mawlamyine?" I asked.

The monk adjusted the crimson robes slung over his shoulder.

"I was visiting a monastery I stayed at twenty years ago. I was looking for some monks I met there once." He paused. "I have a project: I've set up an NGO and was wanting their advice."

"Okay."

"Do you know the girls that ISIS use as sex slaves?"

"Umm, no."

"ISIS keep sex slaves, then cast them off or kill them once finished with them," he said. "Mainly they are Yazidis. Do you know the Yazidis?"

"I don't."

"They live in Iraq. ISIS butchered them a few years ago because they follow a different religion. They killed the men and used the girls as sex slaves. It's not the first time such a thing has happened."

"That's horrible."

"Yes," he whispered. "The girls who survive are obviously traumatised, poor things. Germany and Australia used to accept them as women at risk, not as refugees."

"What's the difference?"

"Women at risk can get full visas and become permanent citizens. It's better."

"Right."

"But recently the governments have stopped accepting them. I don't know why." He shuffled about in his seat. "Some girls still get accepted by other means, but there are over 2,000 of these Yazidi girls and there isn't much they can do if they get cast off and have no family left."

"So what does your NGO do?"

"Well, I want to find out whether the Australian government will accept them again."

"Have you secured funding?"

"I haven't started yet. That's actually why I'm here." He blew his nose. "When I came to the monastery here twenty years ago, some of the monks were clairvoyants. They were obviously clairvoyants: you could just tell," he rasped, nodding and flapping his hands as if to indicate he was needlessly repeating common knowledge. "You see, I don't want to start crowdfunding unless I know my efforts will be successful. I don't want to waste my time, you know?"

I said nothing.

"So I've been to Tibet, where... well. The monks are different there. Buddhism is meant to be about compassion. I didn't see much of that. So I came here, hoping to find the clairvoyant monks."

"And did you?"

"I didn't meet the same monks, but I think some of the new monks may be clairvoyants. However, it's hard to tell because monks are not allowed to reveal their clairvoyance." He coughed and blew his nose again. "And now I'm off to China, where I've met clairvoyant monks before."

This was a definite low point of my trip, and for the rest of the ride I prayed that he would meet a monk who "saw" his project succeeding. However, for better or worse, I did not find out the name of his NGO, so cannot check whether he began crowdfunding.

The bus dropped me at a junction a few kilometres shy of Kyaiktiyo, forcing me to hitch a lift for the remainder of the journey. The driver of the pick-up was a slim, dark-skinned Bamar with caterpillar eyebrows and tight lips. He was oddly loquacious.

"We have big problems in Rakhine State," he said. "Have you heard?"

"With the Rohingya?"

"No!" he spat. "There are no Rohingya, only Bengalis. And they need to be dealt with because they are in contact with IS."

"But the *Tatmadaw* is also driving out civilians."

"That's not true."

"No?"

"No, the *Tatmadaw* are doing a good job. They are just getting the terrorists. If a few civilians get killed, that does not matter."

He wasn't the only one to have changed his mind about the *Tatmadaw* in recent weeks. In October 2017, thousands gathered outside Yangon's city hall to show their support for the military operations in Rakhine State, demanding that then-president U Htin Kyaw condemn international pressure on the Myanmar army. And for the past few weeks, my Facebook feed had been full of praise for the *Tatmadaw* Commander-in-Chief as people wished for the swift expulsion, or even extermination, of every "Bengali."

For most Myanmar, it is simply fact that the Rohingya are "illegal immigrants", since state-run media has preached this for decades, and Westerners who challenge this viewpoint are usually accused of bias. I had raised the question of indigenousness over social media one time and been denigrated for weeks on end.

And so, knowing I would not be able to change this driver's mind about the Rohingya *per se*, I tried a different approach, hoping to highlight the potential dangers of the military's ethnic cleansing campaign.

"But what about IS?" I said. "If the *Tatmadaw* kills Muslim civilians, even accidentally, surely it will make IS angry? Maybe they will even attack Yangon."

"The Bengalis are a big problem," he contested. "They are carrying out terrorist attacks in Rakhine State."

"But what is more of a problem: them or IS?" There was a moment of silence. "If IS get angry and want to cause real harm, where will they attack? Shwedagon? Kyaiktiyo?" Again, he said nothing. "The situation now is bad, but perhaps it could be worse."

He nodded gently. "Yes, but the Bengalis are illegal immigrants. They have no right in our country."

"Even if they are illegal, is that the biggest problem? Are IS not a bigger problem?"

He didn't respond, and the conversation evaporated. I took his silence as a good sign, though I felt my argument had somewhat pandered to the perception of Islam as a "threat". At least I had got him thinking, which was about as good as I could have hoped for.

"Have a great day," he said with a big smile, as I got out and slung my heavy backpack over my shoulders. "Kyaiktiyo is very beautiful."

*

Kinpun, the village at the foot of Mt. Kyaiktiyo, had been defiled by tourism. The centre was divided into a grid of soulless restaurants, tacky souvenir stalls and barren mud patches home to the occasional scrappy tree; waiters hounded passers-by and litter luxuriated in the narrow stream. Except for one eat-drink-shop owner, no one cared that I spoke some Myanmar. Everyone lusted after my money.

"You have to embrace the tackiness," a Brit staying at the same guesthouse told me as I checked into my filthy room and dumped my stuff on the suspect mattress. "But don't stay more than a night."

"How long have you been here?"

"One night. I leave today."

His advice was on the money. I immediately shortened my stay, and soon found immense satisfaction in the primary local product: toy bamboo guns with "USA" stamped on them. They were actually pretty neat – a metal rod wound round to catch a jagged wooden wheel and produce terrific gunshot sounds – but it was the semblance of violence at a pilgrimage site that entertained me most. I bought one for a British friend in Yangon, who shares a similar passion for the absurd and incongruous.

Setting out early the next morning, I learnt that the Buddhist pilgrims were carted up to the Golden Rock in cramped buses like pigs for slaughter. Only I undertook the hike, which offered conversation with friendly residents, superb views of the forested hills, and the chance to watch locals crafting guns, axes and bazookas. After about three hours, I reached the summit, joining throngs of excited locals and a smattering of Westerners. I paid the entrance fee and wandered up the tiled white path to the pagoda, passing tourist stalls, scattered rubbish, rich pilgrims being carried in litters, and young female porters struggling beneath wealthy burdens. Women were not permitted to touch the Golden Rock, a sacred boulder topped with a stupa and precariously balanced on a slanting stone surface, but male worshippers piously affixed gold leaf squares to it.

According to legend, King Tissa in the 11th century regularly visited a hermit, who lived in the mountains. One day, sensing death was near, the hermit gave Tissa a hair of Buddha, which had been given to him years earlier by Buddha himself and which he had since kept safe in his own topknot. The hermit would only entrust it to Tissa if he promised to place it atop a rock whose shape resembled the old hermit's head. The rock had to be enormous, like the wisdom of Buddha.

Tissa – with the help of Thagyamin, king of the *nats*, and aided by the supernatural powers inherited from his father, a *zawgyi* (a skilled alchemist), and his mother, a *naga* (dragon serpent) princess – scoured the ocean floor and eventually found a suitable rock. They shipped it in a magic boat to the summit of Mount Kyaiktiyo, some 3600ft up, and used the single sacred hair to fix it in place. The boat then turned to stone and was named *"Kyaukthanban"* ('Stone Boat Stupa'). A local assured me the hermit head rock was actually floating and that the gap had steadily decreased over time: when his grandfather was alive, he said, it measured almost a foot. He said there was photo evidence. I didn't find any.

After taking a few obligatory snaps, I began the descent, desperate to escape this microcosm of everything I loathed. Was this the Myanmar I had been searching for: one rife with racism and intolerance? I knew it couldn't be, or at least hoped it wasn't. They call Myanmar 'The Golden Land' – which it is: every other company, eat-drink-shop and store is *Shwe* – but I was longing for blander colours. I couldn't take any more. My fondness for Myanmar was dwindling. I now needed to leave it to love it.

I eagerly boarded the first bus for Yangon, where I briefly saw Shwe Ei – the Myanmar I loved but had lost through naïve folly. She reminded me of everything I longed for – beauty, understanding, discerning pride – but which recent weeks had lacked. Four months of travelling had whistled by, but their ending had exposed Myanmar's darker side. And although I promised my friends I would return after Christmas, I wasn't sure it was the truth.

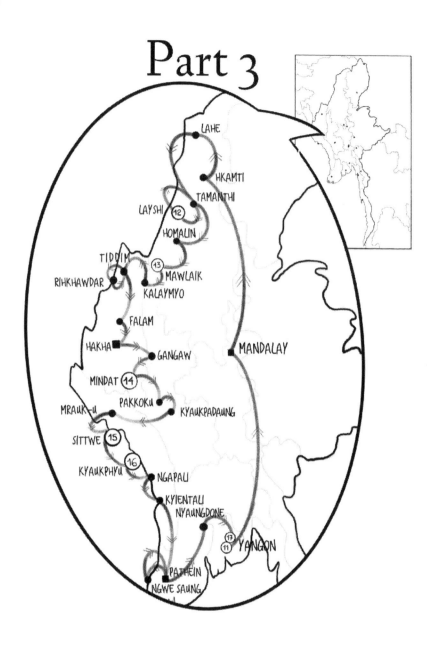

Chapter 11: Into the Naga Hills

The misery of the British winter and daily newscasts about Brexit brought me back. But after almost two months at home, Myanmar felt foreign. Although in England I had read *Ba-Loke-Kya-Ya-Paw!*: *Baa, Moo, What Shall We Do?* to keep up my Myanmar, I had lost my confidence and with it chunks of vocab. I felt detached, and my failure to meet with Shwe Ei while in Yangon compounded my isolation.

I prayed my reservations would dissipate sooner or later and turned my mind to my upcoming trip to Nagaland – a name simultaneously alluring and chilling, redolent of fearsome serpentine deities as well as head-hunting tribespeople. This would be the most unpredictable part of my trip: Lahe, my Nagaland destination, had only been opened to foreigners relatively recently and was not covered by any guidebooks. Over Christmas, I had spent days scouring blogs and internet travel threads in a desperate attempt to find information on the place. But it was all in vain: seemingly no foreigner had been there and written about it. There was a good chance I would be one of the first independent foreign travellers ever to visit Lahe – assuming I made it, for a friend of mine had tried to visit Nagaland the previous year and been arrested…

In theory, I could visit Lahe without a permit – which was all the reassurance required to convince me. And so, after sleeping through one of the nineteen earthquakes to strike Myanmar in the first fortnight of 2018, I took a propeller plane from Mandalay to Hkamti, northern Sagaing Region. At the airport, an unassuming concrete building, stood a few Naga elders in traditional dress: black and red tribal loincloths, headdresses sporting hornbill feathers, and tiger teeth necklaces.

The Naga are an ethnic conglomeration of several tribes native to Nagaland, a mountainous area spread over north-eastern India and north-western Myanmar. My original plan had been to come back from England in time for their renowned new year festival, which had been held in mid-January in Nanyun, but for various reasons I ended up postponing my return. Only a handful of tourists made it to the celebrations, one of them a Frenchman.

"Yezs, I went," he said, staring dreamily into space as we chatted over tea in Hkamti. "It wazs so good, so good." He kissed his curled fingers, then released them like an Italian chef talking about his grandmother's cooking. "The festival wazs so amazing, so amazing."

By the end of our dinner I was extremely jealous, but I later learnt that I hadn't missed a once-in-a-lifetime experience. What the Frenchman didn't relate was the Naga's attempts to modernise. In addition to their distinctive tribal garments, patterned shields and wooden spears, the performers wore big plastic badges – a little like the buckles of WWE belts – and sat on bright pink chairs. Westerners hate plastic because it's shiny and artificial; the Myanmar love it for the same reasons.

The Ministry of Hotels and Tourism had initially stated that a permit was needed to visit Nanyun, but two days before Naga New Year, a festivalgoer told me, the area was opened to independent travellers. Consequently, some tourists paid a total of over $3000 to visit, others under $150. Such instances are common, but Myanmar must improve transparency in the tourism industry if it is to reap the full rewards. After all, travellers can't be expected to drag around bottles of Johnnie Walker with them all the time.

The only way to reach Lahe, one of the three self-administered Naga zones in Myanmar, was via an expensive private jeep and up bumpy orange mountain roads. But Lahe was worth it. At an elevation of nearly 3,400ft, the views of the valley and the evening stars were spectacular. Warthogs wandered between rows of wooden houses, grunting incomprehensible insults at the humans. Everyone wrapped up well in the cold, misty mornings: some donned distinctive black and red Naga blankets interwoven with stylistic animal designs; mothers carried babies wrapped in shawls on their backs. Many residents wore colourful socks with individual toe sections (so they could wear them with flip flops, I later realised), most of the elder women had tattoos of four evenly spaced lines going down from the bottom lip to the chin and nearly everyone wore yellow and red beaded necklaces. The people looked different, almost Myanmar-Tibetan, and were understandably reserved.

Much to my amazement, I had met another foreigner on the plane to Hkamti: David, a 36-year-old American epidemiologist who worked for *Médecins Sans Frontières* (MSF). Knowing their work would interest my editor, I asked David about the possibility of interviewing the MSF Nagaland team. He seemed enthusiastic and invited me for dinner at their lodging in Lahe. In their basic but cosy lounge, countless beer cans crowned the wooden beams running along every wall, reminding me of my student days. Considering they had been there for over six months, the number was not excessive; nonetheless, the questionable decoration choice did little to break the perception of doctors being heavy drinkers. A small wooden table sat in the middle and cushions served as seats.

There were just three of us inside: David, myself and Antonio, the fatherly Italian project coordinator. When dinner was finished, a motherly French doctor and a few others joined us, bringing in with them pasta, avocado and tiramisu. Antonio produced a block of Parmesan cheese brought all the way from Italy.

"This was literally the last place I had been expecting to eat pasta with real cheese," I said. "I was worried it would be three days without any vegetables: I ordered vegetarian fried rice at a restaurant earlier and got... fried rice."

"Yeah, they don't seem to have mastered stepped agriculture here," said David, ladling pasta onto his plate. "Do you know what I mean? In Nepal they have crops, like lentils, growing up the mountainside, but I haven't seen any of that here."

"A meat-based diet then."

We nodded. I tucked into my avocado.

"How is the project going?" I asked.

"It's going well," said Antonio with a smile. "But every village speaks a different language, so treatment can be a lengthy process. And the roads are a challenge: the one up from Hkamti is now okay, but those leading to small villages are bumpy. Sometimes there aren't even any roads, so we have to walk."

"Are there many problems? Malaria?"

"There is malaria," said Antonio, "but we are currently collecting data on malnourishment." He paused to grate parmesan onto his pasta. "One of the most common things I see on the list of ailments is 'bitten by a pig.'" Antonio chuckled. "Bitten by a pig? It seems so absurd. There are tigers and bears in these hills: I thought I might see 'attacked by a tiger', but not 'bitten by a pig.'"

"They mean the sharp teeth on the outside," said someone from the corridor. "What are they called?"

"The tusks?"

"Yeah, the tusks. They are really dangerous."

"Maybe it's a language thing," I said.

"Gored by a wild warthog," said David.

"Tiramisu?"

It was passed round. I took the tray with greedy hands and served myself a large helping, knowing this would be the only tiramisu I would eat for five months. It was delicious: homemade and all the better for it.

"It's a shame you weren't at the new year festival," said Antonio.

"Perhaps you can still visit one of the proper Naga villages," said David, "because Lahe isn't really much."

No matter where you travel to, there is always somewhere better, less touristy, more "authentic."

"You could go to Santon. That's not too far."

It so happened that someone staying at my guesthouse was working near Santon, so I was able to hitch a lift there the next morning. This time there were no kids rolling tyres by the roadside, no shops flying Grand Royal whisky banners; just jungled hills, blue skies, the occasional drifting cloud, stones, and dust. After 45 minutes, we reached a crossroads; the upper fork led to Santon.

"You'll have to arrange a lift back," said the driver. "Or wait on this road for a car, but that could take a long time."

He saluted and left. I turned around and began scaling the dusty track. A group of kids in ragged Western clothes, who had been watching me from behind a bush, giggled and ran up the hill. I smiled, used to this reaction from Myanmar children who rarely saw whiteys. When I reached the brow, thatched roofs reflecting the morning rays came into view; bamboo huts sprawled over a hillside of sparsely scattered trees with skeletal trunks and verdant tops. I spotted a Naga elder in traditional dress sitting outside his hut, but he retreated inside when he saw me. Parents ushered their children into their homes as I passed; every baby cried.

The Santon villagers looked vastly different to the Lahe residents: not only were they filthy from head to toe, the nearest water supply being 20 minutes away by foot, but the women especially had broad faces with wide mouths and round eyes that reminded me of the mermaids in *Harry Potter and the Goblet of Fire*. The elder women had chin tattoos identical to those in Lahe and the girls sported stylish ginger streaks in their black hair. Some of the men carried spears or M1 rifles. Everyone gave me a wide berth.

Already I was quite anxious: this wasn't the comfortable, smiley village stroll I had envisaged but a chilling, estranging reception. If I had been one of the earliest lone foreign travellers to visit Lahe, what was I here? The first? The second? There was no doubt that these people seldom saw Westerners in their village.

Keen to prove I wasn't scary, I tried to charm a clutch of kids by juggling rocks. They were almost impressed but didn't dare descend from their bamboo balcony. They barked words at the ignorant outsider and laughed, though the elderly lady sitting to my left shrieked fiercest. I'm fairly sure they were insulting me.

Ignoring the abuse, I put on my biggest smile and persisted. Then I reached for my camera – sending every child dashing for shelter. They didn't dare return until I had placed my bag on the ground and stepped away from it. Were they merely camera shy, or was there a more superstitious reason for their fear? I knew some cultures believed that cameras stole part of your soul: could they have been afraid of that?

By now, I was feeling incredibly guilty for having turned up to their village uninvited. After a couple of minutes of awkward standing and staring, I tried to teach the kids some English in a last-ditch effort to interact with them. A couple complied by teaching me Naga, but without a common language our conversation was limited.

I began wandering back down the hill, defeated, when someone hatted me with a bamboo cone painted red and yellow. Everyone laughed; it was a nice moment and the hostilities were briefly forgotten. I must have looked a right pillock. The hatter told me I could keep it for K50,000 (£26). I nearly laughed, astounded by his shameless attempt to scam me, but the sight of a spear-wielding tribesman heading my way made me shut my mouth *myan-myan.*

I had tried my all but was evidently still unwelcome. And as I headed back towards the village entrance, a procession of 20-30 weeping women wrapped in blankets followed me. I moved off the path and they strode past in single file, imitating the wails of their elderly leader. Many were genuinely crying and those who weren't held blankets over their eyes to make it look as though they were. Perhaps it was a sort of mourning ceremony, though no one turned to look at them – all eyes remained on me.

A deeply wrinkled though relatively young man wearing a navy sports jacket and smoking an enormous bamboo bong began chatting to me in Myanmar. His eyes were bloodshot and there was little doubt that drugs were doing the talking. He invited me inside his home, where bull skulls hung on the walls: trophies. I was glad the Naga had given up headhunting humans. A fireplace sat on a raised platform, the ceiling had been blackened by smoke and dust particles spiralled through light shafts penetrating the thatched walls.

My host wasn't originally from Santon – that much was clear – nor was his friend who soon joined us. After them came two girls in clean Myanmar attire.

"I'm the village supervisor," said the most smartly dressed in good English. "This is the school teacher," and she motioned to the young lady beside her, whose grey blouse and dark *longyi* made her resemble a Christian nun.

"Do you teach English?" I asked.

"Yes."

"Is that the book you use?"

"Yes."

"Can I have a look?"

"Yes."

The textbook had caught my eye immediately. It was small, pink, and graced with a particularly camp picture of Christiano Ronaldo. Inside were some stellar sentences, including, "These black soles have leather shoes." And, "I would like some powders, large size."

The host offered me *ye-nway-kyan* as I explained that I needed a motorbike taxi back to Lahe. While the girls talked among themselves, the two guys spoke in Myanmar about how to extort as much money from me as possible.

"30,000 [£14.97]," said the smoker.

"I think 15,000 is fair."

The guys began discussing once more while the teacher took selfies with me. Then, much to my dismay, she and the village supervisor left.

"15,000 for the ride, and 5,000 to us for organising it," said one of the guys as he boiled wiry leaves in a spoon over the fire.

What were they smoking? I had imagined it would be opium, but these thin green leaves looked like no drug I had ever seen. Their bamboo bongs were also unusual: each was a perfect cylinder, with only a straw poking out the top. There was no pipe-bowl for burning the leaves, which is perhaps why they first had to be boiled over the fire.

The guys removed the tops of their bongs and poured the leaves in, reinforcing my theory. Then they began slurping – and continued to do so for another 45 minutes, assuring me all the while that my lift was on its way. It eventually came, and after a bone-crunching ride I arrived back in Lahe, having paid double what I should have.

My experience in Santon was similar to Richard's, a Naga New Year festivalgoer lingering in Lahe. He had stayed the night in the local monastery and been invited to Santon by the head monk, who had a house there and educated the children about Buddhism. Although he had been formally introduced, Richard also received a hostile reception. Residents pointed at his money belt with an open hand, refusing to talk to him unless he paid them, and later a village elder stood up and gave a speech, in which he declared that Richard should only be permitted into Santon if he paid. The Bamar head monk, who had moved to the village some months prior, confessed to Richard that the locals recognised him as a religious figure only and did not interact with him on a social level.

Being an unwanted outsider is a truly haunting sensation. Although the Santon villagers had not disliked me personally, I struggled not to take offence at their hostility and must confess that the experience skewed my entire perception of Nagaland. I told a young Indian Naga, whom I met two days later on the boat down from Hkamti, about my reception in Santon and asked whether he thought the residents of an isolated Naga village in India would have been more welcoming. This was his response:

"We Naga have been through much. We have lived here for generations, have our own traditions, our own customs, our own languages and our own culture. We were split up by fighting. Yes, we fought the British. We fought the Burmese army. The Naga remember this. Our fathers told us about it and their fathers before them; so many stories were told to us as children. And we are free. We have delegates at the UN – they recognise us as independent –

and we gained independence from the British one day before the rest of India. We are very proud of this. And we will keep fighting until God comes down and tells us we have been doing it all wrong."

Santon's isolation undoubtedly contributed to the cold treatment Richard and I received, but the Indian Naga's response suggested that pride could also have played a part. After some research, I found that Naga tradition considers each village an independent republic and that foreign concepts, such as a common identity, have historically been met with resistance.

After decades of conflict with the *Tatmadaw*, Lahe, Leshi and Nanyun became Naga Self-Administered Zones in 2008. The National Socialist Council of Nagaland-Khaplang (NSCN-K), who were formed in 1988 and demand "the independence of Nagaland", signed a ceasefire with U Thein Sein's government in 2012. Although some Naga Self-Administered Zones support the NLD, the NSCN-K have refused to sign the Nationwide Ceasefire Agreement, the new government's scheme for pursuing peace, since it does not include Naga in India. Many eastern Naga cling to their history and even reject the 1953 India-Myanmar demarcation of Naga territory.

*

As with Lahe, I had spent much of my Christmas researching boat travel on the Chindwin River, the largest tributary of the Ayeyarwady, which snakes down the north-western edge of Myanmar: was it legal? Easy? Worth the effort?

The answer, as is so often the case in Myanmar, was that I would simply have to find out for myself. The latest guidebooks noted it was technically possible to boat-hop down the Chindwin without a permit, though there was allegedly a good chance you would get sent back by a misinformed immigration officer. A few people on an outdated Tripadvisor thread, however, claimed to have cruised the entire stretch, though they had not provided many details about what lay there.

There's a breed of travellers who never visit places unless they are certain it will be worth the journey. I can understand this – after all, nobody likes to waste their time – but my travelling purpose rarely afforded the luxury of reassurance. "Searching" for Myanmar was often a literal act: i.e. I just had to go to the place and see what I found. The next two weeks would be no different.

My first stop down the Chindwin was Tamanthi, a colourful riverside village and exactly the "authentic" Myanmar I treasure: slapstick movies blaring out of eat-drink-shop TVs, toilet rolls stored inside red plastic High Class dispensers on teahouse tables, honest smiles all around. A girl no older than seven even began talking to me, a lumbering whitey, with genuine interest. I admired her bravery and maturity.

I had read there was a British military base on the river used by Allied forces fleeing the Japanese in World War II, so I set out to find it. By 7th March 1942, Yangon had become a smouldering wreck occupied by the Japanese. Its fall exposed the fragility of the Allies' position and "it was obvious that the whole of Burma might be occupied by the Japanese and that India itself and Ceylon lay under imminent threat of invasion." This was one of the greatest emergencies in British military history, almost comparable to Dunkirk.

The Allies fled for India, but it was to be a bloody and botched retreat. In the hope of inhibiting the Japanese, they scorched arable land, blew up bridges and destroyed oil fields. But the Japanese advance only quickened. By 16th April, the Japanese had penetrated the north of Pin Chaung, Magway Region, where they decimated an Allied attachment and began forming a road block. If the Allied retreat was to progress, the road block would have to be broken. However, the ground was unsuitable for tanks and no artillery support was available.

The task fell to Captain Croft, commanding officer of 'D' Company of the West Yorkshire Regiment:

Croft decided to attack with two platoons east of the Block and one west of it. 'D' Company carried out their advance with their usual dash, though every time they crossed one of the Razor Edges they came under fire. Meanwhile more Japanese were approaching... Without hesitation 'D' Company let the Japs have their grenades and the Block was broken... This was the turning point.[19]

A month later, the Allies reached Manipur, India, where they regrouped before launching a series of successful offensives that resulted in the reclamation of Yangon in April 1945.

---

[19] The above two quotes come from E. W. C. Sandes (1951), *From Pyramid to Pagoda: The Story of the West Yorkshire Regiment (The Prince of Wales's Own) in the War, 1939-1945 and Afterwards*, Parsons.

Only eight Commendation Cards were awarded for services in Myanmar in 1942. One of these went to Major John A.R. Croft, my mother's uncle, though I only learnt of his involvement on Christmas Day 2017 while back in England. It seemed fitting that my subsequent trip down the Chindwin River, roughly retracing the Allies' retreat route, should lead me to the Tamanthi military base, even if it had fallen into utter dilapidation.

I found the barracks without much difficulty and wandered in – only to be confronted by a topless soldier wearing a sky blue *longyi*. He stopped abruptly and gave me an uncertain look. The buildings were so run down that I had assumed the fort was no longer in use, but amazingly the *Tatmadaw* had commandeered it: several soldiers now lived in the rickety wooden huts and perused the old stone bunkers overlooking the river. Only the large stilted barracks, which leant at an ominous angle and whose spiral staircase had collapsed, had been abandoned to ruin.

We stared awkwardly at each other, then both looked down at my large Nikon.

"Can I come in?"

"Okay. But no photos."

I followed him to the other officers, who were sitting round a campfire. They were all smiles and curiosity.

"Here," said the commanding officer, one of the few in uniform. "Army tea."

He handed me a glass of boiling water and an instant tea mix sachet. The small print confirmed that this particular type was only distributed to the *Tatmadaw*. The soldiers were visibly proud of this, as were all the *Tatmadaw* officers I drank tea with during my wanderings, even though it tasted just like any other instant tea mix. It was a suitably bland and uninteresting experience, and I thought about how torturous the scene of a sunburnt descendant clad in a ripped *longyi* and drinking artificial tea would have been for John Croft.

The soldiers invited me for rice the next morning, but I had already decided to give Nagaland another go – this time up to Layshi – so I returned to the guesthouse for an early night. Amazingly, it cost just K2000 (£1.05), the cheapest I ever found in Myanmar, though it was suitably basic: the room was cramped, the wooden bed was furnished with a pitiful mattress and the toilet lay on the other side of the mud drive. The bucket shower had no door, and when brushing my teeth in the dark I accidentally used the water collected from the gutters and intended for the pigs. Fortunately, I kept a spare toothbrush for just such an occasion.

The next day began as many of the cold season mornings on the Chindwin River do: the rising sun scattered warmth through the translucent mist hovering above the water and clinging to trees, recreating an *Apocalypse Now* scene, while women organised their riverside food stalls with sleepy limbs, laying out metal trays of meat and salads on the counter, and men carried goods down to the jetty, ready for pick-up.

The ride to Layshi was also a private jeep affair. I sat beside a friendly ethnic Chin couple, who were equally surprised to find that the *lan* was paved almost the entire way. We stopped for a toilet break at a wooden bridge spanning a stream that fed into a still water basin. My Chin friends wanted some photos, so I posed on the bridge while they clicked away.

Then BANG! A terrific explosion from behind.

I spun around and saw water from the still pool flying into the air. Bubbles rose to the surface at various points, followed by small silver shimmers. A group of half-naked Myanmar guys jumped in and began collecting their catch.

I had only ever seen dynamite fishing in *Crocodile Dundee,* but perhaps it was common here, for our driver ran straight over to help. He returned fifteen minutes later, carrying a clutch of sizeable fish dangling by the mouths from a piece of plant sinew. There was a brief kerfuffle as he decided where to store his dinner, eventually hanging them from the rear-view mirror.

Then we drove off, Bon Jovi translated into Myanmar playing over the radio, fish slopping around in the front: the fisherman's racing dice. It was good fun, though they stank the car out for the rest of the journey. I didn't envy the guy sitting in the front middle.

Layshi was higher than Lahe and colder. The forested ridges, obscured by the haze endemic to many mountainous regions in Myanmar, were steep and impressive; a blue-green river snaked through the valley below. Layshi's cityscape resembled Lahe's – particularly the large football pitch occupying the centre, the only flat piece of ground – and houses similarly sprawled over the hillside.

The sociocultural dynamic, however, could not have been more different: except for a tiny Naga museum and a few embossed shoulder bags, there was no visible tribal Naga influence. There were also plenty of vegetables, the residents were warm and several spoke English. I put the contrast down to Layshi's proximity to India.

I borrowed a motorbike and sped off to find a more isolated Naga community, curious to see how my reception would compare with my previous one in Santon yet equipped with balloons to charm the kids if necessary. It was hazy enough not to bother with sunglasses, but I hadn't banked on a suicidal fly finding me. As I turned a muddy corner, it flew in and nestled itself beneath my eyelid. I extricated the opportunist, but for the rest of the journey my eye itched and watered.

After 45 minutes, I arrived at a terraced village. It was clear immediately that this would not be the eerie experience of Santon. Women wearing *longyis* above their breasts were washing garments beside concrete wells, hanging them out to dry on wooden beams or wire clothes lines. A handful of children were sat beside a thatched house, playing marbles on the baked dirt; they hardly took any notice of me. Shrubberies decorated quaint front gardens and the euphonious trickling of a stream evoked tranquillity. It was a lazy, uninterested atmosphere: idle mountain somnolence.

I wandered along and was invited to sit beside Peter, a middle-aged farmer wearing a bamboo bowler hat.

"What is your name?" he asked in perfect English.
"James."
"And where are you from?"
"England."
"Are you Christian?"

"No, I'm not religious. But I went to a Christian school."

"I understand," he said humbly. "If any of your friends come here, we would be delighted to meet them. I am a pastor and would be happy to speak to them about God."

Peter had been educated in India, as had his friend who turned up a few minutes later with his wife. She carried a baby in a pink frock, who shrieked at the sight of my ghastly pale visage.

Time for the balloons. I blew her up a blue one, which she began using as a dummy. Suddenly a dozen or more kids turned up wanting balloons. I duly provided them. The older ones played volleyball with them and the youngest sucked them – reminding me that I had been glued to the toilet all morning: had I just passed on a fatal foreign illness?!

While I panicked, the baby's balloon popped. She began wailing again, so I puffed up another – only now she had started eating the remains of the last. A quick glance round revealed a village of kids fighting over colourful balloons.

You genius, James.

"I think I'll leave, Peter."

"Thank you for coming. You are welcome back anytime."

I returned to my motorbike and saw in the wing mirror that my eye was now bloodshot and pink.

A quick visit to the Lahe hospital, methinks.

The doctor, after examining my eye for no more than two seconds, prescribed me three eye drops and four antibiotics daily for the next nine days. This was surely excessive – perhaps the excitement of treating a foreigner had got to him – but I accepted the stash of drugs and returned to Viewpoint Guesthouse, where I was the only guest. It was a new building, owned by the managing director of a construction company, and my enormous *en suite* had cost a mere K20,000 (£10.50).

But as I stepped inside that evening, feeling homesick, lovesick and ill, the luxury mocked me. And when I sat down at the desk to write about my experience in Santon, I had a breakdown.

How could I judge foreign cultures and peoples using my Western logic? Suddenly all the travel articles I had ever written appeared nothing better than 21st century colonialism, British impositions; and no matter how hard I tried, I couldn't stop thinking of myself as an ignorant outsider with no right to an opinion.

It was the breakdown of a travel writer, and the first drafts of my Nagaland article violated the first law of travel literature: overall, the piece must be positive. In *Ghost Train to the Eastern Star*, Paul Theroux discloses how miserable he was during the famed railway journey he had undertaken 30 years previously. Like me, he had left his partner to travel – the unopposable force of solo travel had compelled him – and so turning *The Great Railway Bazaar* into an optimistic read had been challenging. I wonder whether his own breakdown in Japan, when he confesses that he's blurred the boundaries of travel writing and fiction, refers to the necessary omissions and amendments he made to prevent his book from becoming a depressing read.

My overall journey round Myanmar was enriching, and things picked up later, but in Nagaland I felt dejected – as I would for the next six weeks. I became a stereotype when I was lonely, asking the country roads to take me home and singing that I only knew I loved her when I let her go. I even called up Shwe Ei in that hotel room and begged her to take me back.

"Don't come back to Yangon for me," she said, soft as ever. "I'm sorry, but I no longer love you... I think of you as a friend and am grateful for the beautiful memories I have of us."

Her response reduced me to tears instantly. Again, I questioned whether I had made the right choice in leaving her: I had never been in such a loving relationship before, yet I had given it all up for months of discomfort and loneliness. Travel suddenly seemed the most romantic and foolish of undertakings, and I spent the evening despairing that my trip would only bring me ill health and regrets.

I felt isolated and unwanted, but over time I realised that Shwe Ei's bluntness had been exactly what I needed: the phone call reminded me that my *chit-thu* was gone and that I would just have to deal with being alone. And though I thought endlessly about Shwe Ei during my travels, especially when I was lonely, my love for her gradually crystallised into fond memories, just as hers had for me.

Chapter 12: Skullball

After a couple of days of illness and cold, I returned to the Chindwin and boarded a long, thin, green motorboat. The cushioned benches inside were cruel and clearly not designed for lanky Europeans. Water sloshed beneath the planked floor, awaiting its opportunity to consume the vessel, while passengers tied plastic bags to the ceiling to charge their phones from questionable hanging power sockets. Electronic cries of "the enemy has been defeated!" punctuated the air constantly.

In her travel memoir *Defiled on the Ayeyarwaddy*, Ma Thanegi states that the younger generations love literature; but she was writing before smartphones were ubiquitous in Myanmar. Today, videogames rule the waves. Perhaps the Myanmar will revert to reading once phones have ceased to be exciting new gadgets – though if the number of phone shops in Yangon is anything to go by, this may be some years yet.

Our departure was delayed by a sizeable delivery of wooden crates containing perhaps 500 tiny chicks chirping in confusion, excitement and fear. They were stacked in the back and proved loud enough to drown out the whine of the motor, though real power resided with our horn-addicted captain.

By mid-morning, it was warm enough to sit on the roof – a male prerogative, for the height was deemed too dangerous for women – which was far comfier than the inside seats. Train or bus travel offers snapshots of life; boat rides provide a continuous film. Quaint wooden huts crowned cultivated riverbanks and sandy shores, watching the river ripple like the folds of a curtain as our boat passed by. Buffalo lazed in the current, children splashed around in uncoordinated euphoria, and women came down in groups to perch on wooden platforms and scrub themselves.

The Myanmar, I believe, take more care of personal hygiene than Europeans, and so it baffles me that they pay minimal attention to personal property. In my experience, people's homes – including those of the rich – are almost always dusty, cobwebbed and messy. Not that this affects the women, who emerge from them in aura of resplendence, their *longyis* sublime, their smiles irresistible, their hair entwined with sprigs of jasmine.

To my surprise, lunch was provided: a polythene box of rice, vegetables and meat, each part wrapped in separate plastic bags. After eating, everyone chucked their rubbish into the water, adding to the copious litter collected by tree branches at the river's edge: a jarring juxtaposition of rusticity and modernity.

"The Burmese are dirty, aren't they?" said one of the crewmembers, seeing me staring at the polythene-flowering trees. An enormous single hair protruded from his only facial mole. Evidently, he, like many Myanmar men, believed it would bring good luck, or that cutting it would cause it to regrow *po-myan-myan*. Its magnificence was such that I had been able to admire it flapping in the wind from halfway down the boat.

I tried to explain that plastic was bad for the environment and might eventually poison the river, but only succeeded in coming across as a pretentious foreigner. Luckily, we were nearing a village and his attention was demanded.

As we approached, a packed speedboat set off from the riverbank and rammed into our side. The boat wobbled violently, water splashed inside, and on hopped a dozen female hawkers carrying metal food trays on their heads and screaming prices. Boys infected with goitre followed them and began scrabbling around for plastic bottles to resell, climbing over seats and skirting along the boat's edges with agility Spiderman would have envied. The cabin was already stuffed and noisy before we reached port – where yet more hawkers poured on to begin barging their way through the crowd in a chaotic free-for-all. Just before the boat set off again, the women and goitrous youths scrambled back to dry land, though a few hawkers lingered to pursue further sales; one entered an hour-long haggling ordeal over a couple of Kachin *longyis*.

These small port stops always followed this pattern and were supremely exciting. Overall, every Chindwin boat ride was roughly identical – the main disadvantage with boat travel: repetitiveness – though a few were unexpectedly *zay-gyi-de* ('expensive', literally 'big market'). In rural, untouristy Myanmar, foreigners must often pay more for transport – partly because many Myanmar believe it is common practice across the globe (it greatly surprised one of my friends to learn that foreigners paid the same price as locals for buses in England), partly because being a foreigner in a recently "opened" country is still a big deal.

Mostly, however, the extra charge is liability cover, for Myanmar transport companies allegedly get into more trouble if a foreigner is involved in an accident. Again, this is a hangover of isolationist, authoritarian rule and likely no longer the case, but people still don't want to take the risk. Chindwin boats are particularly prone to sinking.

After stopping in Homalin, which offered little besides poor value accommodation, I arrived in the verdant riverside town of Mawlaik. Fruit stalls and eat-drink-shops occupied the strand road, gazing out over anchored passenger boats, colourful sampans and the glistening Chindwin. On the leafy outskirts, farmers rode ox-drawn ploughs while kids played chase, threading their ways along the narrow banks of the rice paddies: pleasing agricultural scenes set before a backdrop of rolling hills. A handful of colonial buildings stood scattered around the centre, some neglected but others renovated and now serving as schools or municipal offices. Occasionally, smiley, perfect-skinned teenagers approached me, put their hands together as if in prayer and asked, "May I introduce myself?"

Besides forcing the locals to learn phrases that highlighted their subservience, the colonials built a golf course supposedly modelled on the St Andrew's Old Course, the Home of Golf. Looking past the tropical weeds and pariah dogs, I detected a faint resemblance between the courses' respective opening holes, though I had to stretch my imagination. Members of Mawlaik Golf Club are, in theory, entitled to a discounted green fee at St. Andrew's. Sadly, the Home of Golf told me that they could find no record of this agreement, but the *a-myo-thar* who gave me this golfing info was right about one thing: the fairway grass seeds, which were transported specially from Pyin Oo Lwin, stuck to your *longyi* and became a nuisance *myan-myan*.

I stayed in the riverfront Sone Nay Ja Hotel. It was unclear whether the building was still under construction or if the owners simply rated bumpy concrete floors; otherwise, it was acceptable. The bathroom was tiled and clean, though there was no grating over the drainage hole, enticing a gigantic cockroach to sneak in. It progressed into the bedroom, scuttled up the wall and onto the ceiling, at which point I decided it wasn't welcome.

I grabbed the provided rubber flip-flops and chucked them, hoping to dislodge the cockroach and get us back on level playing terms. It took a few throws, but eventually the flip-flop triumphed. I turned the empty bin over the cockroach and wondered what to do, since I had heard that crushing a pregnant cockroach could cause its eggs to hatch where it died – and this cockroach was so large that it was almost certainly harbouring babies.

"Mwe-lar?" ('Is it a snake?') asked the owner, appearing beside the open door in a mucky *longyi* and revolting tank top.

Not knowing the word for 'cockroach', I shook my head and gesticulated ignorance. Now the owner was intrigued. He stepped forward and turned the bin over.

Just a cockroach, eh?

He put his heel by the creature's head and slowly brought his foot down. The cockroach didn't move, but stoically accepted being crushed into its next life. The owner gave me a knowing nod.

You're welcome.

I spent the next morning in the adjoining eat-drink-shop, typing up my notes. It only took a few minutes for the group of quinquagenarians at the next table to get up and wander over for a look, since using an electronic device with a screen is usually a public affair in Myanmar. A friend of mine once made the mistake of having personal pornographic images on his phone; they came as quite a shock to the novice monk that stole it.

Soon a crowd of nearly ten had gathered to watch me at work.

"Sar-ye saya loke-de" ('He's a writer'), someone muttered.

Everyone nodded, eyes glued to the screen. Then an elderly man with a long nose and grey eyebrows leant forward and prodded it, moving the cursor up a few lines. This appeared to please him.

Do you understand? Men behind me, do you like what I am writing?

They did not understand, which rather nullified the second question. They filtered away and were replaced by three young boys, two of whom took great interest in my tablet. The other, clutching a hacksaw, moved round the front of my polished wooden table and began sawing it. The owner seemed unbothered, so I let the demolition continue until he got bored and left.

Once I was finished, I went for a stroll, absorbing the smiles, the riverside sleepiness, and the smell of fresh fruit emanating from market stalls on the strand road. Suddenly a teenager paused in front of me and put his hands together.

"Excuse me, may I introduce myself? I am Tin Oo. What is your name?"

"James."

"Nice to meet you, James. What is your country?"

"England. Who taught you to speak like this?"

"My English teacher is Mr U Thant Zin," he said, hands still together. "Would you like to meet him?"

Two hours later, I was walking towards a derelict, two-storey wooden wreck plastered with DANGER signs; the balcony looked as though it would collapse under the weight of a single feather. I had timed my arrival for the last fifteen minutes of his lesson, which was taking place in the Victorianesque, ground floor classroom. About twenty pupils sat on basic wooden benches, facing the front.

"Ah. You're here."

The *ingaleik saya* was a relic of the colonial era, who looked as though he had done it all (and probably had). An amber necklace dangled over his bulging belly, which his tank top barely concealed; his glasses were crooked and his hearing aids faulty. His eyes suggested he had seen the Absurd.

"My student tells me you're from England," he said as we shook hands.

"Yes, London."

"Very good. You can help me then."

He leant over and picked up a book on the bench beside him. The effort involved made him huff and wheeze simultaneously – a bizarre sound, which made me think he was about to die, but it turned out huff-wheezes were just his thing. The book was an old-fashioned English language learning guide, which contained example conversations.

"You need to read a few out," said Thant Zin, "so we can hear the correct pronunciation."

They were bland and uneventful – exactly as the dialogues in my German school textbooks had been – and ran roughly as follows:

"Hello, Jane, how are you?"
"I am well, thank you. How are you, Michael?"
"I'm not so well, unfortunately. I've got a terrible headache."
"Oh dear. Have you drunk enough water?"
"Perhaps I haven't. I shall drink more."
"Good idea."

And at the end:

Conversation moves on, probably to discussing the weather.

Well, there's proof that the Brits talk too much about the weather.

After each reading came a stunned silence, and Thant Zin would say, "that's the pronunciation: did you hear?", and everyone would nod.

"Are you going back to England?" he asked, once class had ended.

"Yes, in about four months."

"And will you come back to Burma?"

"One day, I imagine."

"Good," he said, eyes googling, "then please buy the accompanying CD for this book and bring it to me."

He took the book from me and began scribbling the name on a scrap of paper.

"I don't know when I'll be back. You could be waiting a long time."

Undissuaded, he finished writing and handed me my instructions.

"Now you must meet my doctor," he stated, and he disappeared inside his home without another word. Tin Oo, who had lingered, ushered me back onto his moped and drove me to the town clinic.

"Will U Thant Zin be okay by himself?" I asked the tall doctor as I sat down on a plastic chair beside him. "Won't he need help?"

"No," he replied in a cool, smooth tone. "He has a rickshaw. He'll be fine."

I couldn't imagine Thant Zin finding his way into his rickshaw in the dark – let alone managing the drive without crashing – but the doctor was insistent. So we waited and waited, and after half an hour the *ingaleik saya* rolled up in a rickshaw as beaten up as he was. He wore a head torch and a look of maniacal accomplishment.

"This is my doctor," he cough-wheezed, clambering up the small steps with his walking stick. "He is a good man. He gave me my hearing aids."

The doctor smiled shyly.

"I was transferred here from Yangon," said the doctor. "I live in one of the new colonial houses."

"Are you married?"

"Not yet."

"The colonial houses are the only buildings that don't flood," said Thant Zin. "Very clever architects, the British."

Tin Oo excused himself and went home.

"There was lots of fighting here during the Second World War," said Thant Zin. "The Japanese took over Mawlaik for two weeks. Have you seen the District Office?"

"Yes."

"When the Japanese were in Mawlaik, the British restationed their guns on the other side of the river and blew them to smithereens." He beamed at his doctor, who returned another forced smile. "The Japanese who were not killed hung themselves in the district office," continued Thant Zin, his smile growing all the time. "Then the British soldiers paid the Burmese women one *kyat* and the Burmese men two *kyats* to cast the Japanese corpses into mass graves." He giggled and muttered something in Myanmar to his doctor, who shifted uncomfortably.

"What was that?"

Thant Zin laughed, displaying a mouth of missing or crooked teeth – his largest smile yet. "We played football with the Japanese skulls," he said. "We liked the British." He gazed at the doctor's poster of the human anatomy. "Some Japanese families came here a few years ago, looking for their dead relatives."

There was nothing more to say.

Chapter 13: Drink to Death

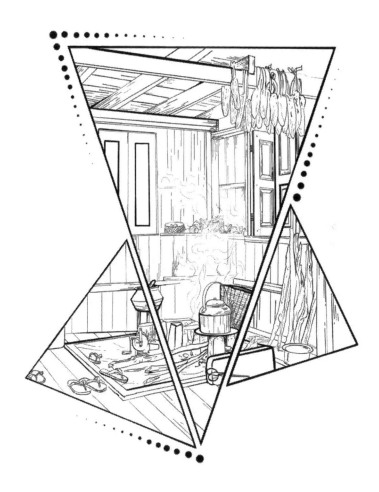

CHIN HOUSE / ချင်းအိမ်

Mawlaik was my last stop on the Chindwin. Although I had enjoyed my riverway odyssey, towards the end I had found myself longing for the Chin hills, which had enraptured me during a brief visit there the previous year. Once again, I would be entering by bus from Kalaymyo, a gateway city on the Sagaing-Chin boundary.

Like Kachin State, Chin was heavily targeted by Christian missionaries during colonial rule. It remains predominantly and devoutly Christian, so I was unsurprised to find "The Lord is My Shepherd" stamped on my flimsy Kalaymyo-Tiddim bus ticket – which he bloody well needed to be the first time I undertook that treacherous journey.

It had been six months earlier, in the monsoon season, and I had convinced two unsuspecting *Deutsche* to join me. Perhaps I should have paid more attention to my Myanmar friends who had warned me not to travel in Chin during the wet season. But I had been too stubborn, so the three of us climbed into the minibus and set off for Tiddim, excited and ignorant.

Before we penetrated the hills proper, the van stopped beside a pair of Christian grave stones. "Amen," and we were off again, Christian rock pounding through the speakers: "Jesus, Jesus, come on and save us!" I later learnt that the prayers had been for a safe journey.

The first hour was graced with sublime views of hillsides layered in mist. Then the *lan* became bumpy and narrow, mud replaced tarmac and we struggled to remain seated as the vehicle blundered along. An old woman behind us puked out the window, then hid her head for the rest of the ride – either in illness, fear, shame, or a combination of the three – revealing her face only when she needed to vomit.

"*Asin-pyi-lar?*" ('Are you okay?') asked a lady in front.

"*Asin-ma-pyi-bu*" ('I'm not okay'), I answered. "I'm scared."

Everybody shrieked with laughter, but my fears were not unfounded. We ripped round boggy corners, often no more than a foot from the precipice, causing the minibus to bounce and wobble. As the music faded, our conversation topics reduced to just two: the beautiful mountains and dying.

Soon the inevitable happened: stuck in the mud, right beside the cliff edge. The driver revved the engine, wheels span and the bus screamed – but we went nowhere. He tried again, but to no avail.

So then he went full throttle: the wheels whizzed like circular saws, mud splattered every window, the bus toppled over towards the edge – and somehow pulled through. The *lan* quickly improved, cue for the Christian rock to return. Jesus was resurrected: we were saved.

Our journey back down a couple of days later proved less fortunate as a four-wheel drive truck delivering boxes of soft drinks to Tiddim capsized in the mud in front of us and landed just a metre shy of certain death, blocking the *lan*.

The crew got out, uninjured, and began removing the cargo from the vehicle. Everyone helped move the boxes, but they lacked efficiency until one of the Germans introduced a chain system. Soon space was clear for the digger, which flattened and widened the track; then somebody produced a rope and connected the vehicles. All were set for the big moment – when suddenly the truck driver ran over to his vehicle and clambered down through the window. He emerged with a bag of betel.

Now we were ready.

The digger positioned itself, raised the hydraulic shovel – and the rope came loose.

Attempt Two. This time the digger uprighted the truck with ease – to the screams and cheers of all – and we were soon underway again. I had been surprised by everyone's nonchalance during the ordeal. It turned out trucks tipping over was not uncommon, nor were landslides, for which prevention measures are still being put in place.

My journey this time around, in the cold season, was less eventful, though we still prayed for safe passage beside the Christian gravestones. The trouble now was not mud but dust, so copious that by the end of every journey I was sneezing orange. Masks were of little help.

"Tiddim" (or "Tedim") describes a local mountain pool and literally means 'bright twinkling' – the effect of sunbeams on the water's surface. The surrounding hills, roughly 5300ft up, basked a soft jade in the sunlight and emanated biblical grandeur. Churches of countless denominations – including Baptist, Catholic, Evangelist and Seventh-day Adventist – dotted the town. Crucifixes adorned households, the Sabbath was kept holy and one believer asked if we would pray for his family, whom misfortune had recently befallen, for God naturally listens more readily to white European atheists than devout

Myanmar Christians. Every day, children praised God in religious private schools from 5-7am and from 7pm onwards.

The Tiddim Chin shared similar looks to the Lahe Naga and were equally reserved, though this time I felt it was because of their faith. On a nearby hill stood a large white cross, which I found an elderly woman walking round, speaking in what sounded like Tongues (certainly it wasn't Tiddim, the local first language). Out of town, women and children lugged huge baskets of logs, straps round their foreheads, hands supporting their backs. I saw this all over Chin State and in other hilltribe areas, including Nagaland and northern Shan. Some of the elder women were hunched and the children were undoubtedly under ten years old. The boys would escape this fate upon reaching adolescence, but the girls would carry these burdens almost every day for decades to come. Myanmar has reasonably rigid gender expectations; and though it varies between ethnic groups, the women always come off worse – as they do in most countries. Seeing these young girls lugging logs nearly broke my spirit, and I will always associate this image with my travels through Myanmar's hill regions.

Tiddim has occupied a meaningful place in my heart ever since I and the two *Deutsche* took a memorable trip to one of its nearby villages during my first visit to the area. As we wandered along the mountain *lan*, admiring the views, a guy pulled up beside us and asked for a photo. A living chicken was sat in a plastic bag hanging off the bike handle, its head poking out.

"Dinner?" asked Flo.

Our friend nodded. "I am a teacher at the school in that village," he said, pointing to a collection of small houses on the hillside about a mile away. "You should come to my school."

It was agreed, and soon we were walking through the gate. The young, ununiformed pupils didn't have academic lessons that day, but undertook physical work – playing football and slicing grass with machetes: the usual Friday fun. Upon seeing us strange white giants, they screamed and ran away.

"The children used to go to school on the weekends, too," said one of the teachers. "But Daw Aung San Suu Kyi changed that."

The kids kept their distance for a good few minutes, despite Emily's best attempts to woo them. Then one brave little girl came and shook her hand, followed by a few daring others. Emily began making funny noises by jiggling her throat, which got the kids in stitches – allowing me to capture a wonderful photo of 30 children laughing away, all toothless or nearly so. It was *hla-de* and uplifting and brings a smile to my face every time I think about it.

"They say her humour is too funny," said the teacher with a grin. "You must be the first foreigners they've ever seen."

After some final photos and many more giggles, we headed off in search of lunch. It turned out the village was too rural to have an eat-drink-shop or a teahouse, but a large elderly lady adopted us and led us into a modest wooden home. A silver kettle sat in the middle of the room on a log fire, a tabby cat curled round it. Sweetcorn cobs hung from the ceiling and light filtered through the open window, illuminating the dusty prints of flip-flops and paws.

The owners were a humble, middle-aged couple with a tiny baby clothed in a pink onesie and a cerulean woollen hat. The mother came over and laid before us rice wine, tea, cookies, and a rice broth traditionally eaten for breakfast.

"What's in the broth?" I asked.

"I'm not sure," said Flo, "but certainly some sort of animal innards."

I tried my best to eat it but felt nauseous after just a few mouthfuls. Emily hardly fared better. Flo of the Iron Stomach ate it all.

When we had finished, our hosts led us outside and slung a traditional head-strap basket round Flo's forehead. He looked ridiculous, but I interpreted it as an honour accorded to him for managing all his food. Everyone had a good laugh.

Photoshoot over, it was time to leave. But as we wandered out the front garden, the husband chased after us and handed me K1000 (£0.52) – probably a significant portion of his daily wage. I declined as politely as possible, stunned by his selflessness.

Myanmar hospitality is legendary. The principle of *bamar-hsan-chin* ('Burmeseness') encourages generous treatment towards guests, and foreigners are seemingly deemed guests even if they live in Myanmar. Friends in Yangon almost always insisted on paying for my meals at eat-drink-shops, and for the first few months of our relationship Shwe Ei wouldn't let me spend a single *kyat* – even though she was a student and I was working.

Of all the wonderful hospitality memories I accumulated in Myanmar, this one in Chin State stood out. Unsurprisingly, we were unable to leave the village without armfuls of sweetcorn.

*

My next stop was Rihkhawdar, home to the mystical Rih Lake. This heart-shaped wonder has a magical, tranquil setting: the water shines a deep blue and the lake is surrounded by rice paddies and forested hills. Its aura is enhanced by its remoteness.

That description is lifted almost verbatim from the 2017 Myanmar *Lonely Planet*, which has somewhat overhyped Rih Lake, probably in order to promote its new section on Chin State. Rih Lake was reasonably impressive, nothing more. Had I visited in the wet season, when the surrounding rice paddies are emerald, not beige, it would have been picturesque. But getting there then would have involved travelling along miles of muddy mountain roads, and I'm not that committed to photography.

In ancient animist tradition, Rih Lake is a gateway to Piairal, the Mizo version of paradise. Despite the dominant influence of Christianity in Chin State and the bordering Indian state of Mizoram, Rih Lake retained its mystical status through the syncretism of Piairal with Heaven. The lake remains a pilgrimage site for Indian and Myanmar Mizo and is a favourite local hangout. I went for a swim in its cool water, stunning a visiting Indian school class and condemning myself to countless half-naked photos with the tipsy headmaster.

The name "Rih" derives from a Mizo folktale. Rih-i had a cruel stepmother, who persuaded her father to take Rihi-i's younger sister into the woods and kill her. Rih-i found her murdered sister and was inconsolable until the spirit Lasi – a lady in a white dress, whom the Mizo fear and still report seeing – disclosed the healing powers of a certain magical tree. Rih-i used one of its leaves to resurrect her sister and another to turn herself into a waterbody, thereby quenching her sister's thirst. She then changed herself into a white mithun, a bovine indigenous to the region, and wandered in search of a safe location. Wherever she roamed, her urine formed *rih note*, small lakes. She came to Sanzawl village near the river Run, but a demon threatened to suck her dry if she settled there. Eventually, she chose her present location and transformed into her most beloved form – a lake, in this instance heart-shaped.

The wicked stepmother is a common fairy tale trope and is found in *Cinderella*, *Hansel and Gretel*, *Snow White* and many others. Since the stepmother is not a blood relative, she is untrustworthy and favours her own offspring, keen they take the riches and the food. In *The Brother and Sister*, the wicked stepmother transforms her stepson into a fawn. In other tales, she convinces her stepchildren to undertake perilous tasks or attempts to have them killed.

In the story of Rih-i, the stepmother has evidently "poisoned" her husband against his daughter – just as in *The Twelve Brothers*, where the wicked stepmother convinces her husband to sentence his daughter to death. In all instances – whether through transformation, murder, masterminding murder, or assigning perilous undertakings – the stepmother threatens to dilute the bloodline.

Fairy tales and folklore may be the widest-spread forms of literature and are among my favourites. I particularly enjoy finding connections between the traditional tales of different cultures, for they remind me that – no matter where they hail from, how they look and what they believe – all people are fundamentally alike, even if our similarities are differently manifested.

After scaling a hill overlooking Rih Lake for some *Tatmadaw* tea, I returned to Rihkhawdar, the closest town to Rih Lake. There, I saw my first tourists in two weeks: a young Italian-French couple. They took a long minibus ride from Kalaymyo; they saw Rih Lake; it was underwhelming; they left. I met them in the only guesthouse licensed to host foreigners. Ben had warned me that this was run by a "terrifying, bearded lady", but she turned out to be merely frightening and a little hairy.

The main downside of the otherwise reasonable guesthouse was the cold bucket showers. In the first five weeks of this leg of my trip, I enjoyed just one hot shower. In toasty lower Myanmar this wasn't an issue, but in Chin State the mornings were chilly and the water freezing.

There's something lonely about the cold: a hot shower embraces you like a lover, but a cold one is an emotionless one-night stand and a bucket means you're doing all the work. The Myanmar word for "to shower" is *ye-cho-de*, literally 'to break water.' My theory is that it evokes how the sheet of water "breaks" as it falls onto the body. But on colder mornings, you just have to be careful it doesn't break you.

Rihkhawdar itself was a dusty town of interweaving streets home to multilingual residents, many of Indian or Chinese descent. The local language was Mizo and a hundred-yard bridge separated Rihkhawdar from the Indian state of Mizoram. Gentle hills enclosed the border towns, creating a shallow bowl that wallowed in the morning mist until the sun rose high enough to pierce it with shafts of divine light. A grand, turreted, sky blue church sat on a hill platform, watching the stories of local lives unfold. From India echoed the screeches of a pig being taken to slaughter, a chilling dirge that reverberated around the hills and curdled the blood.

Border towns tend either to be bland and miserable, feel like the edge of civilisation and be riddled with wraiths whose lives appear shady and mysterious, or to boast the lively dynamic of transnational chaos and perpetual motion. Rihkhawdar was the latter. Until 2015, the sale of alcohol was prohibited in Mizoram, so Mizo people crossed into Myanmar for their fill. If they didn't manage to return before the border shut at 6pm, they had to stumble back across the river or, if the water was high, attempt amateur acrobatics on the bridge – two activities best undertaken sober.

Tamu, the only other border town I visited in Myanmar, was also intriguing. Not only was there a sprawling Myanmar *zay* from which Indians bought copious household goods to transport back to India, usually on their heads and in a hurry, but the endemic *myauk-ngo-thi* (literally 'crying monkey fruit') abounded. Loved by the Indians and loathed by the Myanmar, this large helix-shaped bean looks and tastes like a runner bean and provides a good source of income for both the Manipur Indians and the Sagaing Myanmar: Indians pour into Myanmar to buy the bean, then resell it in India at a premium. I found the *myauk-ngo-thi* cooked for me by an Indian gentleman delicious and suspect the Myanmar's reservation towards it may also have something to do with the cooking.

*

The Myanmar can sleep anytime, anywhere: on a jeep roof, reclined on a stationary motorbike, on the job – I've seen it all. In Kyaiktiyo, one hotel offers family suites, which are literally just empty rooms. The floor is perfectly adequate: some Myanmar merely need a roof over their heads.

As an insomniac, I envy the Myanmar's ability to fall asleep with ease – and nowhere was I so jealous as in Chin State, where I became a pillow for fellow passengers on three consecutive journeys. Perhaps it was the temperature, perhaps it was the dust or the comfortable height of my shoulder; whatever the reason, I made a great headrest.

My third and most memorable friend was an *a-myo-thami* my age from Mindat. It was the second leg of the ten-hour Hakha-Mindat minibus ride and we were sitting in the front row. Her eyelids kept closing and her head kept drooping, only to jerk up again when it touched my shoulder. Each time she apologised and sat back upright, but the sleepiness came back again and again until her eyes were closing for several seconds at a time. Her body started leaning my way like a sapling in the spring breeze, unable to resist the power of Somnus.

I clasped her upper arm and pulled her gently towards me, letting her know it was okay. Her sleepy mind understood; and as she nodded off on my shoulder, her small hand slipped into mine and squeezed tightly whenever we hit a bump – for surprises are scary, even in sleep.

Due to its lower elevation, Mindat was pleasantly warmer than Rihkhawdar and Tiddim. I was finally back on the beaten track and must have seen all of ten tourists in two days. Everyone had come for the same reason: to see the elderly women with facial tattoos. These are typically dark navy and cover the entire face, but the patterns vary with each tribe: spider webs, looping lines, dots, curves; all intricate and defined.

Legend has it that a Myanmar king was so impressed by the local women's beauty that he kidnapped one to be his bride. From then on, families tattooed their girls to stop them being taken either by lusty kings or neighbouring tribes. Another theory is that the tattoos were considered *hla-de* or were simply tradition at the time. Some of the Chin women recall being told by local pastors that only those bearing tattoos would go to heaven.

Just as mesmerising were the women's yellow and blue necklaces that reached down to the midriff, and their wooden earrings decorated with yellow and red beads. These plugs slotted into the earlobe were the size of one's fist and looked desperately uncomfortable; it's little surprise the new generations don't wear them.

A few of these elderly women learned to play a curious traditional instrument in their youth, the nose flute, and I went to see the only one in Mindat still able to. Sat cosily in a spacious loft room, she played a simple melody her mother had taught her in her first year of learning. While her facial tattoo, beaded necklaces and dark garments transmitted an aura of stateliness, her aged fingers worked the flute with a youthful nimbleness. I was encouraged to take photos; and though the light was low, forcing me to use a low shutter speed, the image didn't blur – she remained perfectly composed, nose pressed tight to the embouchure hole. Her breathing was calm and her fingers lithe. She played for three to four minutes, during which we all sat captivated – even her daughter, who must have heard her play countless times before. I gave her a resounding clap at the end.

"*Maw-de*", she said, sitting back upright. I wasn't surprised she was 'exhausted': it had been quite a performance for a 92-year-old.

These women are the last generation to bear such tattoos. The Myanmar socialist government banned facial tattooing in the 1960s – mostly in an attempt to modernise, for Christian missionaries had branded the practice barbaric. Many foreigners lament that this chapter of Chin culture will soon be history, but I think it's for the best, for the girls have their faces tattooed when they are still children and the three-hour process is bloody. We romanticise tradition, though not every tradition is romantic: sometimes it's better off as history.

Most travellers come to Mindat to trek and see the tribal villages, but my debit card had been declined in Hakha and there were no ATMs in Mindat, so I was forced to choose my own itinerary.

I began by visiting the museum on local tribal culture, which I failed to find until an *a-myo-thar* ran out and redirected me to his front garden: the museum grounds. He had a kind, inviting nature, a reassuring, knowledgeable air, and hamster cheeks that dimpled when he smiled.

"We sacrificed a bullock there last month," he said, pointing to a wooden contraption that resembled a medieval torture device. I wasn't surprised.

He led me into the single-roomed museum. Tables stood against the walls and were laden with tribal artefacts, including belts, musical instruments, weapons, jewellery and clothes. On one wall hung the skulls of bulls, bears, leopards and tigers, along with the old-school rifles that had procured them. It was quite a sight.

"These are collected from the tribes around Mindat," he said, "though most come from my family." He picked up a slender quiver and took out two arrows. "Two types of poison arrows," he said, stroking their shafts. "One for animals, one for adversaries." He glanced at me and grinned.

We walked over to a collection of small pots and tools.

"These are all very old. From the Stone Age – one million years ago."

I photographed the "Stone Age" artefacts and followed him to the musical instruments. He grabbed one resembling a lyre and began fingerpicking – dissonantly at first, but then he strummed a minor chord. We exchanged surprised smiles and he gave me an accomplished nod.

"These are from the war," he said, motioning towards a collection of relatively modern bits and bobs, including a willow pattern plate and tins imprinted with German words.

"And these were the clothes of the village chief," he said, taking a floppy beige tapestry from the wall. "The chief always had to wear them wherever he went." He pulled it on over his jacket and was instantly enveloped: there were holes for his head and arms, but otherwise the outfit was a single piece of thick cloth. He looked like a standing carpet.

"2000 *kyats* please."

It was one of the better museums in Myanmar.

In the hope of meeting more tattooed women, I next headed for Baung Te village. The path was steeply downhill, jungled and tranquil. I passed a small cemetery which doubled up as a rubbish dump – rather like the Chinese cemetery in Hsipaw, though not to the same extent. Before I knew it, I had been descending for an hour: that meant a two-hour uphill slog back, and I was only halfway to Baung Te.

As I contemplated giving up, the drone of a motorbike engine made my decision for me. I stuck my thumb out and was soon heading back to town. The driver was an elderly betel fan, who was particularly impressed by my average Myanmar. Suddenly we were at his house.

"Laik-par-one" ('Please come on in.')

I thanked him and stepped inside. He ushered me into his wooden kitchen, where a rickety table stood beneath an open hatch; a sprawling cooking area dominated the far corner. Beside it sat three enormous clay jars, whose ominous contents were connected by a couple of weaving plastic tubes.

I sat down at the table, joining four Buddhist men all smoking cheroots and drinking cloudy concoctions. Two of these kept a low profile, but the two cousins sat opposite me were both "Man U crazy": one of them wore a team beanie, the other an embossed jumper. They were in their late twenties, had warm eyes, slender cheeks, and the most infectious smiles I saw in all of Chin State. Man U Jumper had spiky hair; for all I know his cousin did too, thereby completing their twin aura, but sadly I would never find out.

"Aww, your skin is... white and re'," said Man U Jumper, hitting that glottal stop. "Mine is so black."

My skin was always "white", "red", or "white and red" – never "brown" – and the ghostly ivory skin above my tan lines usually stunned curious Myanmar into silence. As in many Asian countries, white skin is considered *hla-de* in Myanmar. Shwe Ei would even get told off by her mum if she spent too long in the sun.

To acquire fairer skin, the Myanmar use a variety of whitening products, most commonly creams and pills, and almost every beauty product, including shower gel, contains whitening ingredients. In the past few years, whitening injections have also become popular, particularly among college girls and celebrities. A single dose costs between K12,000-K250,000 (£7-£138), depending on the quality (Thai brands are infamous for having side effects), and, according to *The Myanmar Times*, "an individual must undergo at least eight doses, one per week, to see results."

The substance injected is glutathione, an antioxidant found in fruits, vegetables and meats and which is naturally produced by the liver to facilitate numerous bodily processes, including tissue repair. It's also used in oral medicines designed to fight cancer, heart diseases, cataracts and other ailments. These injections are yet to be properly evaluated for consumer safety, and their usage is largely unregulated. Most countries have not approved them.

White skin is a side effect of the shot, as are hives, redness and allergic reactions. Miss Myanmar International 2013 suffered a serious reaction from a glutathione injection and ended up in hospital.

"I thought I would die because I had difficulty breathing," she said in an interview. "I took the injection and it happened immediately. I don't want whiter skin anymore. Now I know my dark skin is more attractive."[20]

As well as being potentially harmful, many of these whitening products have a reputation for turning the skin, well, *blue*. In Myanmar, someone who indulges too freely in such beauty products is said to have a "blue face" (*myet-hnar pyar-ne-de*) – which is perhaps even less flattering than being "white and red."

"Drink?" asked Man U Beanie.

Before I could answer, a large beer glass was filled and thumped onto the table in front of me by a rotund lady who had just entered through the back door.

---

[20]   https://www.mmtimes.com/lifestyle/11469-going-fair-at-any-price.html <Accessed: 14.09.2018>

"What is it?"

"Millet wine."

It tasted good: slightly bitter, with an alcohol content of, I estimate, 20-25%. The lady refilled my glass once I had finished. In the time it had taken for me to drink one, Beanie drained two and a half and the others two each. I drank my second *po-myan-myan*.

They asked me the usual questions and taught me a bit of Chin in exchange for some German. Soon we were embroiled in a haze of conviviality, drinking, joking and butchering foreign languages.

"Where are you going after Mindat?" asked Jumper.

"Rakhine."

"You're going to Yakhine?" he said, mouth agape. It was the first time I had heard someone say "Yakhine" (the corresponding Myanmar character is pronounced "ra" or "ya").

"Yeah, to Mrauk-U first."

"Are you not scared?" asked Beanie. "Of ARSA?"

Everyone stopped drinking.

"I'm not going to that area," I said. "I'll be fine."

The cousins exchanged uncertain looks.

"Why are you drinking?" I asked. It was 10:30am and so, notwithstanding the fact that the afternoon in Myanmar traditionally begins at 11, a little on the early side.

"The mum of one of our friends has just died," said Jumper with a big grin.

Silence.

"Err..."

"The funeral is tomorrow," added Beanie, also grinning.

"Did you... like her?"

The cousins were baffled.

"Of course," said Jumper.

I forced a smile and sipped my wine, prompting the others to do likewise. Then Beanie had the great idea of shoving the plastic tube from the jar of millet wine down my throat and taking a photo of me as I crouched over it like an animal.

"You need to meet my family," he slurred.

He whisked me out the front door, where his purple Kenbo sat waiting. But it wouldn't start – even Jumper's attempts to kick-start it were in vain – so Beanie and I crammed on a single bike with the elderly *a-myo-thar*, who drove us two minutes down the road to a low wooden house on high stilts. An old man with copious nose hair peeked round the door. Then he grinned and bade us step inside.

The living room was haphazardly arranged, with junk lining every surface, bar a couple of chairs in the far corner. A dirty Chin rug lay spread on the wooden floor; graduation photos of family members decorated the walls, as they do in many Myanmar homes.

"This is my grandfather," said Beanie as I sat down. His grandfather displayed a set of white teeth.

"Do your parents live here?"

"No," he said. "They died two years ago in a car crash on Valentine's Day."

It took my inebriated mind some time to clock this.

Beanie said something in Chin to his grandfather, who nodded and disappeared into another room. He reappeared a moment later to give us *ye-nway-kyan* and jaggery, a golden-brown lump of cane sugar eaten with green tea, before disappearing once more.

Sounds of slurping filled the next few minutes, which would have been incredibly awkward had it not been for the tea. Eventually, a shapely lady in her late thirties entered carrying a baby swaddled in a green and white Chin blanket.

"My auntie," said Beanie.

She sat down and smiled at us. She and Beanie talked briefly in Chin, then she pulled up her purple *ingyi* and began breastfeeding her baby. Beanie turned to me and made a camera sign with his hands.

"Photo," he said, pointing at his aunt, who was oblivious to what he was saying. "Photo," he repeated, tapping my Nikon bag.

"Shall we go back?" I suggested, uncomfortable and confused. Why did he think that would interest me?

Beanie grinned, and we left. In a matter of minutes, we were back at the other house, where the number of mourners had swelled. They were all chronically drunk, particularly the Forestry Officer.

"Do you like trees?" I asked him.

He dribbled, which I took for a "Yes, I love them", and we clinked glasses. And so the mourning went on, accompanied by raucous laughter and boundless boozing. The merriness was infectious: the perfect preparation for a funeral.

Buddhist Myanmar funerals can be peculiar experiences for Westerners. *In Twilight over Burma*, Inge

Sargent recorded the bizarre spectacle she witnessed at the funeral of a renowned Shan abbot:

> *Dozens of able-bodied men stationed themselves along the ropes. A deafening blast from a homemade cannon announced the beginning of the tug of war, and dozens of villagers simultaneously tried to pull the cart [carrying the coffin] in opposite directions. At first the forces pulling uphill toward the pyre were ahead, but then the other side gained momentum, dragging the funeral cart back to its starting position. Everybody who had gathered at the funeral grounds became part of the strange contest. Those who could not find space along the ropes waited to take the place of a tired warrior. Women and children provided noisy support. The struggle went on for over an hour until, finally, the funeral cart reached the pyre. Sao explained to Thusandi [Inge's Shan name] that this rope-pulling contest symbolised the struggle between the worldly and spiritual forces for the karma of the deceased. She wondered what would have happened if the worldly forces had won, but she decided against asking that question.[21]*

Instead of mourning the deceased, the Buddhist Myanmar celebrate the completion of another life in the long cycle of death and rebirth. Funerals can be jolly occasions and last a whole week, since it is believed that for the first six days the souls of dead people cannot cope with the fact they have died and so refuse to leave the house. At the cemetery, mourners don't wear formal dress – though

---

[21] I. Sargent (1994), *Twilight over Burma: My Life as a Shan Princess* (Kindle Edition), University of Hawaii Press, pos. 1466-1474.

some may don a jacket or a necktie without a jacket, depending on their own status and that of the deceased – and a coin, called *kudo-hka*, is placed in the corpse's mouth to pay a 'ferry toll' for passage to the underworld.

Chapter 14: Murder and Lies

My travels through Chin State had not been as I had imagined. Having read in numerous books that Chin used to be the poorest region in Myanmar, I had been surprised to find countless clean houses and well-dressed residents. At first, I thought there must have been some mistake – after all, how could Chin be poorer than, say, the Ayeyarwady Region, where many people lived in squalid wooden shacks? – but after some research I learnt that Chin's poverty lay in its food dearth. In addition to inadequate transportation infrastructure, Chin suffers from a bizarre phenomenon approximately every 50 years as flowering bamboo in the jungle attracts rats, which multiply rapidly and subsequently ravage paddy fields and rice barns. Once again, I was reminded that there was much more to Myanmar than I could see with my own eyes.

The next fortnight of my trip would be spent in Rakhine, now the most impoverished state in Myanmar. Rakhine slithers down Myanmar's western edge, a little like Chile in South America, and had somehow always felt like my ultimate destination. Scene of the Rohingya genocide and cursed by a devilishly complicated political landscape, Rakhine is rife with corruption and dodgy dealings. In many regards, Myanmar's future hinges upon Rakhine's. If I was going to "find" Myanmar, visiting it would be essential. The very thought of doing so made my skin ripple and rise with greedy goose bumps.

If you checked the British Foreign Office's travel advice for Myanmar before the August 2017 ARSA attacks, as I did, you would have been strongly advised against visiting Rakhine. If, however, you looked at the Myanmar's Ministry of Hotels and Tourism website, you would have seen that no areas of Rakhine were listed as off-limits to foreigners – part of the government's desperate attempt to claim the region was safe and deny wrongdoing there. Gradually, though, more and more caveats on Rakhine were issued – until only Sittwe, the state capital, could be visited without a permit. Not that this affected me in the slightest: tourism news travels as slowly as political change in Myanmar.

To reach Mrauk-U, my first stop in Rakhine, I would have to overnight in the small city of Pakkoku before catching a night bus from Kyaukpadaung. I had visited Pakkoku before and stayed at Mya Yatanar Inn, run by the grandmotherly Mya Mya and once host to a young David Duchovny. This time, however, it wasn't to be.

"The government has revoked my license for hosting foreigners," she told me in perfect English.

"How come?"

"They said the building is unsafe, which isn't true. Foreigners have always stayed here – my place is well known – but the government now wants them to stay in their fancy new hotels."

"So it's safe enough for locals but not foreigners?"

"Of course," she said, smiling.

It was a shame – corruption had ended a small, charming chapter in local history – but Mya Mya was kind enough to direct me to the cheapest hotel.

The next day began in the idyllic manner of many Myanmar mornings: sunbeams scattered through trees lining the streets, creating a jigsaw of dappled shadows, while nuns young and old, clothed in their distinctive pink robes and turmeric sashes, walked barefoot through town, begging for alms. Rickshaw drivers pedalled along, ferrying *longyi'd* women who were carrying the colourful plastic baskets that are steadily replacing the traditional bamboo ones – a stark contrast to the modest combs and fragrant jasmine entwined in their hair buns. All these sights were contained within the dirty, rectilinear centre of Pakkoku, proving that beauty can blossom in the ordinary.

I took a pick-up to Kyaukpadaung in the afternoon. This was another unremarkable, dusty transport hub. Such places feel forlorn, neither brimming with the optimism of homecoming nor of departure: travelling limbo embodied by ticket stalls, advertising boards and roadside restaurants.

After strolling round town, I returned to the main road and people-watched while munching on a Chinese pear. A tall Myanmar *a-myo-thami* stood nearby, swaying to and fro in waiting. She wore a bewitching lapis *longyi* and *ingyi*, sparkling sandals, and carried a stylish handbag. Her unusual height and classy attire lent her an air of distinction, which contrasted our scrappy surroundings. She must have caught me staring, for she giggled and sidled my way.

"Where are you from?"
"England."
"How old are you?"
"Twenty-four. And you?"
"Twenty-six. Are you married?"
"No. Are you?"
"No."

We exchanged awkward smiles. Then she reached into her handbag and took out her phone, accidentally causing something to spill out and fall on the ground.

It was the Pill.

Her timing was exemplary. We both stared at it, locked eyes – then erupted in giggles. It was a touching moment. Had I been Myanmar, she would almost certainly have been deeply embarrassed; but she presumably guessed from my skin colour that I was also promiscuous and would not judge her for having pre-marital sex.

Still giggling, she picked up the Pill and slipped it back into her bag – at which point a handsome young *a-myo-thar* on a motorbike pulled up beside us. She climbed on side-saddle; and as he pulled away, she gazed back at me, her face etched with a cheeky smile that said, Yes, he's the one.

I was entering Rakhine State at a particularly dark time. In the second week of December 2017, two Myanmar Reuters journalists, Wa Lone and Kyaw Soe Oo, were arrested for possessing top secret documents on the *Tatmadaw's* clearance operations in Rakhine. Within an hour of apprehending them, the police phoned the president's office and sought permission to charge the reporters under the colonial-era Official Secrets Act, which carries a maximum sentence of fourteen years imprisonment.

The journalists' version of events differed considerably from the Myanmar Police Force's, whose witnesses included an officer who had burned his notes for no apparent reason and another who was shown to have the "official" version of events written on his hand.

The plot twist came on 8th February 2018, when Reuters published a report co-authored by Wa Lone, Kyaw Soe Oo and two others on the murder of ten Rohingya men by security personnel in Inn Din village. According to the military investigation, the men had confessed to participating in terrorist activities and were executed by both military personnel and villagers due to a lack of available transportation and prison space. It was the first time the *Tatmadaw* had admitted to wrongdoing in Rakhine State, and few were surprised when the Reuters report found that the murdered men had been teachers, fishermen and students and that an order to "clear" the village had come from high up the chain of command. It was a stellar piece of journalism: not only were Rohingya Muslims interviewed but also military personnel and Rakhine Buddhists who took part in the massacre. It even included photos captured by a village elder.

Media access to Rakhine had been restricted since the clearance operations began in late August – a move condemned by human rights groups as a means for the *Tatmadaw* to conceal its pogrom. Wa Lone and Kyaw Soe Oo eventually received seven years imprisonment, even though one of the police officers who had handed the reporters the top-secret documents testified that the arrest had been set up. The message was clear: those who compromised the official line would be punished.[22]

---

[22] Addendum: the Reuters journalists, Wa Lone and Kyaw Soe Oo, were eventually released under a presidential amnesty on 7th May 2019, having spent more than 500 days in prison. Government spokesman,

The situation for the Rohingya had not improved either. The arrival of almost 700,000 refugees into Bangladesh by mid-January 2018 had transformed Kutaplong into the world's largest refugee camp. There had already been an outbreak of diphtheria and, with the monsoon season approaching, preparations were being made for the management of corpses.

The governments of Bangladesh and Myanmar agreed to repatriate the refugees over two years, beginning on January 23rd, though only Rohingya who could provide tangible proof of their residency would be repatriated – a difficult task for a largely stateless community.

From the outset, the Myanmar government was accused of apathy. The 23rd of January came and went, without any refugees returning to Rakhine State. Myanmar claimed it was ready for repatriation, but officials from both the UN and Bangladesh argued that the safety of the refugees could not be guaranteed, that the temporary repatriation camps near Maungdaw had not been completed, and that many Rohingya were unwilling to return. *The Global New Light of Myanmar*, a state-run newspaper, subsequently published an editorial called 'Good Friends Really Needed', in which it accused Bangladesh of slowing down the repatriation process and condemned the international community for labelling Myanmar with "new titles, so that inconveniences and problems [could] be created."[23]

Zaw Htay, said the pair were freed after their families wrote to Aung San Suu Kyi.

[23] http://www.globalnewlightofmyanmar.com/good-friends-really-needed/ <Accessed: 09.08.2018>

The editorial made no mention of the refugees' safety or wellbeing, which encapsulates the core issue of the repatriation process: few Myanmar want the Rohingya back. The government's vagueness, apathy and lack of transparency reflect this: of the first 8,032 Rohingya Muslims to complete the repatriation forms, only 374 were verified. Myanmar accused Bangladesh of providing insufficient information and claimed to have found three "terrorists" among the applicants.

For those refugees who do make it to the temporary camps in Maungdaw, houses constructed of inferior timber await them. They will share the area with recently relocated Buddhist Rakhine, beneficiaries of the Ancillary Committee for the Reconstruction of Rakhine National Territory in the Western Frontier – a private scheme funded by Rakhine donors that seeks to create a "Muslim-dry" buffer zone between Maungdaw Township and Sittwe, the Rakhine State capital. Amnesty International also recorded that the *Tatmadaw* were building helipads, roads and security installations over razed Rohingya settlements nearby.

*

Mrauk-U revealed itself as the most touristy place I had visited in a month – I saw over ten tourists – and the most impressive. As former capital of the Arakan Kingdom, which ruled Rakhine State, Chittagong and Bangladesh from 1430-1784, Mrauk-U abounded with magnificent red brick temples and stupas, many crowning picturesque hilltops. The temple interiors were home to elegant stone carvings of Buddhas, sinuous dancers, fighting peacocks and countless other wonders. The buildings oozed majesty, vividly evoking the Arakan Kingdom's former glory, and herdsmen urged their livestock along rural roads, adding a sense of timelessness.

"I've come to the most touristy place in Mrauk-U and there are only three people here," said Ellie as we sat atop a *taung-paya* and watched the sunset. Ellie was a South African-born Bristolian with a modest afro, twinkling eyes and a euphoric disposition. She had one more week in Myanmar but was thinking of overstaying her visa – the only penalty for which is a fine of $3 per day.

"Mrauk-U is the most touristy place I've been in five weeks," I said.

"I didn't like Bagan," continued Ellie. "Too many people, and the atmosphere was artificial. Mrauk-U is much nicer."

I nodded my agreement, gaze locked onto the sun dipping below the horizon. We remained silent for the next ten minutes, watching the sky transform into a series of purple, amber and turquoise swathes. Pockets of fog spread between the trees and town, weaving one large, translucent spider's web, and small stupas stood proudly, enjoying the twilight before darkness swallowed them. Gradually, the pale lights of people's homes flickered on, anticipating and mirroring the emergence of pin prick stars.

"They call that fog in all the sunrise and sunset photos a morning or evening 'mist'", said Ellie. "But it isn't, is it? It's pollution: smoke from bonfires."

"Yeah, I expect so," I said. "People warming themselves up at the coldest times of day."

Ellie nodded. "But its atmospheric and good for photos."

She was right, though the atmosphere by day in Mrauk-U was eerie. On 16th January 2018, just under a month before I arrived, eight Buddhist Rakhine protestors had been shot by security personnel. In protest of the police's decision to cancel the 233rd commemoration of the fall of the Arakan Empire, thousands had gathered in downtown near the ancient temples. According to witnesses, the protesters destroyed property, including a motorbike and some plastic chairs, after which police fired into the crowd. Two weeks later, the town administrator was murdered.

Knowledge of this recent bloodshed turned sightseeing into a blind, sinister activity, and I couldn't help wondering whether the red patches covering the ground were blood or betel, so I resolved to leave. Unfortunately, since Mrauk-U was a tourist destination, the transportation prices to Sittwe were absurd. The boat there cost K26,500 for foreigners, K5,000 for locals, and the bus K10,000 for foreigners, K2,000 for locals. Feeling particularly stubborn, I sought an alternative – which there always is in Myanmar, providing you look hard enough.

I walked to the downtown bus stop, hoping to catch a passing coach and haggle a reasonable price. But Fortune was being more favourable. Opposite the bus stop sat a blue Htoo San Co., truck bound for Sittwe. Naturally, the young Rakhine driver, a chill dude sporting a Myanmar football shirt, offered me a lift.

As we cruised along, listening to quality Myanmar driving tunes, I felt pretty chuffed with my small victory. I sat there enjoying the ride past lakes layered with lily pads and over timeless rivers, wishing I were in a pre-plastic Myanmar. As we neared Sittwe, the roadsides became an almost unbroken line of Buddhist women holding out silver donation bowls, Buddhist flags were ubiquitous, and pagodas were being constructed on every other hilltop. Then came numerous *Tatmadaw* bases, and outside of each stood a red sign bearing the following message:

တပ်မတော်အင်အားရှိမှတိုင်းပြည်အင်အားရှိမည်

'When the Tatmadaw are empowered, every nation will be empowered.'

    I jacked up the shutter speed and took a picture. The driver glanced at me but said nothing. Then he stopped the truck and explained I would have to find another lift to the city centre, for he was turning off shortly.

    A white pick-up with three large elderly women sat in the back soon appeared and I climbed in. We set off, but a motorbike caught up with us *myan-myan* and told the driver to pull over. There was muffled talk in Rakhine, then everyone turned and stared at me. One of the women pointed at my Nikon bag and barked something in Rakhine – which is closely related to Myanmar, but I didn't understand. The driver turned around and headed back towards the military checkpoint.

    I whipped out my camera, memorised the message and deleted the photo. My heart was a jackhammer, my mind a mess; I could only think of how stupid I had been to photograph a *Tatmadaw* base in Rakhine State.

Yet we passed through the checkpoint without stopping and pulled over a minute later. I clambered out the back – to find the Htoo San Co., truck driver jogging my way and smiling.

I had forgotten my camping mat.

Sittwe was an abomination of stinking streets, dilapidated buildings and suspicious glares. The strand road *zay* offered hacked-up stingrays and sharks by day, gloom and desolation by night. Neighbourhoods previously home to Rohingya were now spectral ghettos, ghosts of the former apartheid system, and trucks packed with armed *Tatmadaw* soldiers passed regularly through the city centre, leaving little to the imagination. The only impressive building was the ransacked Jama Mosque, which had been closed since the 2012 sectarian violence. I was banned from taking a photo.

Everyone I know who's visited Sittwe shared my experience, but I met a couple of American tourists who, like others, had heard the Rakhine capital was an elegant port city steeped in remarkable colonial history. They were equally disappointed to discover that it was actually a fetid prison hemmed in on the western side by the Bay of Bengal and on the other by *Tatmadaw* bases. It was probably the single worst place I visited in all of Myanmar and I caught food poisoning almost immediately, depleting the last remaining Christmas fat reserves I had so desperately accumulated in England.

While walking through the cramped downtown alleys in search of a guesthouse, wheedling my way round rickshaws and people carrying bundles of dried fish or baskets of goods, I felt myself being gently tugged round. The small dangling string of my camping mat had untucked itself and got caught on a passing motorbike.

As I slowly spun, utterly helpless, I fumbled desperately at the air and whimpered for the driver to stop. But it was in vain. Suddenly I was pitched into the air. There was a loud crash followed by a scream. I landed on my backpack, bum pressed up against the motorbike, feet pointing to the sky.

Someone ran over and helped me to sit up. There were red blotches on the road – curry – and the driver, a girl younger than ten, was shrieking.

To my great relief, she was only in shock. In fact, neither of us had been injured: my backpack had cushioned my fall and she had not been crushed by the motorbike. Still, I felt awful; and although everyone acknowledged it had been bad luck, I could detect animosity in their eyes.

Feeling outcast, I did the most expat thing imaginable: I escaped to Sittwe's only Western-style cafe, ordered pizza and spent the day writing. It was the single best decision I made in Sittwe (besides leaving early the next morning) and the pizza soothed my self-deprecation immeasurably.

*

Two days after I left, three bombs went off in Sittwe, injuring a security guard and a passer-by. The subsequent arrests reflected suspicions that the Arakan Army (AA), an insurgency group who claim to safeguard Rakhine national interests, had carried out the attacks. The bombings came two weeks after the nationalistic Arakan National Council refused to sign the Nationwide Ceasefire Agreement.

"Rakhine" means 'one who maintains his own race', and Rakhine is the only Myanmar state in which an ethnic political party won the most seats in the 2015 elections. Support for the triumphant Arakan National Party was palpable in Sittwe, where their campaign boards vastly outnumbered the usually ubiquitous NLD ones.

Rakhine State's ethnodemographics were transformed by the conquest of the Arakan kingdom in 1784 by Bamar kings, and by the influx of Indians with colonialism. Many Rakhine nationalists remain bitter about both "invasions" and regard themselves as the victims of both Burmanisation and Muslimisation. One eat-drink-shop owner told me the Bamar were of inferior intelligence and that she only liked Aung San Suu Kyi because she was the daughter of Aung San, her "favourite person in history." She said the government had done little to aid Rakhine State, the poorest in Myanmar, and that their rejection of NGOs and foreign food handouts had condemned many Rakhine to malnourishment.

The Rakhines' devotion to their identity has earned them a reputation as nationalistic, and the Bamar even tell the following joke about them: "If you see an ethnic Rakhine and a cobra at the same time, kill the Rakhine first."

Chapter 15: Soon Forgotten

It's amazing how experiences shape your perception of a place. Diarrhoea, the camping mat debacles, Sittwe's general filth – all these (actually rather minor) setbacks had turned me against the place and made me desperate to escape.

In Lahe, Richard had advised me to visit the Rakhine city of Kyaukphyu, so that's where I headed next. The boat there was costly but divine. We set off before sunrise, trashy Myanmar comedy playing loudly over the TV. As it grew light, the captain ushered me onto a titchy plastic chair on the bow – where I sat alone, chilly but enraptured, watching fishermen cast silhouette nets into the wine-dark sea. Flanked by fecund fields and gliding egrets, we rode into rosy Dawn. Colours spilled into the firmament like oil paints over a canvas, illuminating verdant islands shrouded in the morning gloom and transforming the strait into a mini archipelago.

As we approached port, Soe Moe, a rotund Myanmar chap who smoked and chewed liberally, joined me on deck. I could see in his eyes that he had taken a liking to me, and sure enough he offered me a lift to a comfortable guesthouse. He had excellent taste: Yadanabon Motel was probably the best value Myanmar guesthouse I ever stayed in, and the staff warmed to me like family.

Once I had dumped my stuff, Soe Moe insisted on showing me the sights, and afterwards he treated me to a seaside meal replete with quality whisky. We dined slowly, as delicious food and drink merits.

Soe Moe was one of the good guys – his heroism lay hidden beneath his betel habit – and I returned to my guesthouse sated and fulfilled. Then, after a lengthy nap, I went out for another explore.

Kyaukphyu was the perfect remedy to Sittwe. The town was divided into a series of clean streets, the beaches were *shwe* and the residents so generous that I hardly spent a dime. To keep karma flowing, I bought 120 pens and rulers for a local high school and handed them out on the morning of a state examination. I *thanaka'd* up and dressed in my best *longyi* for the occasion. The pupils accepted the donations with bashful smiles and a soft "thank you" or *"kyay-zu-din-par-de."*

I made various similar donations across Myanmar, hoping to give something back to the country whose people had been so kind to me. For me, travel is not about destinations but connection – forming an emotional attachment to a country and its people. Being charitable, I have found, is one of the best ways of doing so.

Every evening in Kyaukphyu, I hitched a lift to its western beach, where locals gathered to play football beneath a crimson sunset, using driftwood for goalposts. I didn't go a single night without being invited to join someone's picnic. Like everywhere in Rakhine State, women carried towering silver water jugs on their heads, the crowning piece of the town's rustic aura. Both the men and women in Kyaukphyu were *hla-de*, far more so than in Sittwe.

Kyaukphyu occupies the northernmost point of Ramree Island, which was captured by the Imperial

Japanese Army in 1942. Following an offensive three years later, the Allies reclaimed the island, compelling Japanese soldiers to flee into the mangrove swamps. British soldier and naturalist Bruce Stanley Wright recorded what happened next:

That night was the most horrible that any member of the M. L. [motor launch] crews ever experienced. The scattered rifle shots in the pitch black swamp punctured by the screams of wounded men crushed in the jaws of reptiles and the blurred worrying sound of spinning crocodiles made a cacophony of hell that has rarely been duplicated on earth. At dawn the vultures arrived to clean up what the crocodiles had left.... Of about one thousand Japanese soldiers that entered the swamps of Ramree, only about twenty were found alive.[24]

The fabrication lies in the language – no report is so literary – and historians and zoologists have dismissed the crocodilian massacre as a sensationalist urban myth. Not only does the testimony of other soldiers differ, but it's doubtful the mangrove swamp ecosystem could have supported such a large population of saurians. Still, it's a good story – even the Guinness Book of World Records snapped it up, labelling it the highest "number of fatalities in a crocodile attack."[25]

The saltwater crocodiles of Ramree Island have since been hunted to near extinction; a local told me that

---

[24] Quoted by F. McLynn (2011), *The Burma Campaign: Disaster into Triumph, 1942–45*, Yale University Press.
[25] N. Kynaston (ed., 1998), *The Guinness 1999 Book of Records*. Guinness Publishing.

any stragglers found are shipped to Yangon zoo. He may not have been a reliable source, but he wasn't joking. That was a bit of a downer, for I was harbouring the peculiar (English) desire of getting myself into at least a spot of crocodilian bother.

By my third day I had become quite popular in town – the advantage of being the only tourist and of speaking some Myanmar – and was spending much of my time with Kyaw Oo and his three buddies, who had begun chatting to me on the beach one evening. Kyaw Oo, like one of his other friends, was an electrical engineer and wealthier than most Rakhine. He rode a powerful Thai-made motorbike, travelled to Yangon and Shan State occasionally and spoke reasonable English – usually an indication of having attended a private school. He hoped one day to travel as I was, but he didn't earn enough for that.

Once I felt I knew him well enough, I asked what he thought of the Rohingya situation – a topic I otherwise avoided discussing with Myanmar friends for fear it would strain our friendship.

"It's very bad what's going on," he said, slumping his shoulders. "So much death."

"Do you think it will affect tourism here?" I asked, having seen various hotels and resorts under construction on nearby beaches.

"Yes. It's bad for the country. Bad for business." He sighed. "I just want it to end."

I had my answer, so I asked about another local issue.

"And what do you think about the Kyaukphyu special economic zone?"

Kyaw Oo exhaled and pulled his jeans up. He was muscly and handsome, and his every word rang with sincerity.

"We have electricity now – and it's really cheap in Kyaukphyu, because of the pipeline. Lots of places in Rakhine don't even have electricity."

This was true. Over half the households in rural Rakhine State report using candles as their main source of lighting. The national average is one in five.

Kyaw Oo looked out over the moonlit sea, towards the indistinct bulge of a distant island.

"But I do worry it will pollute Kyaukphyu. It's beautiful here," he said, gesturing towards the ocean with a solemn passion one can only feel for one's home.

Kyaw Oo was referring to the Shwe Gas crude oil pipeline, which became operational in April 2017. Agreements to build the crude oil pipeline and a parallel natural gas pipeline were signed in 2008 by China and Myanmar's military government. Myanmar Oil and Gas Enterprise – which a four-year investigation conducted in the 1990s by a team of research analysts for *Observatoire Geopolitique des Drogues* found to be "the main channel for laundering the revenues of heroin produced and exported under the control of the Myanmar army" – take a 49.1% stake in the project; China National Petroleum Corporation takes the rest.[26]

In a similar manner to how they bulldozed Bagan, forcing its residents to relocate, the junta cleared space for the oil pipeline by confiscating thousands of acres of land.

---

[26] D. Bernstein and L. Kean (1996), 'People of the Opiate: Myanmar's dictatorship of drugs', *The Nation*, 263 (20): 11-15.

Amid economic marginalisation, land grabs and cronyism, violence broke out against ethnic Rohingya. And as the military moved in, compelling over 125,000 Rohingya to flee for Bangladesh in 2012, Myanmar state agencies appeared to foster the clearance campaign "to divert populist anger away from the devastating impact of the pipeline project."[27]

These projects, along with a £5.4 billion Kyaukphyu deep-sea port plan, are part of China's One Belt, One Road (OBOR) initiative, which aims to develop new trading routes with Europe, Africa and Asia. Although the Malacca Strait is the shortest transport route connecting China to these trading networks, China fears it is open to piracy and naval blockades. Resource-rich Rakhine has therefore become a focal point of OBOR.

But China's just the half of it. India also has oil interests in Myanmar, and its Act East policy, the counterproject to China's OBOR, similarly seeks to take advantage of Rakhine's geostrategic location. State-owned Indian oil and gas companies have been active in Rakhine since 2004, and in July 2016 India announced the creation of a Sittwe Special Economic Zone (SEZ), rivalling China's Kyaukphyu SEZ. Neither India nor China have condemned the military clearance campaign; and with China invested in Rakhine, Myanmar can count on their power of veto at the UN.

Religious persecution has dominated headlines about the Rohingya, allowing the dodgy dealings of

---

[27] https://www.theguardian.com/environment/earth-insight/2013/apr/26/fossil-fuel-secret-burma-democratic-fairytale <Accessed: 25.06.2019>

corporate projects to slip under the radar. The extent to which extractive sector development and power generation projects have contributed to the displacement of Rohingya villages cannot be measured accurately, but there is little doubt that Rakhine is proving a lucrative state for multiple players – legal, illegal and crony.

*

Besides substantial litter, the only unpleasant part of Kyaukphyu was the stone mosque, which had been ransacked and left to ruin. A police officer allowed me to probe around inside. It had become the town rubbish dump.

Kyaukphyu used to be home to the Kaman, Myanmar's only officially recognised Muslim ethnic group. Following the outbreak of communal violence in 2012, Kyaukphyu officials moved the Kaman to IDP camps outside the centre. They are still languishing there, having never received a clear response as to whether they will be allowed to return to their homes.

Under the 1982 Citizenship Law, the Kaman should qualify for citizenship and be permitted free travel. In reality, acquiring the documents from immigration is tricky. To leave Rakhine State, Muslims must carry a National Verification Card (NVC) and use it to apply for Form 4, which grants travel outside Rakhine State. However, Kaman report that the process gets deliberately slowed; some have been waiting for their NVC for over three years.

Most Myanmar parrot the false notion that the Rohingya are the only persecuted Muslims in Myanmar, since they are "terrorists" or "illegal immigrants." This is either denial or ignorance, for Myanmar Muslims of all ethnicities face at least some degree of discrimination. This comes through most clearly in the country's bureaucracy. Thida, a twenty-five-year-old Muslim girl and dear friend of mine, recently picked up her national identity card. It cost her K300,000 (£166) and she's labelled "Myanmar-Bengali", even though her family has lived in Myanmar for generations. In contrast, it cost Shwe Ei, a Bamar Buddhist, just K30,000 (£16.60) – a price that included "tea money", a small and usually necessary bribe, for faster service. The standard price for the national identity card is K5,000-10,000 (£2.76-5.52).

Thida is training as a tour guide, but she worries that getting a job will be difficult due to her ethnicity and religion. She can tolerate being called *"kalar-ma"* in Yangon by racist onlookers, but she could not bear unemployment.

"I want to be independent," Thida told me. "I don't rely on my parents' money now and I don't want to rely on a husband's in the future. However, I don't think it will be easy to find a job as a Muslim. There are very few female Muslim tour guides in Myanmar."

Thida is multilingual, enjoys reading and always wears her *thanaka* in the same way: a dot on the nose, one on each cheek and one between the eyes. She hopes one day to live in a more Muslim-friendly country, but first she needs the money to move out of Myanmar – a Catch-22, you might say.

I had been expecting my twelve-day trip through Rakhine State to be plagued by Islamophobic slurs and conspiracies, yet the only person to raise the ongoing unrest in conversation spoke with genuine sorrow and impartiality, neither using the terms "Bengali" nor "Rohingya", just like Kyaw Oo. Nonetheless, the destroyed mosques, ubiquitous Buddhist flags and residents' collective silence on recent issues suggested a sinister dynamic: the place of Islam in Rakhine State was not being contested but erased from memory. While many Rakhine simply wanted the conflict to end, others wanted to end the conflict; the two were worlds apart.

Chapter 16: Career Advisors

Travelling alone brings out the contemplative side of you – a side I never knew I had until I went to Myanmar. Some travellers shun loneliness, but I personally enjoy these quiet periods and their concomitant self-reflection; bus journeys in particular provide welcome relief from the daily emotional and physical drain of travel. I spent most of mine staring out the window, thinking back over my time in Yangon, the friends I had made there and everything I had learned, while watching the outside world blur by in a Picassoesque collage of colours and activity that mirrored the restlessness of my own mind.

On the bus out of Rakhine State, however, I could only dwell on the region's troubled and uncertain future. While some Rakhine were evidently sympathetic towards the Rohingya's plight, the overall community had been turned against them by nationalistic rhetoric and values. It was another manifestation of the tension between individual and group behaviour – a chasmal contrast proving harmful for all the region's residents. And although I held fond memories of the flawless hospitality I had received from Soe Moe and Kyaw Oo, they were tainted by the knowledge that I, an outsider, was more welcome in Rakhine than the native Rohingya, who were being banished from their homes.

It was amidst these sombre thoughts that Michael, a skinny Rakhine with the countenance of an honest gentleman, sat down beside me and jerked me back into the travelling world with the strangest of conversation starters.

"I was reading an English book yesterday," he said. "But I didn't like it."

"Oh, why not?"

"I just can't understand these writers who talk about two things happening in different places at the same time," he said, looking exasperated. "How can they know about two things happening at once?"

"So long as they've done their research, they could write about loads of things that happened at once."

"I'm talking about fiction."

"Fiction...?"

"The writer cannot be in both places at once," he stated, with an incensed shake of both hands, "so they cannot possibly know what is happening to people in those places at the same time."

"But it's not real," I protested. "The author creates those people and decides what happens to them and when. They could write about 50 people if they wanted."

"You mean the writer is up in the sky and has an open plan view of everything?"

"Err, sure... I guess you could put it that way."

Michael gave me a stern, quizzical stare. "I prefer stories in which one event happens after the other," he said.

"Do you read a lot of English books?"

"I do, normally short stories."

"Your English is good."

"I'm a private English teacher." He sighed. "It's a shame the youth cannot speak very good English these days."

"The military regime banned teaching it in schools, didn't they?"

Michael nodded. We fell silent for a minute, and I returned to watching the straggly trees and bushes of the slashed-and-burnt Rakhine Yoma.

"And what do you do?" asked Michael.

"I'm a travel journalist."

"Are you writing about Myanmar?"

"I am."

"And are you writing a book?"

"Yes." I paused. "The story is strictly chronological: it's a travel book."

"Good," he said, looking genuinely pleased. "Will you talk about Rakhine State?"

"I will. What do you think about what's happening?"

"I think the government needs to stop lying," he spat, shaking his hands rigorously again. "I know what's really going on – I read *Frontier* and the BBC. I know how bad it is."

Michael was presumably referring to the government's propaganda campaigns and their denials of ethnic cleansing. Many of the Myanmar official outlets, including a social media page run from Aung San Suu Kyi's office, had dismissed reports of alleged atrocities committed against the Rohingya as fake news – a term the Myanmar have latched onto and readily apply to independent reports that factually differ from those produced by state media. A Myanmar acquaintance, who lived in England for four years and now runs an English language course, even attempted to discredit the BBC on Facebook by only partially quoting one of their articles then writing "BBC" beneath to make it appear like poor journalism.

"We need to work with the UN and we need independent media access to Rakhine State," said Michael. "Otherwise, we will never have the truth and things will only get worse."

Michael was evidently well educated and intelligent, even if the ontology of literary fiction stumped him, and we chatted for most of the journey. His opinions on the Myanmar news outlets and the international community aligned with my own; not many people's in Myanmar did.

After disembarking at the Yangon junction and hitching a ride with a jolly truck driver, I arrived at my comfortable hotel in Pathein, the capital of the fertile Ayeyarwady Delta in the southwest of Myanmar. An adolescent boy cleanly clothed in a green *longyi* and white *ingyi* showed me to my room – and everything in it.

"Here is the bed. Here is the fridge. Here is the aircon. Here is the telephone. If you have problem, you call 807. You have nice face." And he left.

Pathein offered the city bustle I had missed over the past six weeks yet retained a small-world feel. There was also 24/7 electricity, unlike in rural Chin and Rakhine, where electricity was limited to the evenings. Pathein's riverside setting, though not especially attractive, was good for people-watching and the sunset. Ferries and sampans cruised through the sparkling reflection of the blood red sun, watched by residents strolling towards the night *zay*. Across the river lay a village, where I was warmly welcomed and force-fed watermelon.

Pathein is renowned for parasol production. Myanmar's parasols come in a variety of profound colours, including crimson, mauve and magenta, and are traditionally made using paper, though crafters have also started producing ones of cotton, silk and satin to meet the demands of Chinese and Japanese customers. You can visit the family workshops and watch the crafters produce their masterpieces – unless you arrive on a national holiday, the bane of every traveller, as I did. Fortunately, it also happened to be the evening of the Opera Musical, which would no doubt be entertaining for unintended reasons.

I was ushered in gratis and sat down beside the seminarians. Christian nuns and government officials occupied the front two rows, which were reserved for VIPs, and the public filled the rest. A large stage dominated the front of the auditorium, which I suspected was a collection of badminton courts. The air was so thick with mosquitoes that everyone was complaining about them. The organisers waited until every seat was filled, delaying the start time by an hour. But that was okay: I knew I was in for a treat.

The first act was a dance performed by four boys and four girls all dressed in bold colours that matched their partner's. They must have been around eighteen years of age, but the performance resembled a primary school talent show. They wore enormous, artificial smiles. The audience loved it.

Next, a violinist played a plaintive tune over a video of Myanmar landmarks projected onto the screen behind him. This was followed by a speech from the Minister of the Ayeyarwady Division, then a video about a Christian youth initiative helping impoverished African children. The focus, however, was not on those being helped but the helpers: Asian youths who had been looking for meaning in their lives, or who had not been on good terms with their parents but had found happiness through Christian altruism. The African communities figured more as portals through which the youths found bliss, rather than as humans crippled by disease, malnourishment and war. The audience loved this too.

Unsurprisingly, the video was followed by a "tribal" dance performed by the same eight teenagers. The boys wore scant "tribal" costumes and wielded spears and shields embossed with simple achromatic patterns. Clothed in pretty pink dresses with red cummerbunds and sporting plastic Tanzanian necklaces, the girls looked a little more tasteful. They danced to Shakira's *Africa*, making primitive grunts in time with music; the choreography was equally basic. And yes, the audience loved it.

Things took a turn for the better after this. The four girls took to the stage and sang a couple of Christian hymns, followed by the four boys. The audience whooped and cheered and demanded an encore. After a hushed discussion with tech, *Take me Home, Country Roads* began playing. The boys sung it proficiently, nailing the melancholic longing of the chorus. As they sang, some spectators, especially members of a Chinese tour group, stood up, climbed the stage stairs and slapped K5000 notes into their hands. This merited great applause each time, and soon people were getting up from all over the hall – causing the clapping to become almost constant.

But John Denver had only whet the audience's appetite, so after another hushed discussion with tech, *Hallelujah* came on – the original Cohen version. The singers really shone this time. One in particular had a booming voice inexplicably tinged with a Bavarian accent, which imbued the verses with an uplifting fullness, distinct and substantial. He was duly rewarded with several K5000 notes – this time stuffed behind his ears – for apparently the truest way of showing appreciation is with money.

*

Having recently finished reading *The Beach*, a scathing critique of backpacker culture, I opted for a spontaneous beach trip to Ngwe Saung. En route to the bus station, I passed through one of those many pagodas in which you cannot wear shoes, but through which you may drive a motorbike.

The reason shoes are prohibited in pagodas is to show respect: unlike the holy complex, shoes are unclean; furthermore, whatever lies beneath your shoes is considered symbolically "lower" than them. On this logic, surely motorbikes should also be banned?

"There were no motorbikes in Buddha's day," joked Ko Ko, a Buddhist friend of mine. Like Shwe Ei, he disapproved of the practice but acknowledged it was commonplace. Both Ko Ko and Shwe Ei were university-educated, compelling me to theorise that adherence to the strict rules only was a by-product of Myanmar's rote-learning school system.

It's a truism often forgotten by foreigners that locals can be disrespectful too. Perhaps as a result of how Western holiday companies market travel abroad, especially their emphasis on the importance of the traditional and spiritual customs of foreign cultures, we expect the people of these countries to be consistent and predictable in their actions, forgetting that they, like us, are only human. Hypocrisy can deter travellers from exercising proper etiquette, but you just have to bite your tongue – remembering that not every worshipper is representative of their country and religion – and be all the more vigorous in demonstrating respect.

When I arrived at the bus station, I was forced to pay the tourist price and then crammed into the back corner of the minibus. It soon became clear that we would not be departing for some time, and the bus was filled with mosquitoes, so I climbed out. That's when I noticed that my fingernails had reached a length comparable to the men's in Laos.

Repulsed, I clambered up the minibus ladder, rummaged through my backpack, took out my nail clippers and got to work. As I perched on the roof and clipped my nails into a static stream of broken glass, plastic bottles and sweetcorn skins, heads turned and people gathered round. I had understandably become an object of great curiosity, a lanky white troll.

After a mosquito-filled two hours squeezed between four guys and with a toddler sprawled across me, I arrived at Ngwe Saung. But the beach was not what I had been hoping for, and I realised now that I had been spoilt with Dawei and Ngapali. There was almost no shade, and motorbikes, quadbikes and depressed donkeys bearing middle-class Myanmar patrolled the sand endlessly.

Disillusioned, I sat down at a beachside eat-drink-shop and began writing an article due for the following week. But the words wouldn't come, so I took to procrastinating on my phone instead – only to find Shwe Ei had posted a picture of herself bathing in the Ngwe Saung shallows.

My stomach churned. Did I want to meet her? Although I was slowly getting over her, I wasn't sure I was ready to see her in a bikini.

Eventually, I decided against it and prayed instead that Shwe Ei would take my advice of learning to swim in the shallows, where the salt would make it easier for her to stay afloat. Few Myanmar, especially Yangonites, can swim, which means the deep end of city swimming pools are often empty. In Yangon, I had tried to teach Shwe Ei to swim but had left to travel just before she got the hang of it. One time, hoping to speed up her progress, I had quite literally "thrown" her in at the deep end to see if she would sink or swim. She sank. It wasn't my proudest moment.

"You're on holiday. You shouldn't be working," said a white American pensioner sat at another table.

"I'm a travel journalist."

"Then life's pretty good, isn't it?" he said. "You *must* be happy."

There was a pause. I looked at him with unresponsive eyes. He bumbled on:

"You're young. How old?"

"Twenty-four."

"Baby, baby, baby," he cooed, shaking his head slowly. "You've got life by the bum when you're young. You don't realise it, but you have. My daughter is like you – works from her laptop and can make money all around the world. You're a lucky boy – you may not know it now, but how many of your friends are doing what you're doing?"

"Not many."

"Exactly, the world is an oyster for people like you." He leant forward, elbows on the table. "But you know which two jobs are recession-proof? Medicine and Law Enforcement. Just a tip, you know: you need to *have* money to *spend* money. Everything else can come second." He grinned. "You may not know it, but you're in a great position and employers will love that you've been to Myanmar, whatever you do. It may not seem like life is ideal right now – but trust me: you've got life by the bum."

He looked candidly into the distance, head inclined upwards, and began rubbing his chin.

"I saw something on a T-shirt in Thailand once: 'I use the wood of bridges I've broken to light my future.' I think it's one of the best things I've ever read. Neat, huh? That's what you need to think about."

He fell silent and gave me a warm smile that I didn't return. I couldn't decide which part of this bizarre exchange was most infuriating – that he had seemingly ignored my reply about how few of my friends were doing what I was doing, that he appeared to believe the very act of visiting Myanmar somehow guaranteed future job security, or that the phrase is "burn" and not "break" your bridges, rendering his pseudo-philosophical T-shirt doubly redundant. More than anything, however, I was stung by his assurance of how "lucky" I was. Travelling, a privilege though it may be, isn't just fun and games – especially in rural Myanmar – and I was still feeling pretty low at this point. You cannot simply adduce another's happiness from their job title and surroundings. Oh, and you grab life by the *balls*, not the bum.

*

I returned to Pathein the next morning and took a bus to Nyaungdone, a small town on the Ayeyarwady River. In just one day I would be back in Yangon, which was a pleasing prospect. Travelling down the western edge of Myanmar – through Nagaland, Chin State, Rakhine State and the Ayeywarwady Division – had been the most draining leg of my trip so far: not only had it been the longest, but loneliness and illness had been constant companions. Nonetheless, I was pleased with what I had experienced – I felt I had really begun to penetrate some of the deeper issues troubling modern Myanmar – and I was looking forward to learning more about these topics when I travelled up north. For now, however, I needed a relaxing break.

The bus to Nyaungdone was eventful, as most regional buses in Myanmar were. I bought the last ticket, but naturally they stuffed more passengers onto titchy plastic stalls down the aisle. A TV at the front played modern Myanmar music videos, many erotic. One featured a stylish couple dressed in edgy black clothes, delving into the world of drugs. They were cool for cats and didn't care what others thought of them. The rock song ended with this exact message:

So Dangerous! ! Please don't use drugs anymore

Not long later, a young girl in front of me puked into a clear plastic bag. Her mum tied a knot in the sick bag and attached it to a clip on the edge of the aisle chair. It swung back and forth hypnotically as the bus bumped along. No one could take their eyes off it – especially not those sitting in the aisle, for whom it swung at face height.

After an hour, the bus stopped to collect passengers, among them a large lady in a floral *longyi* and lime green blouse, who was carrying a large watermelon.

"*Par-ye-thi-ga gyi-de-naw?*" ('That's a big watermelon, isn't it?').

"*Ayan gyi-deh*" ('It's so big').

"*Be-hma htar-ya-ma-le?*" ('Where can I put it?')

"*Ei-dar-go ei-di-hma htar-lo ma-ya-bu. Ayan gyi-pe*" ('Well, you can't put it there. It's just too big').

"*Kine-pay-par one-naw*" ('Just hold it').

"*Dar-pay-me ayan lay-de!*" ('But it's so heavy!')

The owner protested, but the watermelon was clearly too massive to be stored anywhere. She slumped onto her stall and sat cradling it in visible discomfort, muttering *"lay-de."* And so the bus trundled on, with everyone either watching the swinging sick bag or chatting about the inconvenient watermelon – a curious contrast to the serene rice paddies outside, stretching to the horizon.

As in several Asian countries, 'rice' (*tamin*) is a synonym for food, breakfast, lunch or dinner. According to the Myanmar Rice Federation, the Myanmar consume more rice per capita than any other nation. One suspects the source is biased – other studies have placed Myanmar fourth – but there is no doubt that the Myanmar really love rice.

I reached Nyaungdone around 2pm and was invited to overnight by the head monk in a local monastery, but immigration had other ideas and ordered a motorbike taxi to drive me to Kay Khaing Oo guesthouse. This was run by the tall and gentlemanly Peter Lwin, who wore a drab green jacket over a clean white shirt and moved around with an unhurried, reassuring ease that has always eluded me. He won my trust immediately by convincing the taxi driver to give me back K1000 and became more generous with every hour that passed.

"My friend, do you drink whisky?" he asked with a Myanmar smile.

"Sure."

"Can you ride a scooter?"

"Yes."

"Then take mine."

"Thanks. See you tonight."

I drove towards the centre, shabby rice factories on my right, grassy embankments on my left. A handful of men and women were loading crops onto the back of a rickety wooden cart, struggling to push it up the bank. I parked up and offered to help, stunning them into inactivity.

"Myanmar-lo ya-lar?" ('Can you speak Myanmar?') asked a middle-aged man in a ragged T-shirt and torn navy *longyi*. Then he said, *"Kyanaw ayin-ga naing-nan-char-thar-dacho-go myin-hpu-de. Pyi-daw kyanaw-ywar-go-le thu-go peik-chin-ke-de. Da-pay-me kyanaw-ga ingaleik-saga ma-pyaw-bu. Kinbya lar-thin-de"* ('I've seen a few foreigners before and have always wanted to invite them to my village, but I don't speak English. You must come').

And he abandoned the cart without a word to his friends and bade me follow.

We strode along a narrow path towards a looming copse, his natter constant, rapid and barely intelligible. As the track broadened, his impoverished hamlet appeared. Although the copse was spacious, the wooden huts were cramped and their stilts suspect. There was no electricity nor modern building materials, and the entire community shared a single well whose water looked contaminated. In a few months, the dry season dust would become sludgy mud and the living conditions would further degenerate.

My host took me to his house and offered me *ye-nway-kyan* from a fetid mug. I couldn't resist his eyes, so took a few sips (this may have been the cause of another bout of dysentery I was to suffer upon returning to Yangon). He apologised for not having any food to give me but promised his aunt would. So we went to her hut, which, like his, contained neither chairs nor mattresses – only bare planks and a few blankets.

His aunt was skinny to the point of malnourishment, had perfect teeth and a toddler on her lap. She warmed to me immediately, and I to her.

"Be-ga lar-le?"

"En-ga-land." (The closest phoneme Myanmar has to the English "g" is *ga*, hence the three syllables.)

"Aww, En-ga-land, En-ga-land," echoed children lurking in the shadows. Auntie gave a young girl some money and sent her off in a rush of hand movements and half-uttered commands. She returned a minute later with coffee mix and several cakes packed with preservatives – prestigious food for the prestigious guest.

Everyone was staring at me expectantly, so I pretended to relish the artificial flavours. My hosts were all smiles and offered to buy more food, but I managed to convince them I was full.

"Kyanaw-mi-bar-twe-ein thwa-ya-aung" ('Let's go to my parents' house'), said Aung Soe, my original host.

So that's where we went, only now I had a following of a dozen scruffy children. My curious sandals, and the rigmarole of removing them before entering somebody's home, intrigued them no end. They waited outside as I climbed the small bamboo ladder and into the home of Aung Soe's parents. They must have been forewarned of my arrival, for a cup of fake coffee as well as a plate of identical cakes sat waiting on a red rug.

"Ingaleik lu-myu" ('He's English'), Aung Soe told his parents. Their faces glowed.

"Ba aloke-loke-le?" ('What work do you do?') asked the father.

"Sar-ye-saya loke-de" ('I'm a writer'), I answered.

"Aww, very good," he said in English with a giggle.

"Hman-lar?" ('Was that correct?') his wife asked me.

"Hman-de" ('It was').

"Be-lo thi-le?" ('How did you know that?') she asked her husband.

"Taw-de" ('I'm clever'), he said with a chuffed grin.

"Ayan taw-de" ('extremely clever'), I added. We all laughed, and the surprise English-speaker patted his chest.

When we left, I found my number of followers had doubled and even included a few mothers clutching babies. The journey to the next hut began, this one home to a couple of village elders. People gave me quizzical looks as our entourage passed, but the kids answered them with shrieks of *"Myanmar-sagar pyaw-dat-de! Myanmar-sagar pyaw-dat-de!"* ('He speaks Myanmar! He speaks Myanmar!'), encouraging others to join.

After my fourth instant coffee and yet more sweet cakes, Aung Soe and I left the elders' hut and returned to the hamlet entrance. Our group now numbered over 30; excited screams of *"Myanmar-sagar pyaw-dat-de!"* reverberated all around and kids jumped up and down with the enthusiasm of someone who's been miraculously cured of paraplegia.

We reached the final hut I was to be a guest at and climbed inside, followed by several children. I was seated in the only chair I had seen in the last two hours and treated to yet more prestigious artificial coffee and cakes. Hmmm. The children formed a semicircle round me; the rest stood on the path outside and peered in.

"Yo-shin kyi-ne-ya-tha-lo-pe" ('It's like watching a film), giggled the hostess, an elegant *a-myo-thami* in modest traditional dress. *"Da-gyi"* ('You're head of the village'), she joked, and echoes of *"da-gyi"* went around the semicircle. *"Be-hmar-ne-le?"* ('Where are you staying?')

"Kay Kaing Oo guesthouse," I replied, and I explained that I had wanted to stay in a monastery but hadn't been allowed.

"Di-hmar ne-lo ya-de!" ('You can stay here!') boomed Aung Soe, pointing at the sleeping area inside the hut.

Surely he knew that was illegal? I turned to our hostess, who nodded and smiled.

"Di-hmar ne-lo ya-de," he repeated. *"Kalay-twe-go inglaleik-sa-thin-naing-thar-lo ywar-lu-gyi-ne twe-pi ywar-*

hmar loke-hpo loke-at-dar-twe-le pyaw-naing-bar-de." ('You can teach the kids English and talk to the village elders about what needs to be done in the village').

Aung Soe rambled on, his eyes no longer imbued with warmth alone but also expectation. Had he mistaken the *da-gyi* joke and actually granted me a position of importance in his hamlet? The look on our hostess' face suggested so, and I now realised that her nods and smiles were symptoms of *ah-nar-de*, a Myanmar code of conduct which, among other stipulations, prohibits contradicting in public those of superior age. The kids were also still grinning, though I don't think they had fully understood.

I said I had to go, and the crowd gradually dispersed. Aung Soe was despondent as he accompanied me back to the road. Then with a firm handshake he wished me goodbye and told me I could visit again anytime. One day, perhaps, I shall.

I returned to Yangon the next day, hideously hungover after dinner with Peter – who insisted on paying for everything, simply because I had been able to order the dishes in Myanmar – but elated. The *da-gyi* episode in the hamlet, followed by Peter's boundless hospitality, had reminded me of why I had chosen Myanmar: not only was travel there full of quirks, but the people cherished interaction with foreign travellers. They saw me as proof that Myanmar was changing – a joy to experience, even if I knew that political progress was going to be arduous – and my ability to speak (mediocre) Myanmar signified that foreigners could take a genuine interest in their country, whose underdevelopment sometimes embarrassed locals.

So I ended the penultimate leg of my journey on an emotional high, looking forward to my impending visit to Sri Lanka, which people only seemed able to praise, yet yearning to see more of Myanmar. My final trip round the country would take me to the war-torn Kachin and Shan states – a prospect that got my nerves tingling, and a chance for me to dig deeper into the complex issues stalling Myanmar's peace process.

Part 4

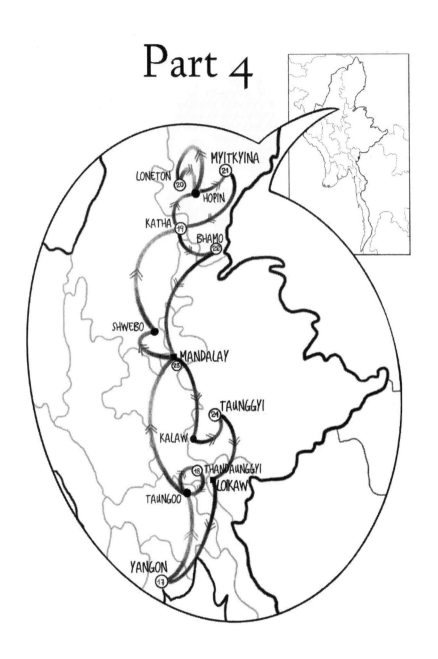

Chapter 17: Water, Water Everywhere

THINGYAN (WATER FESTIVAL) / သင်္ကြန်

I returned to Myanmar with a new appreciation for both the country and my travels through it. Sri Lanka was beautiful, its cuisine exquisite and the people welcoming, but the high level of tourism had made penetrating its culture a challenge – unlike in Myanmar, where the lack of tourist infrastructure meant it was bursting at the seams, eager to ravish the curious traveller.

My return to Yangon was carefully timed for the most distinguished event of the year, *Thingyan*, the Buddhist water festival which falls in mid-April, lasts four-five days and marks the end of the Myanmar calendar. Like *Songkran* in Thailand, *Thingyan* is celebrated by throwing water on people to wash away their sins, allowing them to start the new year "clean". It's also the peak of the hot season, making it a great time to cool off.

Buddhists use the final few days of the year to accumulate merit by observing the Eight Precepts and by performing good deeds, such as donating money or freeing caged birds. Swearing or getting angry during *Thingyan* is a big no-no.

Captain Symes, a delegate of the East India Company who was sent to Myanmar on a diplomatic mission in 1795, provides the fantastic following account of a *Thingyan* festival he witnessed:

To wash away the impurities of the past and begin the new year free from stain, women on this day throw water on every man they meet, and the men are allowed to throw water on them in return. This permission to throw water on one another gives rise to a great deal of harmless merriment, especially amongst the young women, who, armed with large syringes or squirts and vessels, try to wet every man that goes along the street, and in their return receive a wetting with the utmost good nature.[28]

But alas, the days of chivalrous wettings have past. My friends had portrayed *Thingyan* as a constant soaking contaminated with inebriated brawls; most foreigners had left the country to escape the festivities and every Myanmar friend told me they would spend all four days inside, only emerging once for a ritual "cleansing".

Anxious and intrigued, I bought a water pistol on the eve of *Thingyan* and teamed up with two Belgians, Axel and Jokè: unsuspecting tourists stranded in Yangon. The first day was underwhelming – minimal madness – but the intensity of the celebrations increased as the festival reached its climax. People patrolled the town wearing plastic phone holders round their necks and carrying water guns, buckets or plastic bottles, ready to wash away sins. *Pandals*, special marquees rigged with hoses and/or stages for dancing and singing, were set up at the roadsides to drench passing traffic. They ranged from municipal concert stages, the largest being at Sule Pagoda, to modest marquees erected by shop owners. For the latter, friends and family revived rusty motors and pumped water into troughs or paddling pools, which in turn supplied high-pressure hoses. Axel and I foolishly refilled at one controlled by an excitable man armed with a fire hose, who

---

[28] M. Symes (1800), *An Account of an Embassy to the Kingdom of Ava: Sent by the Governor-General of India in the Year 1795*, W. Bulmer and Co. As quoted in: Aung San Suu Kyi (1997), *Letters from Burma*, Penguin.

sprayed us in the face at close range. We were lucky he didn't burst our ear drums, an endemic *Thingyan* threat.

The greater emphasis appeared to be on getting wet as pick-ups fitted with bamboo frames and packed with celebrants cruised through town, stopping before *pandals* to be purified. These trucks were especially popular with teenagers and young adults, who rode around carrying guns, syringes, buckets, and even canisters of fake snow. This was a product of overexcitement: the fake snow stung my eyes, did not absolve me of my sins and had poor range. The festival spirit had evidently consumed the Yangonites, almost all of whom are desperate to see real snow. Personally, I would ban the fake snow.

Many middle-class Myanmar now favour the *Thingyan* mini EDM festivals, perhaps the newest addition to the traditional celebrations, and enormous public foam baths have become a hit. Axel, Jokè and I took part in the Yangon Splash Walk, which had been organised by young Yangonites wishing to showcase how *Thingyan* has changed since the Bagan era. However, we three tall Europeans proved to be far too tempting a target, so we spent most of our time with watery eyes.

Symes recorded that no dirty water was thrown during *Thingyan* 200 years ago and that everything was cricket. Today, some cruel splashers fill their guns with cold water and people spray motorbike drivers with high-pressured jets; in extreme instances, these falls prove fatal. The drunk driving and high adrenaline also lead to accidents, and in Yangon seven died and 830 were injured during *Thingyan* 2018. Naturally, theft and violent crimes prevail, though educational activities carried out prior to

Thingyan 2018 resulted in the crime rate reducing on previous years.

Overall, I was impressed by the decorum exhibited. There existed an unspoken amnesty over chucking water at diners and those evidently not prepared for getting wet, though special exceptions were made for whiteys. In downtown, Muslims were respectfully ignored – heart-warming to see, for tensions between Yangon Muslims and Buddhists had been strained in recent months.

New president U Win Myint announced a *Thingyan* amnesty and conditionally pardoned over 8500 prisoners, including 36 political prisoners. Most of the beneficiaries had been convicted on drugs charges, others for violating the Unlawful Association Act or the Military Act. Among the released were two Kachin pastors who had been convicted under charges of unlawful association in October 2017 for assisting visiting journalists. However, many political prisoners remained behind bars.

*

I celebrated the ending of *Thingyan* with explosive diarrhoea and vomiting, symptoms of food poisoning, and by delaying my departure for Thandaunggyi, a former British hill station in Kayin State. Eventually, I reached Taungoo, a transit town on the old Yangon-Mandalay highway. Flat, bland and baking, Taungoo was dominated by non-descript concrete buildings and dotted with modernised Victorian doll's houses painted in ghastly colours and furnished with shiny metal balustrades – the homes of the burgeoning middle-class. Its only saving grace was an empty lakeside park, where I sat down and spent twenty minutes meditating, allowing the refreshing evening breeze to massage my acned visage.

Taungoo is renowned for its numerous areca palms, and when a Myanmar receives unexpected good fortune, they are likened to a betel fan receiving a paid trip to Taungoo. I was not so lucky, for I arrived Saturday evening and the morning pick-up to Thandaunggyi did not run on the Sabbath. I toyed with the idea of renting a motorbike and heading there myself, but did not fancy my chances against 41°C. That left me in a pickle, for my article on Thandaunggyi was due in three days.

So the next morning I started walking along the main road, hoping to catch a lift to Thandaung ('Iron Mountain') and from there to Thandaunggyi ('Big Iron Mountain'). Sure enough, a barking oldie on a motorbike soon found me.

"Where you go?" he shouted.

"Thandaung."

"Aww, yes. I go. I take you."

I thanked him and climbed on. He turned around and drove back to Taungoo.

"Sorry, but I'm going to Thandaunggyi."

"Yes. There is bus. I show you."

"No, it's not running today. Please drop me here," I pleaded.

He waved his hand to say, "trust me", and drove to the town's tiny bus station. A white pick-up was being loaded with boxes of energy drinks and a man lazed in the driver's seat of a black hatchback. Everyone stared as we approached.

My driver parked up and began speaking to the strapping young men loading the pick-up, displaying such a hunger for information that his eyebrows danced as he spoke.

"Aww, there is no bus because it Sunday."

What a surprise.

"Are you going to Thandaunggyi," asked the *a-myo-thar* in the hatchback. He was a stocky guy in his early thirties with dark skin and an apathetic demeanour. His hair was cropped to the left, he wore authoritative gold rings on his middle and index fingers and oozed mystery.

"Yes, are you?"

"I am," he answered in faintly accented English. "I can take you for 5000."

"Great. When are you leaving?"

"I don't know. I have to wait for my wife."

"Where is she?"

"In hospital."

There was an awkward silence. Neither his eyes nor tone betrayed any emotion.

"Err, okay. Perhaps I will look for another lift."

"Give me your phone number," he said. "I will call you when I'm leaving."

"Good idea."

He fished an Oppo out of his jeans pocket and I gave him my number.

"What's your name?" he asked.

"Kyaw Thu." He nodded his approval. "And yours?"

"Joker."

Of course.

"Thank you, Joker... Let me know."

He nodded. I turned around.

"Money! Money!" barked the oldie.

"How much?"

"1000."

I sighed and gave him the cash, mainly because I had been impressed by his tenacity in uncovering what information he could.

"Wait," I said, "that's way too much. Give me 500 back."

He nodded and consented. Then I left the bus station to resume my original plan of hitching to Thandaunggyi. Hitchhiking is not a concept in Myanmar, though people regularly give strangers lifts – it's part of the close-knit community mindset. I met a few Europeans hitching around Myanmar during my travels, but personally I felt Myanmar could do with the money and so only hitched when I had to, ready to pay if the driver asked.

About 200 yards down the main road to Thandaung, a black Land Rover stopped for me. It was owned by Zaw Zaw, a benevolent plump Shan who had been educated in Russia and later worked as an assistant physics lecturer in Moscow, Mandalay, China and India. Although Zaw Zaw was turning off in a few miles, he took it upon himself to find me a lift to Thandaunggyi, as if it were a noble quest entrusted to him by the Queen of England.

Sure enough, halfway through a cup of tea, Zaw Zaw spotted a pick-up heading our way and ran out to intercept it. After a quick discussion with the driver, he waved me over.

"This is Peter," said Zaw Zaw. "He will take you to Thandaunggyi. Let's get your stuff."

"Okay, thank you. Does he want money?"

"It's okay, it's okay," said Zaw Zaw as he unlocked his Land Rover. "I'll pay."

I grabbed my backpack and introduced myself to Peter, a Christian Karen with hypnotic hazel eyes and a humbleness that made me take an instant liking to him. He was married and owned a petrol station in Thandaunggyi, his hometown.

"Thank you, Zaw Zaw," I said, "but I can pay."

"No, no. Let me," he replied, handing Peter K5000. "If you have time when you come back, message me."

"Of course. Thank you very much."

Zaw Zaw beamed and waved me off. He was one of the good guys, and his selflessness would put me in a good mood for the rest of the day.

It was a smooth ride in the cool of Peter's pick-up. We glided along forested roads to Thandaung, where Peter stopped for a late breakfast of *mohinga*, a fish soup and possibly the favourite dish in Myanmar. While he ate, I sat down beside a uniformed policeman wearing pink flip-flops and playing Candy Crush, then photographed an *a-myo-thami* in an immaculate black and gold dress as she piled bouquets of flowers onto her motorbike. She was a florist, and almost every *pan* in each bouquet would likely become an offering in a pagoda. This is one of the few remaining uses of real flowers in Myanmar: they are rarely given as gifts, and plastic flowers are preferred as decoration. Preserving natural beauty is a privilege of wealth: in Myanmar, almost every flowering branch is stripped, and its flowers sold – leaving one for the sake of aesthetics would be considered wasteful. I understand this mindset but mourn the devastation.

Peter finished and we set off, up the narrow twisting road and into the Kayin hills. Colourful lizards scuttled across the concrete; birds flittered between thin branches flapping in the breeze. As we approached Thandaunggyi, hillsides dotted with boulders and sparse tea trees appeared, though they lacked the majesty of Sri Lankan plantations. As in Chin State, churches were everywhere, though in recent years several pagodas had sprouted on nearby hilltops. The road wound along the ridge, past tasteful two-storey homes made of concrete or wood and modern churches perched on grassy ledges, finally climaxing with Naw Bu Baw Mountain, whose LED-edged crucifix lit up after dark.

The town abounded with Bed and Breakfasts. These local businesses were beneficiaries of a hotel licensing scheme introduced in 2016, which sought to revive Thandaunggyi as a tourist destination. For many of these families, running a guesthouse – which by law must consist of a minimum of ten rooms – would have been too expensive. The experiment has been successful: the lodging revenue now goes straight to the Karen community and the number of tourists is steadily increasing, even though Thandaunggyi was only opened to overnight visitors in 2015.

I stayed at Khaing's Villa, where "bed and breakfast" meant bed, breakfast, lunch and dinner. My room was a clean *en suite* with a cosy bed and a view over the garden of sagging tree branches. The B&B's matriarch was 96-year-old Nancy Khaing, a keen storyteller, who enjoyed befriending guests. Although largely restricted to her bed or chair, she was lucid – her age was the only piece of information she ever repeated.

"There used to be lots of tigers here," she told me over a cup of Kayin coffee. "They came right into town and preyed on the cattle. Sometimes we watched them from our classroom as they ate calves in the street."

Nancy spoke in a euphonious lull and her English was perfect, having been educated by American missionaries. She was one of the few remaining Myanmar to have enjoyed a quality education before the junta deported overseas teachers and Burmanised the school curriculum. The teaching of local languages was prohibited while new textbooks referred pejoratively to the ethnic minorities – labelling the Mon, Shan and Karen "colourful insurgents" – and glorified the ancient Bamar kings. To foster an obedient generation that would not question authority, and by extension military rule, critical thinking and independent thought were discouraged and the education system was degraded to one based on rote-learning.

This legacy lingers. Pascal Khoo Thwe, who through a chance encounter with scholar Dr. John Casey came to study at Cambridge University in 1991, noted how challenging he found voicing his own opinion in essays. Similarly, in the first few months of our relationship Shwe Ei would agree with anything I said; if I contradicted a statement she made, her opinion swiftly adjusted to fit mine.

This changed over time, as Myanmar education will also. Launched in February 2017, the National Education

Strategic Plan seeks to abolish rote-learning and establish a 21st-century education system with critical thinking, child-centred learning and interactive classrooms at its core. Aung San Suu Kyi, who presented the plan, said the education reforms would be "extremely important to Myanmar's social and economic development"; UNICEF called the plan's inauguration an "historic moment". With any luck, the next generation will be the best educated in Myanmar history.[29]

"Are there any tigers left?" I asked Nancy, knowing I would be dreaming of tigers that night.

Nancy smiled. Then the cat jumped on the table and began sniffing the biscuits. Nancy barked at it in Karen, leaning forward and swatting her hand in a display of energy that only frustration can breed.

"I don't think there are many tigers left," said Nancy, once the cat had fled. "But about three months ago, two brothers in a nearby village went hunting in the jungle. They came back with two bears, made merry that evening and had a feast. Then they said, 'we will go hunting again.' So they did, only this time they didn't come back." Nancy paused for breath. "When villagers went to look for them, they found the two corpses unmutilated. The bears hadn't eaten them – they had just wanted to send a message."

Nancy's eyelids started to flutter shortly after recounting this tale, so I went for a wander round Thandaunggyi, equipped with my camera in the hope of taking photos suitable for an article. The Karen residents resembled Shans in appearance – the men had rounded

---

[29] http://investvine.com/myanmar-revamps-education-system-ditches-rote-learning/ <Accessed: 09.08.2018>

faces and broad shoulders while the women were short and shapely – and had mostly shed their traditional clothes. Only the tasselled Karen bags remained popular, though one clothes store offered the whole range. The Karen dresses may be the prettiest garments in all of Myanmar. Cut above the knee and suited to the women's slender frames, they are decorated with simple, elegant designs that neither jump off the fabric nor retreat from the eye. Many are tasselled and the colours often bold, complementing the dresses' vivacious yet dignified aura. I have worn dresses before and even own one – a gift from friends who had noted my predilection for them – and in Thandaunggyi I seriously considered buying an enchanting, grey Karen dress with white pin-stripes and black tassels. But alas, I was too colossal.

It was one of my most rewarding village strolls. First, I stopped in the stately red brick tea factory founded over a century ago by the British and now run by the *Tatmadaw*. After all the "army tea" I had been forced to drink in military bases across the country, this felt like the conclusion of a pseudo-spiritual journey of discovery. The fact that they were making green tea and not the 3-in-1 tea mix I had usually drunk with soldiers made the experience less meaningful and thus somehow more fitting. The tour was roughly what I had expected: welcoming officers, broad smiles, and dated equipment mostly imported from India and now giving up the ghost. One soldier, while kindling the furnace, spawned a fierce fireball that turned the room into a sauna and very nearly consumed him.

I then headed to the outskirts, where I took a pleasing photo of children playing in an old cement mixer, before heading to Naw Bu Baw Mountain. This was the busiest area in Thandaunggyi, a pilgrimage site for Christians all over Myanmar. At its foot, local tourists fed plastic bags and bottles to two monkeys chained to trees, no doubt believing that other primates valued plastic as highly as we do. A set of newly painted red stairs led up the hill of short, healthy trees, passing small chapels containing crucifixes and sparkly pictures of Christ the Lord. A group of cheeky Karen girls aged seven-fourteen dogged my ascent, asking me where I came from, what my name was and whether I was a virgin. I prayed virginity was not a prerequisite for climbing the holy mountain and continued to the top, where the views of the Dawparkho mountain range were at their finest: bushy jade trees, interspersed by the occasional building or dirt road, covered the hillsides, which rolled beneath a pale blue sky and into the distant haze.

After a short rest, I descended and stumbled upon two large abandoned concrete buildings that occupied prime positions on the hillside. The windows were smashed, rubble covered the floors and the grubby walls were graffitied.

"I love you Law Eh," read one scrawl. *"Min-go chit-de"* ('I love you'), read another.

I had visited expecting to see needles and had found messages of love, along with black line drawings of happy couples. It was a heart-warming surprise, and a moment later I walked in on a teenage couple getting kinky in a cramped, burnt-out storage room whose floor was littered with broken glass. It was the last place anyone would choose to make love, but then there was nowhere else they could go: the woes of imposed premarital celibacy.

Keen to explore the lush surroundings, I set out the following morning with Ya Zar, a reserved Karen who had practically begged me for employment. He was stocky and smooth-skinned, with a downturned expression and an amiable air. Although he was powerfully built and wore a sheathed Karen knife at his hip, he seemed gentle and caring. I asked to visit a local waterfall I had read about, compelling him to switch from his shiny Honda to a beaten-up hunk of junk with exposed wires, no wing mirrors and a smashed display panel.

"Are you sure?" I asked.

"Yes. This is much better," said Ya Zar, tapping the strong metal frame on the back of the seat. It was passenger support: we were in for a rough ride.

I hopped on, then we drove along the main *lan* before turning down a narrow, poorly concreted path. It was so steep that I couldn't stop myself from slipping down and getting snug with Ya Zar, who was having a tough enough time already with the driving. When we finally turned onto a flat dirt track, the bike broke down, and for the next ten minutes Ya Zar fiddled around with a USA-flag screwdriver. His frustration showed as he began slapping his beloved, but his efforts paid off and we were soon able to continue.

Having turned down a perilous, dusty track that I had taken for the remnants of a landslide, we entered the jungle proper: canopy blocking the sunlight, tree trunks protruding from dense thickets, dark green leaves of every shape and size, straggly branches reaching out to tear at our skin and clothes. A track had been hacked away through the undergrowth – so narrow that I felt claustrophobic and so steep that Ya Zar had to put his feet down; I was even forced to dismount a couple of times. I was glad not to be driving, for I would probably have pissed myself with terror.

Ya Zar, confident yet barely in control, steered round the dodgy corners, occasionally asking me to shift position – either to rebalance the bike, or because he did not want me bumming him (I could empathise on both levels). He bumped down a particularly steep, rocky hill, twisted round a sharp corner – and crashed into a dusty bank.

"Sorry, sorry," he said, flustered. We had both come off, and Ya Zar's right leg was trapped beneath the bike. Fortunately, the bank had been soft and we had not been going *myan-myan*. I was hardly even bruised.

"No worries," I told him. "I didn't lean as I should have."

Ya Zar was embarrassed, but I smiled to reassure him. He got the machine going again and we trundled down the final few sections, coming to a short wooden bridge spanning a small creek. A couple of middle-aged forager-farmers were down here, their motorbikes laden with crops and bamboo shoots, their clothes ragged and dirty. All wore Karen knives at their hips.

Ya Zar parked up and waved for me follow him down a small track that led to the waterfall. The first part was easy, but then the undergrowth thickened. Soon Ya Zar was hacking through bushes and towering grass with his blade.

For some curious reason, which did not mirror my experience of travelling in Myanmar, I had imagined our journey to the waterfall would be a roadway cruise followed by a countryside amble and so had not donned proper walking shoes. Naturally, the clamber down to the waterfall was as steep, slippery and challenging as the motorbike track. The descent demanded sliding into bamboo thickets and clasping onto jutting roots, and proved too much for my trekking sandals, which finally escaped Samsara. They had been reborn several times through the blessings of staples, cable ties and super glue, but their good karma had finally triumphed. Now they are in nirvana, no doubt deploring the shoddiness of sartorial existence.

My immediate fear was not of injuring myself going barefoot through the jungle but of losing my twenty-month sandal tan – two dark square patches on the top of each foot, edged by porcelain skin. Their colour was indistinguishable from dirt and I had become deeply fond of them. But to my great relief, my fears were unfounded: six weeks of sun would not prove nearly enough for the untanned parts of my feet to turn the same shade as the tanned squares. Even now as I write this – almost two months later, back in the UK – my glorious sandal tan remains visible.

Since it was the dry season, the waterfall was not raging. However, it was still a good experience and I cooled off in the plunge pool. The surrounding jungle was lush and looked as though it held many secrets. When we returned to town, I told the Tourism Information Centre, a small office tacked onto Star of the East guesthouse, that foreigners would enjoy undertaking multiday jungle treks.

The owner grimaced.

"We would have to negotiate with two governments: the Karen National Union and Naypidaw," he told me. Fighting, it seemed, was still raging between the *Tatmadaw* and the ethnic Karen militia, even though both parties had signed the Nationwide Ceasefire Agreement.

Before bed, there was time for one last chat with Nancy. Like Thant Zin in Mawlaik, she was one of the few remaining Myanmar who had lived under colonial, military and democratic rule.

"Life was good under the British," she told me. "We played with the British children sometimes, but the British were very proud and would often keep themselves separate from the Karen. Proud like the Germans," she said, wagging her finger.

"Actually, German pride has fallen because of the holocaust," I said.

"Oh really?"

"Yes, I used to live there. Many young Germans still feel guilty about Nazism, though some are starting to become patriotic once more, for Germany is accepting lots of refugees from Syria."

"How interesting," said Nancy in her sonorous tone.

"How was life during the military years?" I asked.

Nancy waved her hand in a manner that said, "How could you even ask that question?!" and rolled her eyes.

"Ne Win was a bad man," she said, grimacing. "Than Shwe was worse."

That was clearly all I was going to get.

"No! No!" she shouted at the cat, which had jumped on the table to inspect the sweet shortbread. Nancy cried in

Karen and swatted it away, her venomous energy confirming that she would be alive and kicking for a few years yet.

"And what do you think of the new government?" I asked. "How are things today?"

"Oh, I'm very optimistic about our new government," said Nancy with a beatific smile. "Things are much better now. Visitors can come to my home and I can chat with them. I'm always interested to meet them. Even the soldiers respect me," she said, gesturing in the direction of the *Tatmadaw* tea factory. "They know how old I am. Did you know I am 96 years old?" Nancy closed her eyes and leant back into her seat, an image of old-age bliss.

"Yes, they treat me well. You've never met Burmans like them."

Chapter 18: What Would George Have Said?

Following a gruelling train ride from Taungoo, I arrived the next evening in the stifling and godforsaken city of Mandalay – again. Worst of all, I had three days to kill because of a scheduled meeting. Two of these I spent writing, but for one I followed a rewarding *Lonely Planet* cycling route. At the end, I settled down in a riverfront pagoda to read my Kindle. Three young children kept coming over to stare at the sunburnt whitey wearing a *longyi* and clutching a mysterious electronic device, giggling when they got close.

"ROAR!"

They gazed at me, bemused, but did not flee. It seems I could not be scary, just odd.

Realising I had left my phone in my bicycle's front basket, I wandered back to the pagoda entrance. It was gone.

I searched frantically through my rucksack and non-existent *longyi* pockets, flapping like a startled hen. Nothing. So I asked the man selling barbecued chicken feet, who was positioned by the parked motorbikes. Sure enough, he opened a draw of his stall-on-wheels and took out my Vivo. I thanked him and leant forward to accept my phone, but he didn't offer it.

"You cannot leave your phone there," he said, shaking it at me. "Someone might take it."

"I know, I'm sorry. I just forgot."

"If you leave your phone like that, someone could just walk in and steal it!" he barked, brow furrowed and eyes narrowed.

It seems we were not going to become Best Friends Forever.

"I'm sorry. I left it there by accident."

"What's happening?" asked a rotund, wrinkled *a-myo-thami*, looking from me to the barbecued chicken feet seller.

"The foreigner just left his phone in the basket of his bicycle," he said.

"Why did you do that?" she asked severely.

"I didn't mean to. I forgot it!"

She exchanged glances with the food seller. A handful of other adults came over to ask what was up. The news that I had left my phone unguarded did not go down well with them either.

"Look," I said. "It was an accident: I meant to put the phone in my bag but forgot. Can I please have it back? I'll go."

Everyone looked at each other unsurely, then at me suspiciously, but eventually the barbecued chicken feet seller returned my Vivo. I left immediately.

The Myanmar are renowned for their honesty and theft is rare. In my eighteen months there, I never once had anything stolen. iPhones get stolen – stories of how much they cost have reached Myanmar ears – but otherwise all agree that the Myanmar are an exceptionally honest folk.

Why, then, had these people berated me for leaving my Vivo in my bicycle basket? It was one of just two or three occasions in Myanmar that someone had got angry with me, and I can only imagine it was because I had left my phone easily exposed to theft – within a pagoda complex. Presumably, stealing something from sacred ground would be abominable. Perhaps they had been furious that I had offered the temptation, worried they might slip into sin. Just a theory.

As usual, Mandalay was only serving as a transit point. For this fourth leg of my journey, I would make my way through Myanmar's heartland and up to Kachin, its northernmost state, before looping back down through Shan and Kayah, which both sit on Thailand's northern border. Myanmar was now in the suffocating grip of the hot season, with temperatures regularly exceeding 40°C, and I had much travel ahead of me.

With the aim of reaching Katha, a small riverside town near the Kachin State boundary, I travelled to Shwebo, a former royal city situated roughly 65 miles northwest of Mandalay and renowned for its fragrant *thanaka*. On board the train, hawkers clutching baskets of *thanaka* logs proved popular as Kachin residents heading home stocked up for the year. A small rat scuttled around the carriage, sniffing at people's belongings and prefiguring the presence of a rodent on every train journey I would take from now on – or perhaps it was the same creature each time, spying on me. Outside lay barren fields of cracked orange soil; goats fed on whatever greenery remained, unable to reach the plush foliage of the surrounding trees but desperate to survive the hot season. Thatched bamboo huts made occasional, welcome appearances, emerging unexpectedly from the unforgiving thickets. This bleak, agricultural pattern continued until we passed a large lake of modest white lilies and towering rushes that created narrow channels, through which fishermen paddled their sampans, just as their ancestors had before them.

When we arrived in Shwebo, I first had to undergo the ritual of learning that none of the cheap guesthouses accepted foreigners; so by the time I reached Sann Tinn hotel, I was sunburnt and sweaty. I went straight for a shower – and was stunned to find two Chinese-made condoms stuffed in the soap dispenser. I guessed it was the influence of the owner's Chinese roots, for otherwise sex is a taboo subject in Myanmar – condoms were even banned under Ne Win. They retain a social stigma today because of their association with the sex industry, though are now widely available and can even be bought on street corners in Yangon.

If the first concomitant ritual of visiting an untouristy Myanmar town is finding a guesthouse that accepts foreigners, the second is getting accurate information on how to leave the place. I asked the owner of Sann Tinn hotel what time the bus for Katha left. He told me 8:30am, by minibus only, and that I could not wait on the road outside, which led to Katha, but had to go to Shwebo's main station. This seemed questionable, so I asked in an eat-drink-shop. The staff, five bashful young ladies dressed in pink polos, assured me that coaches left regularly and that I could wait on the road outside. Once I had finished eating, I returned to the hotel and asked a different member of staff, who was quite certain that, being a Sunday, the only bus left at 7pm.

Once again, it seemed hitchhiking was going to be the most reliable form of travel.

Having awoken early and traipsed onto the road outside, I caught a lift to the main junction, where I stood in the shade of a large billboard that read, *Protect us from Dengue Haemorrhagic Fever*. The first hour passed by, with me only getting thumbs-ups from passing drivers.

"The bus to Katha will come in 30 minutes," said a plump noodle seller, waddling over from his stall across the street. "A big, yellow, aircon bus. You can wait with me."

I thanked him, but by now was desperate to get moving. A beaten-up bus stopped, and I made it understood that I wanted to go to the junction 50 miles north. The ride was the slowest of the slow: acrid black smoke billowed out of the exhaust pipe as we trundled along, and we twice stopped for tea. As I sat drinking Premier coffee, a yellow aircon coach ploughed past.

Finally, after nearly two hours, we reached the junction and I disembarked into a village of modest homes, struggling trees and DIY teahouses. The heat had taken control and the dust was copious. Fortunately, I wasn't waiting long: a betel-chewing trucker transporting oil drums offered to take me, as did a family driving a white jalopy. They had been the first cars to appear, had stopped at the same time and were both turning off 60 miles shy of Katha. Suddenly I had a choice of two lifts – a complete contrast to Shwebo, where countless drivers had sped by without glancing at me. It was the age-old story: true honesty and selflessness resides in the rural, where community remains essential.

I thanked the trucker and jumped in the jalopy, knowing it would be a faster ride. The elder brother relegated himself to the back seat, where his sister sat cradling a baby, which burst into tears at the sight of me. We all laughed. The driver handed me a can of Shark, then sped along the single road that wound through a characterless landscape of rufous soil and low, scrappy vegetation. The sky turned a pessimistic grey, but the air remained still and undoubtedly just as humid. The land seemed desolate and lifeless, but the occasional appearance of wooden huts or ploughed earth reminded me that it was someone's lifeline – even if that person was unknown and invisible to me.

We reached the junction in two hours and I stopped for fried vermicelli. Half an hour later, two buses bound for Katha appeared.

"Belauk-le?" ('How much?') I asked the young money collector.

He didn't respond. I heard someone inside the teahouse repeat my question, followed by a reply of *"ngar-tauk"* ('5000'). Finally, when boarding the bus, I got my answer.

"Chauk-tauk" ('6000').

I shrugged, but halfway through the journey plucked up the courage to say that 6000 was too much. The money collector was not pleased, but duly reduced it to 5000. As is usually the case in Myanmar, the dispute was immediately forgotten, and we kindly wished each other goodbye at the journey's end, around 4pm. The 190-mile hitch from Shwebo had taken 9 hours – not bad by Myanmar standards.

*

"*Burmese Days* is a good book, but even better are Orwell's second two about Burma: *Animal Farm* and *1984*."

So runs a common joke made about the days of military rule in Myanmar. Naturally, of Orwell's "Burmese trilogy" only *Burmese Days* could be bought, since its anti-colonial overtones were thought to validate the junta's Burmanisation project.

Burmese Days was Orwell's first novel and, quite frankly, is a bitter, uninspiring read. Based on Orwell's experience as a colonial police officer in Katha, it concerns a British teak merchant disillusioned with British rule yet self-conscious of propounding it. In this regard, it is not a book about Myanmar but Orwell's own confession of how he was unwillingly sucked into the exploitative world of colonialism. When it was published in the 1930s, Orwell was deemed to have been unfairly critical of colonial society. Nowadays, many agree he was too scathing of Myanmar culture, and it infuriates expats that *Burmese Days* is the only book most travellers in Myanmar read.

Of course, parts of the novel are relatable and insightful: in particular, Orwell captures the expat's love-hate relationship for the country they live in, as well as the isolation felt upon returning home after long periods abroad. It's easy to find equivalents to his colonial characters in contemporary expat society, for the racism, snobbery, and refusal to engage with local culture linger.

Unfortunately, bitchy, unpleasant comments about Myanmar are also rife throughout the novel, even if it was progressive for its time. The natives are regularly likened to animals and fixed as racially inferior through cultural stereotypes, such as the servants being lazy. The narrator's complaints are damning and often petty as he hardly has a good thing to say about the country.

Orwell sought to empathise with the Myanmar by exposing the colonials' pretentiousness – which he was partly successful in doing – but what comes out most strongly is how much he hated living abroad. In his own words, "the English of the East ... lead unenviable lives; it is a poor bargain to spend thirty years, ill-paid, in an alien country, and then come home with a wrecked liver and a pine-apple backside from sitting in cane chairs".[30] For Orwell, serving in Myanmar was a form of exile, and his unhappiness was compounded by his detestation for his unbearable colonial colleagues. Ultimately, I'm unsurprised *Burmese Days* came out as it did and hardly blame Orwell for being so damning. I only mourn that people treat the novel as gospel just because he wrote it.

I arrived in Katha (pronounced "Qatar") on the full moon of Kasone, the day that Buddha was born, attained Enlightenment and finally passed away. To celebrate, Buddhists throw water on banyan trees. Everyone in Katha wore their best traditional dress, meaning the *paya-gyi* was full of adorable, excited children, smart men and elegant women.

I was plucked from the crowd and led by the arm to a mystical, twisting banyan, whose perimeter was decorated with small Buddha statues. There was great excitement at seeing the *longyi'd* foreigner joining in the fun and I was soon surrounded by young men and women

---

[30] G. Orwell (1974), *Burmese Days* (Kindle Edition), Mariner Books, pos. 3039.

equipped with selfie sticks. One of them whacked the whitening setting up to full, turning me into a ghost. I'm not sure I threw the water on the tree correctly – the ubiquitous smiles gave nothing away – but I greatly enjoyed doing so and the struggles of my nine-hour hitch were quickly forgotten.

Rejuvenated, I went for dinner at a popular street stall in the town centre.

"Bar-sar-ma-le-go Ingaleik-lo be-lo pyaw-le?" ('How do you say, "what will you eat" in English?') said one of its owners to a lady beside her.

"Ma-thi-bu" ('I don't know'), she replied. *"Thi-lar?"* ('Do you?').

"Ma-thi-bu," said another.

The three women looked at each other in silence.

"Shan hkauk-hswe sar-me," I said with a big grin.

They laughed, relieved, and prepared a delicious bowl of Shan noodles, which came with copious pickled vegetables – one of my favourite Myanmar foods. Once I had finished, I went to the riverside for sunset, expecting to find young couples perched on benches and snuggled behind umbrellas. In Myanmar, public displays of affection are a big NO – even holding hands is considered scandalous. To get around this, couples get intimate hidden behind umbrellas, for love is more powerful than the rule of law.

On this occasion, however, I found just one lonely soul on the riverside bench: an off-duty policewoman wearing a green and gold matching *longyi* and *ingyi*, looking out over the mighty Ayeyarwady with her hands in her lap. She appeared peaceful and contemplative, and I was initially afraid that my presence might disturb her. But when she saw me, she smiled and began chatting.

After the usual introductions, I asked if there were many policewomen in Katha. She beamed, displaying perfect teeth, and said there were perhaps more policewomen than policemen. Then we both turned our gazes to the river and watched children upstream charge into the water screaming, people carrying baskets of food to moored passenger boats, guys squatting by the edge smoking cheroots, and, eventually, hundreds of stars emerging.

One of the reasons I was in Katha was to write an article on the buildings that appear in *Burmese Days*, so I set out the next morning in search of them. After visiting the police commissioner's house, Orwell's former residence, I went to the Deputy Commissioner's Office – the grandest structure still standing and comparable to the colonial mansions in Pyin Oo Lwin, albeit not as magnificent. Originally Mr Macgregor's residence, its interior was filled with colonial-era pictures, including photos of elephants dragging enormous teak logs, and with information boards in Myanmar about George Orwell. The upstairs was dusty and decaying.

One hundred yards down the road sat the 1924 tennis club and the British club. The latter, now serving as an association office, was a half-timbered structure whose upstairs had been renovated.

"This is the old bar," said the association officer, gesturing towards a cramped, cobwebbed room containing broken fans, empty petrol cans and a shiny red Yamibisi motor. The downstairs classroom, by contrast, was the original and had been well maintained. I smiled at the sight of cheeky drawings on the blackboard, proof that school children are the same the world over.

The concrete tennis court, now home of the Kan Thar Tennis Club but originally part of the British Club, was dark green, edged red and enclosed by towering trees. The lines had been repainted, but the court needed resurfacing and the net looked to be a colonial relic. When I arrived, a children's training session was underway. Watching them was a fit and healthy *a-myo-thami* wearing Western clothes and a string necklace: one of the club's ten regular members.

"We play every evening at five," she said. "Do you want to join?"

I did, so I returned later in walking shoes and shorts. Although I had not played in years, I was optimistic that I could avoid making a complete fool of myself. The lady who had invited me was the first there, now in blinding pink tennis attire.

We began rallying. I did not rip the court up, but most of my shots landed in – which was about as good as I had been hoping for. Gradually, other players arrived, all men. I came off to allow a doubles match to begin – and realised just how much better than me they all were. My host had clearly been going easy on me, for she could smash low forehands over the net and serve with speed. She exerted full energy on every shot and won her first service game to love. The score was counted in English, but deuce was a "tie" and foot faults were myths.

When the set was over, won in a tie break, they came off and I began rallying with a latecomer. After a failed underarm serve, I leant on the net to collect a ball – and collapsed. The net had broken. In fact, the thick wire inside the white lining had snapped.

You idiot, James! You've destroyed the single nice legacy left by your countrymen! What would George have said?

Had I been a native in the colonial days, I would surely have received numerous lashes. But my hosts assured me it was "no problem" and began repairs. Still, I felt flaccid as I watched them try to slide the frayed end of the wire back through the lining. It wasn't happening, despite everyone's best efforts. Someone disappeared into the clubhouse, now a storage room, and returned with pliers and tape. He squeezed and wrapped the end, then tried again.

Failure.

What had I done? Why couldn't I even manage a game of tennis, without screwing things up?

There was a pause as people discussed what to do. Over twenty minutes had already passed – valuable playing time, with the light fading. The same guy went back inside and found a pair of scissors. There were nods of agreement as he cut the lining to make more space. Then they tried pushing the wire through once more.

"*Hswe! Hswe!*" called the eldest.

They pulled and pulled until somebody was able to grasp the end with a pair of pliers. Success. The wire was reattached to the poles and play resumed. I left immediately and went for a massage.

Things did not improve back at the hotel, either, as I blocked the squat toilet with loo roll before locking myself out of my room.

"Ah, no spare key," said the other owner, slumped over a wooden chair. "No matter."

He disappeared round the side of the building and came back with two long, flexible pieces of plywood, which he fixed together with a rubber band. Then he grabbed a screwdriver and hammer from a toolbox and headed upstairs.

"This room?"

"Yep."

I wondered what his plan was, for the open windows above the door were mosquito-screened. Using the screwdriver, he removed a piece of the wooden window frame and tore away the screening, making me feel even guiltier and yet more useless. My room lay at the end of the corridor, beside the window, which he promptly opened. Then he climbed on its lower inside railing, put his left foot on my door handle and poked the hooked stick through.

"Where's your key?"

I climbed up to have a look. It was no surprise that he hadn't been able to see it: I had left it in the most inconvenient place possible, right at the back of the room, behind a plastic bag and atop my tablet, which was poised precariously on the edge of the table.

We swapped places again and the manoeuvre commenced. I couldn't see what he was doing, but I heard several disconcerting thumps as things fell on the floor (please not my camera!), followed by the rattling of a key.

"Ahah!"

He pulled the plywood back slowly, threading its rear end through the corridor window. The key was almost within reach, when I heard a "rattle" followed by a "thump."

The manager slapped his forehead and tried again. I soon heard him hook the keys, then he began withdrawing the plywood.

Rattle. Thump.

"Hmm."

Attempt Three. This time he didn't thread the back of the plywood through the window, but let it bend up the wall – until it snapped.

Rattle. Thump.

Yet by a stroke of luck the plywood had snapped into the ideal length. The manager tried again and retrieved the keys almost instantly. I thanked him and went inside to flop onto my bed and bury my face in my pillow.

This incident was the newest in a stellar saga of incompetency. Over the past few months I had become a sloppy traveller, leaving knives in hand luggage, not bothering to haggle and forgetting clothes in guesthouses. Quite simply, I had travelled too long and too hard and burnt out. Although I was still enjoying myself, I was on my last reserves and really had to make an effort with everything I did. The days of bliss, when travel becomes indistinguishable from everyday life, had come and gone. My body was feeling it too as I had lost considerable weight and was covered in bruises and scars.

I've learned that the best way to deal with failure, which for me includes sheer idiocy, is not to punish yourself but to treat yourself – otherwise life just wears you down – so I went for a good meal and another massage the next evening. Over my final weeks of travelling, I would become increasingly lavish, staying in cosier and cosier hotels, eating more and more Western food, and paying for fancier transport every time.

Chapter 19: Crocodiles, Flowers and Hornbills: A Natural Metaphor

Kachin: one of the Myanmar states most affected by civil war and socioeconomic marginalisation. That's what I had read and that's why I was heading there. In this part of my "search", I wanted to find out for myself the extent of the damage inflicted by internal conflict and its impact on the region's residents. Luckily, I had friends in Myitkyina, the state capital, who would be able to aid me in doing so.

Of course, my research would be greatly restricted, for foreigners were only permitted to visit a few Kachin destinations. One of these was Indawgyi Lake – which tourists could only travel to by train, for apparently the authorities feared the Kachin Independence Army dacoiting road vehicles. (Was a slow locomotive not an easier target?) The prospect of a hideously slow train ride did not get me bounding up and down with excitement, but little did I realise that the Katha-Indawgyi Lake journey would be the most eventful of my entire trip.

The train left from Nabar, twelve miles west of Katha, so I waved down a packed songthaew heading that way. An *a-myo-thar* was duly relegated from his seat and forced to sit beside the driver, allowing me to squash on the wooden bench. My fellow passengers were either all befriended or simply treated each other as such (it's often hard to tell in Myanmar). Among them was a dude in a leather punk jacket, a mother with a sprig of plastic yellow flowers in her hair, and your "everyman" Bamar cradling a dog. Further up sat a gentleman with a chicken on his lap, which kept shooting nervous glances at the furry predator.

Following a brief betel stop, we set off at full throttle. This seemed cue for everyone to begin teasing the dog – twisting its ears, patting its head, putting their hands in its sharp-toothed mouth – and for the toddler to pat its head with an enthusiasm bordering on abuse. The dog yelped in response, then made a sudden dash over people's limbs, towards the side railing, and attempted to throw itself onto the *lan*.

There was a frantic kerfuffle, but two guys managed to restrain the suicidal *kway* in the nick of time. Then the teasing resumed. As we rode on, the sky darkened and sinister clouds moved in, announcing their arrival with a rumble of thunder.

"*Mo-ywar-daw-me*" ('It's about to rain'), mumbled the mother.

It seemed the perfect time to pull over and help another songthaew driver repair his vehicle. Once again, the *kway* made a burst for freedom, running into a field of cabbages. This time it evaded its captor for ten minutes by weaving between the wooden posts marking the field's perimeter, but eventually its great escape came to an end. Rather amazingly, they fixed the songthaew in fifteen minutes and we reached the train station just before the heavens opened.

I traipsed across the mud carpark and bought a ticket. On the platform, women squatted with bamboo baskets of cultivated crops at their feet, staring at me curiously, while toddlers in pale frocks or tiny *longyis* flitted around, engrossed in smartphones or tugging at their parents' clothes and pointing at the foreigner. A teenager wearing baggy jeans and a Barcelona football shirt took a few final bites of his apple and kicked it onto the train tracks, which were now being pelted with raindrops. They were the usual station scenes: the behaviour of tired waiting.

I had been told the train would come at 10am by the guesthouse manager, at 09:15 by the songthaew driver and at 09:30 by the ticket seller. And in a moment of inspiration, I thought of a way to work out the actual time it would arrive.

Using the calculator on my phone, I found the mean time of those given, which turned out to be 09:35... And, would you believe it, a train pulled in at exactly 09:35. My chest swelled and I nodded gently to acknowledge my own genius – until I realised it was a mere cargo train, thus shattering my theory on how to determine rail timetables in rural Myanmar, along with any lingering hopes of making it into the School of Sophistry.

My train eventually arrived at 10:43 and I nestled down in the first-class carriage, adjacent to a monk sat in the lotus position, smoking directly beneath the "NO-SMOKING AREA" sign. He wore a thick Vans beanie and polarised sunglasses; the handles of his grey sports bag were tied with a USA-flag handkerchief.

Five minutes into the journey, as we rocketed along at nearly 15mph, a chunky topless *a-myo-thar* standing behind the railside thickets looked towards my window – then bolted for the train. I leant out the window and saw him jump on a lower carriage.

Great, I thought, an immigration officer coming to pull me off the train.

He entered our carriage with purposeful strides, determination etched into his face. Yet he bypassed me and walked towards the doorway.

I relaxed and returned my attention to the rain outside falling diagonally, slicing through the morning air, but soon heard commotion from behind.

"*Kale! Kale!*" ('The baby! The baby!') someone shouted.

The mystery man was now wearing a red shawl containing a *kale* on his back and leaning out the door.

He was going to jump.

The lady who had been carrying the baby stood beside him, looking on with an odd neutrality. She looked classy, clothed in a turquoise silk *ingyi* and a Kachin *longyi*, but something about her body language wasn't right.

The guy jumped. Everyone peered over.

Impressively, he landed on his feet, baby intact. While I watched him push his way through bushes lining the railway track, there was a soft crash – and the lady crumpled onto the ground outside, only narrowly avoiding being crushed by the wheels.

What had happened?

I asked the man sat opposite me, who said that the guy was taking the baby back to its mother, who lived in a nearby village.

So what about the lady in the silk *ingyi*?

My co-passenger shook his head. No idea: she wasn't related to the child, nor did anyone know her, and now everybody was throwing wary glances at her.

Apparently, she had stolen the baby.

Despite my many subsequent enquiries, I failed to learn anything more about this inexplicable baby-theft; and in just a few minutes everything was forgotten – once again proving that travel consists of moments of madness interspersed by normality.

I spent the next few hours reading my book and stretching my legs outside whenever we stopped, which was often. Two-thirds of the way to Hopin, the transit town for Indawgyi Lake, a one-legged beggar on crutches came through the carriage, asking people for money. But when he reached me, he merely offered me betel, grinned, shook my hand, then continued on his way.

He was followed by a middle-aged Kachin with terrible breath and a missing incisor, who sat down opposite me, cross-legged, and began talking quickly and incomprehensively. In addition to his questionable manners, he had a penetrating stare and an unkempt, almost windswept appearance. He was a peculiar individual, and I was hardly surprised when he reached into his brown jacket pocket and handed me a pale sticky dough ball, which had no taste and was unpleasant to chew.

"I'm sorry, but I don't like this."

"Ea' i'! Ea' i'!" he barked, hitting every glottal stop.

I tried again, then protested more.

"Ea' i'! Ea' i'!" he repeated before moving to sit beside the monk and observe me.

He kept such close watch that I only managed to chuck a tiny bit out the window. Once I was finished, he retook his seat opposite me and resumed talking incomprehensively – now joined by a smiley lad in a filthy green sweatshirt, who wanted my number. The other guy rambled on, his breath stinking out the space between us. I tried everything to signal my wish to be alone: I got my phone out; I looked unenthused; I was unresponsive; I even went so far as to put both earphones in and select ambient techno right before his eyes. And yet he persisted, displaying all the mettle of an Arthurian knight in a Monty Python sketch.

Following disagreement on Rakhine State, my tormentor left me in peace and went to sleep. A few minutes later, his smiley friend disappeared too. Then my phone buzzed with an email from my mother.

`Hope you're not going here,` it read, with a link to a BBC article on the recent escalation of fighting in Kachin State.

The conflict between the Myanmar military and the Kachin Independence Army (KIA), which formed in the late 1950s/early 1960s and seeks greater autonomy for Kachin State, had taken a sharp turn for the worse in early April, with almost 7,000 people being displaced by mid-May. In the months leading up to April, the *Tatmadaw* had purchased six Su-30 fighter jets from Russia and conducted test-firing operations in the Ayeyarwady Region, arousing suspicions that they would subsequently target the KIA. Sure enough, Kachin natives were soon reporting devastating airstrikes.

`All fine. Nowhere near Kachin State,` I wrote back. I don't think my mum will ever stop worrying about my travels.

At long last, having suffered through several of those seemingly reasonless stops endemic to travel in developing

Southeast Asian countries, we pulled into Hopin at 19:22, having averaged a fierce 7.5mph over our 65-mile journey.

*

You can get into any conversation in a teahouse, which is why everyone in Myanmar adores them. I sat down the next morning in Hopin opposite a skinny 20-year-old Buddhist Kachin, who wanted to know if I was travelling to Indawgyi Lake to see the *paya-gyi*. I said I would visit the pagoda, but the lake itself was what attracted me most.

Huh? How could anyone be more interested in the lake than the pagoda?

It was a common confusion: for Buddhist Myanmar, a pagoda's serene setting – be it hilltop, lake or forest – merely lends the religious site tranquillity and is no attraction itself. Of course, for non-religious tourists, like myself, the pagoda was just the cherry atop a delicious cake.

My breakfast partner then leant closer and let his voice fall to a hush, fearing eavesdroppers. Eyes jittering, he began asking about sex and penises. However, since I am a proper, honourable gentleman who considers even the very thought of sexual conduct a heinous sin, my Myanmar vocabulary was not sufficient to understand his question. Seeing my incomprehension, and visibly desperate for an answer, he brought up a Facebook page filled with pictures of penis enlargers.

Ahah! Now I understood! I quickly assured him that Europeans did not use penis enlargers – their penises were just naturally bigger.

But no! This was not his question! He glanced around and squirmed on his seat. A bead of sweat formed on his brow. He scrolled through his phone and brought up a new Facebook page, this time of women using strap-ons.

Once again, I thought I had the answer. But no! Apparently, his question was not about lesbians using dildos either! It concerned men, and he subsequently began speaking about pain upon getting an erection. We never got to the bottom of his sordid mystery, and today I still wonder what on earth he could have meant.

I arrived at Loneton, a village on the western edge of Indawgyi Lake, around mid-morning by pick-up. A long wooden walkway led to Indaw Mahar Guesthouse, the only licensed guesthouse in the Indawgyi area. Raised on short stilts, it occupied an idyllic spot by the edge of Myanmar's largest natural lake – a dozy giant fringed by emerald rushes and embraced by hills swaddled in cotton wool clouds. Birds that looked ordinary from a distance, but upon closer inspection revealed plumages of dark sapphire, silver and jade, perched on bamboo poles by the lakeside with their wings spread, enjoying the breeze that tickled their feathers. Common Coots and Ruddy Shelducks cast fleeting shadows over the water while small fishing boats below them carved gentle arcs. Each morning, children released ducks from their lakeside enclosure and herded them into the water. The fuzzy outlines of Indawgyi's distant shores beckoned to be explored.

There are several versions of the lake's aetiological myth and all bear a resemblance to Noah's Ark and the flood story in the *Epic of Gilgamesh*. According to one, a great city populated by the Htamanthi, ancient relatives of the Shan Ni, occupied the natural basin. One day, the Dragon King issued a warning that in seven days he would flood the area and transform it into a giant lake. An old widow heard him and tried to tell people, but nobody would listen.

"Oh, this widow," they said. "She's just yearning for a husband. We don't believe her."

On the seventh day, the widow took her meagre belongings, her buffalo and her grandchild and fled to the hilltop. As she struggled up the mountainside, a tempest lashed the land and sent thunderbolts flashing across the sky. When she looked back, the basin was flooded and the city submerged. After death, the widow became an angel and returned to the lake's edge, advising the peoples living there to build a pagoda on the water. As proof of this, the widow's footprint is preserved in the lakeside village of Lwemun.

In another version of the myth, the Dragon King was angered after children ate eggs laid by the Dragon Queen, which they had found near the river. He flooded the city as punishment – which is why the barking of dogs, as well as the singing and laughter of the drowned residents, can still be heard.

According to a third variant, the city was filled with immoral people and only the widow was deemed worthy of surviving the deluge. After the flood, the residents transformed into fish with human teeth, though they have since all perished.

In the three cultures' flood myths, the timeframe of seven days plays an important role: God tells Noah to enter his ark seven days before sending the deluge; in the *Epic of*

Gilgamesh, Utnapishtim takes seven days to build his boat and the rain lasts for seven days; and the widow of Indawgyi is warned seven days before the storm strikes.

The Gilgamesh flood myth is lacunose, like the epic itself, but the Indawgyi one appears fractured: in the official, first version, no reason is given for the Dragon King sending the deluge. Punishment for eating the Dragon Queen's egg, conversely, is a rationale, as is the purging of an immoral city. Perhaps two or more of these tales were originally a single, "full" myth, which has been split by time.

"Hello," said someone from behind me.

The speaker was Carmen, a Dutch national studying the language Shan Ni, a variant of Shan spoken in some of the local villages. She had medium-long brown hair, broad shoulders and was confident in her abilities and beliefs. She was knowledgeable on Myanmar culture, a rarity for expats, and interested in local politics. Carmen was also the third Westerner I had seen in a week, which was infinitely more than I saw during many weeks of my trip.

The owner, an amiable, orbicular ex-soldier, walked onto the veranda and began gesticulating at Carmen, who understood immediately.

"Do you know about the fighting in Kachin State?" asked Carmen, walking over towards a map of Indawgyi Lake on the wall.

"Partly. I expect you know more."

"So villagers have been displaced to Nyaungbin," she said, pointing towards a village at the lake's northern tip, "by fighting in Chaung Wa. The KIA have planted landmines on military routes near Konmana," a village 2.5 miles north of us, "and the residents of Maing Naung," which lay six miles south, "reported hearing gunshots the other night. If you want to visit this area," she said, indicating the northern quarter of the lake, "you need permission."

Okay then.

"There's a military checkpoint at the end of the road. And you can't enter the jungle without a guide because of landmines."

Myanmar is one of the few countries not to have signed the 1997 agreement on banning the use of landmines, and in 2017 ranked last in a survey of countries trying to eradicate them. Of the 298 casualties in 2016 from landmines, over half were in northern Shan State, where residents regularly go foraging in the jungle for food or medicines. Britain-based NGO Halo Trust has been running Mine Risk Education events in affected areas of Shan State, but sometimes villagers are scared away by the presence of armed ethnic groups or the *Tatmadaw*. Although the Nationwide Ceasefire Agreement commits signatories to stop laying landmines and undertake de-mining activities, it does not explicitly ban possession of them.

The 2017 Landmine and Cluster Munition Report found that the *Tatmadaw* and 17 armed ethnic groups in Myanmar were using landmines. Late in 2017, Myanmar wrote to the International Campaign to Ban Landmines, reporting that the Commander-in-Chief of the *Tatmadaw* had announced a ban on landmines. However, there was no mention of any timeframe nor of geographical extent.

"How long have you been here?" I asked Carmen.

"About a month," she said. "I'm supposed to be here until August, but I might have to leave if the fighting gets closer."

We had a coffee on the veranda and talked about her project. Shan Ni, said Carmen, had never been properly studied.

"Are there no colonial texts you can use? I know linguistic studies were conducted."

She laughed and shook her head.

"A few missionaries wrote about it, but they had no linguistic training: sometimes they were writing about more than one language at once, without realising. They were also really racist."

"So how do you conduct your research?"

"I go to villages with an English-Myanmar translator and we ask Shan Ni-speakers to tell a simple story or to translate sample sentences. It's hard to find people in these villages, who still speak Shan Ni." Carmen sighed and waved her arm longingly towards the north of the lake. "There are still villages that speak Shan Ni as a first language, but they are all in the conflict zone."

After coffee, I walked to the lakeside to take a few snaps. Along from our guesthouse, uniformed *Tatmadaw* soldiers were sat by a wooden jetty, smoking and chatting. I trod over the lush grass towards them, pointing at my camera. They nodded, so I stepped onto the jetty, joining soldiers washing their uniforms.

What were they scrubbing out? Dirt from the jungle? Sweat? Blood?

I would never know, but I took an evocative, jarring photo of a soldier striding across the jetty to clean his clothes, past an arched bamboo pole draped with drying military uniforms, backdropped by the glittering lake and majestic hills.

"Where are you from?" asked one *sit-thar* in a strong accent.

"England."

"Aww."

"Do you like the Premiership?" I asked, hoping to tempt him into conversation. "Which football team do you like?"

He shook his head, then pointed at himself and mimicked pulling the trigger of a rifle. I think he was trying to say that he only understood how to shoot.

Because of the strong military presence, Carmen and Suzanne, a young Yangonite working on a project for Flora and Fauna International, had developed code words for speaking about the current situation: *Tatmadaw* soldiers, by virtue of their dark green uniforms, were "crocodiles", KIA insurgents "sparrows", IDPs "hornbills" and landmines "flowers", thereby adding an incongruously natural twist to the conflict. I said they should go full metaphor and speak of crocodiles "preying on" sparrows, hornbills "migrating" and flowers "blossoming", but my suggestion was deemed too literary.

"Any news today?" Carmen asked Suzanne, who worked closely with some of the local villages.

"Several villagers in Maing Naung reported hearing more gunshots last night," she said in a hushed voice, "but the bangs did not last long. And others said that two crocodiles were killed by flowers in the jungle."

"There are protests going on in Myitkyina," Carmen said to me. "Are you following the Kachin Youth Movement page?"

"No. Should I?"

"Have a look."

I got out my phone and tried to load the Facebook page, but the internet was poor.

"Are you with Ooredoo?"

"Yes."

"That's why it's slow," said Carmen. "Apparently the locals refused to let Ooredoo put up telephone towers here, because Ooredoo are from Qatar – a Muslim country."

Really? How petty. Even though I was quite used to hearing such information by now, it still came as a shock and made me reflect on the poisonousness of Islamophobia in Myanmar.

I switched to my MPT SIM and brought the page up. It showed pictures and videos of young people rallied in Myitkyina, the Kachin State capital; a newsfeed provided updates on the conflict. This rally would swell to a protest of over 5000 people calling on the government to rescue villagers caught in the warzone, many of whom the *Tatmadaw* were allegedly preventing from fleeing.

"If the fighting gets too intense here," said Carmen, "Suzanne and I we will leave together on my motorbike and go to Myitkyina – which will be safer, even if there are protests at the moment."

Chapter 20: The Police State

Once I had exercised my British prerogative of becoming a lobster while kayaking, I left tranquil Indawgyi Lake, honoured to have visited perhaps the most beautiful place in Myanmar, yet concerned for the residents' future. A German couple, who had arrived in Loneton the day after me and had been surprised to discover they were near a conflict zone, offered me a lift back to Hopin on their Boxers. As we rode, I admired my sunburn in the wing mirror, occasionally casting my eyes over the forested hills swathed in heavy fog that seemed unsure of whether to let the looming rainclouds take charge. We zipped along, rarely dipping below 40kmph, and narrowly avoided a slender black snake wriggling across the asphalt.

Why did the snake cross the road? Probably because it lacked the mental faculties to know what it was used for – otherwise it might have thought twice after seeing its squashed cousins.

The Germans dropped me at Hopin train station, whose ticket officer demanded an English lesson.

"If I have eating, I will stay here," he said, trying to translate my sentence of *"sar-pi-yin, pyan-me."*

"When I have eaten," I said.

"When I have eaten – *ma-hoke-bu*. When I have eating..."

"When I have eaten, I will come back."

"When I have eaten, I will come back," he repeated.

We both grinned and he wrote me a ticket. Then an *a-myo-thar* in a blue sports jacket came over and spread an enormous log book before me.

"We have to use this," he said, sounding tired and irritated. "It's all in English."

He scanned his finger across the headings, among them "Passengers", "Consignor" and "Wharfage of demurrage charges." He sighed and shook his head. I felt his pain.

The train to Myitkyina mostly transported cargo, meaning there were only two passenger carriages. The benches were wooden but not uncomfortable; many were piled with cardboard boxes and plastic baskets while sacks of rice, cabbages and other crops blocked the hallway. A little rat scampered across the floor, sniffling at people's shoes and enjoying the general filth. No one used the overhead racks: they were simply too disgusting.

The passing scenery on this journey was unspectacular and frequent downpours gave them a melancholy tinge. When we paused at one station, I eagerly stuck my sunburnt arms out in the rain and watched tangerine sellers beside the platform don translucent cagoules while guys scrabbled for shelter beneath a large truck carrying felled timber. Glum, revealing scenes.

Shortly after the train began moving again, a friendly-looking, round-faced teenager in an orange anorak sat down nearby and started pumping tunes at high volume out of his phone. Naturally, nobody uttered a word of complaint, for the "national trait" of *ah-nar-de* forbids imposing on others. Fortunately, his choice was melodic metal, which I personally enjoy, so I spent the rest of the ride listening to ripping guitar solos and Myanmar harmonies, watching the wet world slip by.

Myitkyina, Kachin State: I had finally made it. But what was I going to find? Would my "search" here be at all successful, or would I get kicked out *myan-myan* because of the current difficulties?

My first impression of the state capital was of a city with a vast disparity of wealth: simple, squalid homes ringed the centre, which boasted several banks and towering hotels – among them the ominously named Cartel Hotel. Except for a couple of newly surfaced main roads, the streets were potholed and uneven; the one outside my guesthouse was even flooded, for roadworks carried out two months previously had compromised the drainage system. Opposite a Buddhist monastery stood an elaborate building of elegant yellow walls with orange trim. I assumed it was a crony hotel, but it turned out to be a grand Hindu temple – a pleasant surprise. On the balcony, a young girl watched Hindi music videos on her phone, allowing Indian melodies to diffuse through the evening air and imbue it with invisible beauty.

The Kachin were generally broader in stature than the Bamar and fairer in complexion; many were of Chinese descent. At a catwalking practice session, which took place in the building adjacent to my guesthouse, I saw why the Kachin were renowned for their looks: everyone's facial features were striking, the women voluptuous and the men handsome.

Like many of the hill regions, Christianity thrived in Kachin State. The Christian Kachin I met were warm and jolly, declared Jesus head of the household and would probably have sprayed WWJD on their cars – only that phrase seems to be reserved for Americans.

Outside my guesthouse was a cosy, international eat-drink-shop, whose only customer was a bulky white quinquagenarian who looked fed-up with life. He looked UN to me. A few minutes later, a white number-plated jeep pulled up nearby, confirming my suspicions.

"Excuse me," I said, walking over to his table, "but do you work for the UN?"

"I do."

"I just ask, because, well, I was wondering about trying to visit an IDP camp. Some friends told me that if I could visit any IDP camp in Myanmar, one near Myitkyina would be my best bet. Just some unofficial advice, of course."

"Well, I can give you some official advice," he boomed, leaning back in his chair. His voice was gruff and his accent faintly Irish. "As you may know, you are only about 70 kilometres from a warzone. Now, you may say it's only recently escalated, but then this is the world's longest-running civil war."

Actually, the conflict between Karen rebels and the central government was, but I didn't interrupt.

"In your hotel you will see a red signboard that lists the areas in Kachin State you can visit, areas for which you need permission – which means you won't get permission – and the areas that are off-limits. Almost all the IDPs are in the off-limits areas." He took a sip of water. "Even if you do make it to an IDP near Myitkyina, it probably won't be representative of the others. You see what I mean?"

I did.

"Now," he continued loudly, "why those places are off-limits can be argued. Maybe it's for your safety – after all, there is serious fighting going on – or maybe it's because they don't want you to see what's really happening. Who knows?" and he waved his hands flamboyantly, which told me he was rather enjoying himself. "But if you really want to talk to an IDP, why not the sex worker on the other side of the block? Hell, that's part of the informal economy!"

I shuffled around and looked across the *lan*.

"I'm not keeping you standing for no reason. I'm about to leave," he said, finishing his water. "And don't be fooled: every step you take, every move you make, they are watching you."

Did he just quote Sting at me?

"It may not look like it, but your movements are being very closely monitored."

I was not sure how I felt about him quoting The Police at me, but gave him the benefit of the doubt and decided it was meta.

"Anyway, I hope some of that has helped," he said as he stood up and reached out to shake my hand. "Wow, that's some sunburn." He started walking towards the UN car, then stopped and spun round.

"One tip I can give you is that the owner of this restaurant speaks good English and isn't afraid to talk."

I saw him twice more; on neither occasion did he make eye contact. However, I took his advice and had dinner at the international eat-drink-shop, hoping to engage the owner in conversation. He was of Chinese descent and moved onto the topic of the KIA-*Tatmadaw* conflict without prompting.

"You see, the *Tatmadaw* are up here from South Burma and don't know the terrain. That's why they want to stay in the villages and won't let the villagers leave."

"Why not?" I asked.

"So they can make the villagers cook for them, carry their stuff..." He didn't need to finish the sentence. "There is food being sent," he said, arms folded across his chest, "but the *Tatmadaw* won't allow it through to the IDPs. The chief minister of Kachin went out two days ago and brought back 120 IDPs, then about 140 yesterday, but it's very slow because they have to travel by boat."

I was unable to verify his numbers, but he was right that evacuation operations were underway, initiated by the chief minister. The challenging, mountainous terrain was partly why the conflict in Kachin State had been running so long: the *Tatmadaw* lacked the knowledge to operate in it successfully, nullifying their advantage of superior numbers. Surely, their Su-30 fighter jets would soon change that.

*

„Die gefährlichste Weltanschauung ist die Weltanschauung derjenigen, die die Welt nicht angeschaut haben."
('The most dangerous world-view is the world-view of those, who haven't seen the world.')

I was wearing a T-shirt emblazoned with this quote from Alexander von Humboldt when I set out to fill my Myitkyina agenda, assisted by a Kachin friend's brother and his *chit-thu*. Today, although I still think there is truth in the aphorism, I find it slightly pretentious – after all, not everyone has the chance to travel. On this day, however, wearing the T-shirt seemed appropriate, since the sentiment really did fit with my Myitkyina plans. I had resolved to travel round Myanmar because I was fed up of learning about the country second or third hand – I wanted to see it for myself – and of nowhere was this truer than of Kachin State, about which I had read so much. Here, I really hoped to experience what was going on first hand and let this knowledge inform my own *Weltanschauung*.

Our first point of call was a drugs rehabilitation centre. Kachin State is suffering from an addiction epidemic, with mainly young people hooked. Most take "yaba" (Thai for 'crazy medicine'), methamphetamine pills whose ingredients are readily available in Myanmar. As demand has risen across Southeast Asia, meth labs have sprung up all over Myanmar, particularly in Shan State. Often no more than a bathroom in someone's house, they easily avoid detection.

Yaba is the scourge of modern Myanmar and is destroying lives in the border regions. Driven by poverty, unemployment and marginalisation, many young Kachin have begun taking yaba intravenously. Worst of all, due to inadequate sex education, social taboos surrounding condoms, needle-sharing, and addicts' unwillingness to tell their spouses, HIV/AIDS is rife. According to Dr Tun Tung Brang from the Substance Abuse Research Association, 40-50% of users in Kachin State are infected. All over Myanmar I had seen signs reading 'Drugs Free School.'

We first visited a government rehabilitation centre, whose outside wall bore the message: *Yes to life, No/Never to drugs.* The idea of a journalist poking his head round and talking to patients did not go down a treat, but some guys loitering outside told us to try around the corner. My friend drove me to a two-storey wooden building and tiptoed inside. A moment later, he waved me over.

Suddenly I was in a Pat Jasan office.

I had read about Pat Jasan and was both nervous and surprised to be admitted into their district headquarters; my first thought was whether they would let me interview them. Backed by various churches, Pat Jasan, a Christian anti-drugs vigilante group made up of thousands of Kachin residents wishing to take matters into their own hands, conduct various drugs-elimination activities, including destroying local opium crops, arresting drug dealers and sending addicts to faith-based rehabilitation centres. Allegedly supported by the KIA, Pat Jasan (Kachin for 'fighting against drugs') are militaristic and wear army-style vests and helmets. They have come under criticism from human rights groups for flogging drug dealers and for their harsh rehabilitation methods. These include the "detox room" – a small cage that all Pat Jasan clients must spend two solid weeks in during the initial withdrawal process; they are not given relief medicine, are often restrained and must defecate inside. As of autumn 2016, Pat Jasan have no official authority but remain operational.

The Pat Jasan district head made it clear from the outset that he did not want to be quoted, so we spoke off-the-record. But what I will say is that his arrogant aura of self-certainty, as well as the photos on the walls of members dressed in khaki uniforms, suggested Pat Jasan were hardly saints.

With my skin crawling from the interview, I headed back to my guesthouse, stopping for lunch in a bakery which deserves a mention. Western-style bakeries are becoming popular in Myanmar, though naturally every cake, sandwich and bun comes with extra added sugar. This bakery offered a good range, including pizza, blueberry pudding, chocolate cake and Dia Bread, my single favourite food name in Myanmar. This is a standard sliced white loaf, but few Myanmar would eat bread lacking in preservatives and artificial sweeteners. That's why it's called Dia Bread, short for Diabetes Bread (for only diabetics would eat it).

Later, I met up with Ko May Be, the brother of another friend. May Be was a tall, healthy Chinese-Myanmar in his late twenties. He was Catholic, married to a Kachin lady and owned a motorbike shop. The seriousness of the situation in Kachin State was revealed by how quickly he began talking about it.

"There are three governments in Kachin State: the NLD, the *Tatmadaw* and the KIA," he whispered, eyes scanning the street. "The *Tatmadaw* want to weaken the NLD – that is why they are fighting the ethnic groups. Aung San Suu Kyi's government has only been in power for three years but has almost 60 years of military rule to cope with. Every country criticises her. The UN are no good either, making criticisms when it's so complicated."

May Be fell silent as the waitress laid our kimchi on the table.

"And what is the fighting in Kachin State about?" I asked.

"You know there is lots of jade and amber and teak going to China?"

I did.

"Do you know about the Ledo Road?"

I didn't.

"It is a road that goes from India, straight through Kachin State and into China. It has not been used for years, but now China wants to reopen it. That's why there is so much fighting in the jungle: the *Tatmadaw* want to rebuild it."

"So that they can send resources more easily to China?"

May Be nodded. The Ledo Road, later renamed the Stilwell Road, was built by the British during WWII to deliver supplies to China after the Lashio-Kunming Burma Road had been cut off by the Japanese. Currently, all the jade, amber and teak from Kachin State first travels to Mandalay, then along the Burma Road to the border town of Muse – roughly 630 miles total. If the Ledo Road were reconstructed, it would shorten the journey from Myitkyina to Muse by over 400 miles. In June 2016, Beijing suggested India, China and Myanmar establish a joint dialogue to restore it. India, however, is hesitant, for it fears that the road will result in Chinese goods flooding the Indian market and that it could be used by ethnic insurgents in Northeast India, who have hideouts in Myanmar.

"It is all about China," said May Be. "The KIA and the *Tatmadaw* are both working with them, because China is rich. China wants the fighting to continue: they want to take control of Kachin State."

I put this last remark down to sensationalism, but he was right that China was playing a political game – part of which included delivering weapons to insurgent groups.

Exactly how China wants to influence Myanmar politics remains a controversial, complex topic.

"You know," said May Be, "we pay taxes to the state government – that is good, 'white money' – but also to the KIA. They levied taxes off me last month." He pulled out his phone and showed me an official-looking document with his signature on. "Someone came into my store, put the form on the counter and laid his handgun beside it."

"How much did you have to pay?"

"Five laks [£272]. They did the same in many shops, sometimes asking for 10 laks."

"Do people here like the KIA?"

"Why did they have to put a gun on the counter when taxing me?" he replied, incensed. "Only the uneducated Kachin support them. I have to be careful around my wife's family, for they are Kachin and like the KIA."

May Be finished his drink and leant closer, hands on the table, his expression even sterner.

"Do you know about the drugs?" he asked. "The *Tatmadaw* allow an open border, but the KIA traffic drugs too. They take them to Rakhine State, then the AA [Arakan Army] traffic them to Bangladesh."

This was not the first time I had heard about methamphetamine and opium trafficking, which has become a huge problem in Myanmar and is inextricably linked with the civil wars. Among those arrested in 2017 in Rakhine State were a Buddhist monk carrying 400,000 yaba pills, three Rohingya men attempting to smuggle 800,000 such pills into Bangladesh, and two *Tatmadaw* soldiers hiding almost two million yaba pills in their military vehicle. On 24th August 2017 – just one day before the Arakan Rohingya Salvation Army (ARSA) attacked police outposts and triggered the brutal *Tatmadaw* retaliation – the Advisory Commission on Rakhine State published a report on local drug trafficking, noting that ARSA were using trafficking revenue to fund violent activities.

I found no reliable evidence to support May Be's claim that the KIA were trafficking drugs, but it is generally believed they do and there was good evidence to suggest the AA, their allies, had dirty hands. The *Tatmadaw* are also not clean and many say they encourage trafficking to cripple the ethnic minorities' sense of worth and weaken armed insurgent groups. It's likely that all these claims are true, but historically the *Tatmadaw* have been portrayed as the enemies and the ethnic militias as freedom fighters – literature documenting crimes committed by the latter, excluding perhaps by ARSA and the United Wa State Army, remains relatively scant.

"Some of the officers in the KIA are billionaires [in *kyats*: that's millionaires in pounds sterling]," said May Be. "They are no longer fighting for freedom." He paused and took a deep breath, placing his hands flat on the table. "I believe in Myanmar as one country. I believe in Aung San Suu Kyi. If only the ethnic groups would have faith in her government, we could have peace. But now they just want money. Shan State is going to become part of China." He sighed, nodding to the waitress for the bill. "All the ethnic leaders are liars."

May Be paid for us, then escorted me to the cinema.

"I cannot join. But let me take you to an amber market tomorrow," he said.

"Thank you so much – for everything. That would be wonderful. 9am?"

He nodded.

"Enjoy the film."

I had come to see *The Mystery of Burma: Beyond the Dote-Hta-Waddy*, keen to test out the theory that the cinema in any country provides a unique insight into its culture. Everyone was bubbling with excitement and had bought enough rations to survive a zombie apocalypse, just as they did for any journey exceeding an hour. The sound of mouths munching on cakes, crisps and other foods was overwhelming, and within minutes the carpet was strewn with sunflower seeds. Expectations were particularly high, for *The Mystery of Burma* was part of the new wave of Myanmar movies that aimed to meet international standards (hence the English title).

After everyone in the cinema had stood for the national anthem, prompted by the appearance of the Myanmar flag on screen, the trailers began. First, the traditional Myanmar films that you see on bus journeys – wealthy people living in villages or small towns, getting into humorous situations with their friendship group – followed by one for *Avengers: Infinity War*. The contrast was colossal: the room vibrated with the orchestral music, special effect explosions promised action and excitement. No one understood the English jokes, but they enjoyed any slapstick and were captivated by the spectacle.

Finally, the film started. Some of the audience watched with bated breath, others video-called their friends to show them the screen or talked on the phone. After a tense opening scene set in ancient Mandalay, we moved to modern-day Paris. Ko Htet Paing – a muscly, handsome Myanmar Tom Cruise – was "friends with benefits" with a red-headed *mademoiselle*. He was also an antiques dealer, as his father had been.

After learning that his parents had been murdered, Htet Paing returned to Yangon, devastated and confused. The film was careful not to show any of the grottiness of Yangon, making it appear a flourishing, developed city.

Htet Paing arrived at his parents' home, nostalgic, mournful and perplexed; this is when the English subtitles really came into their own. Two policemen entered and began explaining what had happened, asking the protagonist if he knew anything. Htet Paing sat down before the window and put his head in his hands, soft light falling on his face.

"I believe that they lived in the peace of mind at all times ever, since I came to life."

The policemen understood his pain, but they had studied the crime scene: it was undoubtedly "a vengeance."

What was Htet Paing to do? He went to town and bumped into a friend, Elvis, who turned out to be the film's jester. Elvis embodied the transition between traditional Myanmar comedy and Hollywood and was easily the best character. He asked why Htet Paing was upset and confused.

"I don't know what the heck's going with my life. My parents were murdered. That hurts!"

Aww, now Elvis understood.

"That's brutal," he agreed.

The trio was complete when Htet Paing realised a beautiful young woman – played by Ah Moon, who had been chosen, said director Arkar, not to make the film "hot and sexy", but just to play the part of a "normal girl" – was following him at Bogyoke *zay*. Her name was Saung and her father had also been murdered. In fact, her and Htet Paing's "pops" had been friends and had even searched together for an enormous ruby once owned by King Thibaw. But "wicked George", an Englishman who had been part of the expedition team, had betrayed them, eager to have the ruby all for himself. It was *he* who had masterminded their murders and now he was after the "national treasure" – could Htet Paing, Saung and Elvis stop him?

And so began a Lara Croft-like adventure of unconvincing high speed chases, solving ancient puzzles and being helped by selfless Myanmar. The Englishman was greedy and spoke no Myanmar, but he was determined, and having a European in the film was a strong statement of intent. The subtitles couldn't decide whether to be in white, illegible black or just disappear entirely, but like everyone else I was quickly hooked. Being a miserable British sod, however, I didn't roar with laughter, nor scream with fear or enthusiasm, unlike my fellow spectators.

The final scene took place on the frayed rope bridge of a cavern beneath a secret Bagan pagoda. Saung had discovered the ruby, but "wicked George" had a knife to her throat. Htet Paing stepped tentatively across the planks, then gave the rope a sly twist, throwing George off balance and forcing him to release Saung. Then he snapped the rope – and down fell the English thief, landing with a cracking thump.

Saung and the "national treasure" were saved. The cavern began caving in, so Saung and Htet Paing escaped to level ground, where they heaved themselves onto a low red brick wall, a proud pagoda of the same colour forming the backdrop, fringed by lush trees on either side. Both were gradually recovering their breath. Htet Paing's tested muscles were bulging. Saung reclined – her hair back, her slender leg arched casually, her white vest accentuating her curves.

Then it cut to photos of their wedding three months later.

Myanmar isn't yet ready for the Hollywood snog.

The Mystery of Burma went down a treat and put all in a visibly good mood. It wasn't going to win any Oscars, but I had enjoyed it for a whole other reason.

It's about identity! I wrote in my notebook.

Believe it or not, the story was loosely based in truth. When the British dethroned King Thibaw in 1885 and sent him into exile, they stole over 167 of his favourite treasures – including, he claimed, the Nga Mauk, a giant ruby. In 1964, the plunder was returned to Myanmar as a gesture of good will, but the Nga Mauk was not to be seen.

In 2017, British filmmaker Alex Bescoby and Soe Win, one of Thibaw's great-grandsons, travelled to London to see if they could find the stolen ruby. The suspected culprit, still infamous in Myanmar, was Colonel Edward Sladen, a decorated veteran of Indian and Myanmar campaigns who spoke Myanmar and would oversee Thibaw's packing for exile. As evidenced by a list signed by a British political officer on 29th November 1885, Thibaw entrusted "1 ruby ring known by the name of 'Nagamauk'" to Sladen for safekeeping during his passage to India. The

British ignored later pleas from Thibaw for his ring to be returned.

Soe Win's uncle took up the search for the ruby, believing it had been cut into smaller pieces and embedded in the Imperial Crown of India. The rubies in this crown do come from Myanmar, but then so do most of the world's rubies.

Upon seeing the four 1.5cm rubies in this crown, Soe Win was convinced it was the Nga Mauk quartered. Bescoby, however, decided to keep hunting. His journey took him to the "Political and Secret" collection of the India Office Records, held in the British Library. There, among the dusty tomes, he found three drafts of a letter written by Sladen to the Viceroy, replete with rephrasings and deletions. Due to the chaos of the day, Sladen writes, Thibaw made "no attempt at handing over particular items or a given quantity of anything."

The colonel's diary, however, suggests a different story. In the entry from 29th November 1885, the day after Thibaw's surrender, Bescoby found twelve full lines blacked out – the only part of the entire diary that had been redacted. Using multi-spectral imaging, some of the text could be recovered. A few intriguing words jumped out:

Kings asks me to receive over... Regalia – I agree – asks me personally to take K...

... King's Nga Mauk? Unfortunately, the next three words were illegible. Determined to find the truth, Bescoby followed a lead suggesting Queen Victoria had bequeathed the ruby to Princess Louise, Duchess of Argyll. But here his

hunt came to a frustrating end, for the wills of royal family members remain sealed.

The richness of Myanmar soil is a source of great national pride and the Myanmar treasure the quality and quantity of their jewels – that's why countless companies are called *"Yadanar"* ('Gem'). Myanmar still decries Sladen's theft and mourns the loss of their royal ruby. In Soe Win's words, "The Nga Mauk reminds us of what we had, and what we could do. It reminds us that once we were a proud, independent nation with a rich history. We have nothing to show from that now to teach the next generations in Myanmar."[31]

The Myanmar lost their sense of national identity during colonial rule, particularly after King Thibaw was dethroned and exiled. That's why the junta attempted to restore a "pre-colonial" Myanmar: by deporting foreigners, encouraging the practice of traditional activities, such as *chinlone*, and renaming the British-named streets after famous Bamar kings, the government hoped to revive the country's nationhood.

Can it, then, have been mere coincidence that *The Mystery of Burma* constantly referred to Thibaw's ruby as the "national treasure" and that it was an Englishman who sought to steal it?

Of course not. The Nga Mauk had been symbolic of Myanmar's national identity and "wicked George" of the British imperialists. This was not merely an action movie, but a critical and patriotic analogy, which screamed: *The*

---

[31] The above quotes, as well as most of the information concerning the Nga Mauk, come from https://www.bbc.co.uk/news/resources/idt-sh/who_stole_burmas_royal_ruby <Accessed: 07.01.2019>

British stole our nationhood and now we must recover it! Once I realised this, my respect for the film increased significantly.

As promised, May Be took me to the amber *zay* the next morning. Situated in a concrete business park, it was hardly different to a fish *zay*: beneath two corrugated iron roofs, each roughly a quarter the size of a football pitch, sellers squatted behind spread blankets piled with dark orange rocks or stood at modest tables of amber goods. There were no fancy glass cabinets nor classy shops that corresponded to the cost of the items on sale. The first area was for amber jewellery, amber *thanaka* and other amber products, the second for unclean, uncut stones. Some pieces were translucent even in the shade; others resembled bits of charcoal. Men and women, mainly of Lisu or Chinese blood, were squatting round with torches examining the stones.

"Most of the ambers mines are in KIA territory," said May Be as we sauntered past the tables and rugs. "You pay 10 laks [£544] to enter them and bring back amber to Myitkyina."

An *a-myo-thar* wearing a blue Lisu Students T-shirt passed me his torch and gave me a crash course in gemology.

"There are two types here," he said. "Diesel orange and diesel red."

I plucked a stone and inspected it. Sure enough, the light passed through it a dark orange. My *saya* passed me another stone, which lit up dark red. Simple enough.

"And what are you looking for in these rocks?" I asked him, pointing at a handful of darker pieces he had picked out.

"A dark green colour," he said, passing one over.

Under the light, veins in the stone glowed dark green, like jade.

"So the green makes them valuable?"

He nodded and put the piece in his string pouch.

"And how much do these pieces cost?" I asked, nodding towards the six or seven raw stones he was buying.

"260,000," he said. That's £141.

I looked around, watching people flick through thick wads of *kyat* and haggle with amber sellers. I was out of my element, surrounded by jewellery and stacks of cash.

"Amber is used in traditional medicine," said May Be. "Good for blood circulation if you hold it close to the body."

A Chinese-Myanmar woman approached and showed me a small, uncut piece containing a spindly spider.

"150,000 [£82]," she stated.

She was followed by a short, scruffy man, who fished a piece of amber the size of my little fingernail out of a baggie. It was pretty and held a perfectly preserved, tiny bird's egg.

"How much?"

"$200 [£151]," he answered.

"Who buys this mostly?"

"The Chinese," he said. "But also Germans." Perhaps he had seen my T-shirt emblazoned with the German quote.

The amber may have been 'big market', for me, but compared to jade it was cheap. Myanmar is the world's largest producer of jade and a study found that in 2014 alone the business was worth up to $31 billion (£24 billion) – equivalent to nearly half of Myanmar's GDP for the entire year. Of course, most of the money goes to military elites, drug lords and cronies.

"Here, a present for you," said May Be, handing me a thin, turquoise felt cushion. "It's an amber cushion: those rounded parts are stuffed with amber granules." He unzipped the top to reveal them. "Good for your sleep," he said. "It helps me."

I thanked him, wondering how he knew I was an insomniac. His purchase, I felt, also encapsulated the local attitude towards the precious stones business: it was dirty, bloody and criminal, but that was just something you had to accept. Few people at that *zay* could afford to be picky about how they made their money.

Chapter 21: Relocation, Relocation, Relocation

Because of travel restrictions and Myitkyina's eerie atmosphere, I chose not to stay a third night. Foreigners were prohibited from travelling from Myitkyina to Bhamo, south-eastern Kachin State, by boat or bus for safety reasons, so it was back to Nabar by train. I had planned to leave in the evening, imagining I would arrive in time for the 9am boat from Katha to Bhamo, but the ticket salesman had other ideas.

"You will arrive in Nabar at midnight and won't be able to get to Katha, where the only guesthouses for foreigners are."

"But the journey from Nabar took me over seventeen hours," I replied. "Surely I'll arrive in the morning?"

"This is the fast train."

That's what travellers call "pernicious optimism." However, he wasn't to be swayed, so I boarded the midday Myitsone-Mandalay Express. As we trickled out of Myitkyina, two policemen entered the carriage and began talking to the conductor, who was tidying a nearby first-class seat. One officer bent over and whispered in his ear, pointing furtively my way. The conductor's glance flicked up and we briefly locked eyes, then he nodded to his superior.

Keep an eye on him.

"What would you like for dinner, sir?" asked a skinny teenager in jeans.

Well, well, this was an improvement on the Myanmar trains I had ridden thus far! I ordered noodles and began reading my book, now hopeful that the ticket officer had been correct. The train was busy, mostly with people bound for Mandalay. At the front sat an entourage of saffron-robed monks, who bought food from almost every hawker that passed.

My noodles arrived at 6pm in a polystyrene box, which I took into the eat-drink carriage. With grimy walls, metal tables, men drinking beer, and no women, it was roughly what I had been expecting. Four monks from my carriage were already scoffing egg fried rice, casually flouting Buddhist precepts.

I sat down and was immediately confronted by a toned, topless, tattooed dude sporting a ponytail, who took away my food without explanation. The mystery was solved ten minutes later, when he returned carrying a plate of *hkauk-hswe-kyaw* with extra fried eggs, chopped raw red onions and a homemade sweet chili sauce. He gave me a betel-tinged smile and a cool, knowing nod. What a gentleman.

I ordered a *biyar* and the conductor whacked on Lay Phyu, one of Myanmar's best musicians. While speakers smashed out rock, jagged lightning forks split the outside darkness and an awesome deluge assaulted the train, turning the carriage into a testosterone-filled party wagon. As we bolted south, the electric storm rolled by, punishing those not aboard the Party Express and illuminating forests for split seconds at a time, transforming them into the haunting abodes of unseen horrors. We were expressing it Myanmar monsoon style, and boy did it feel good.

An *a-myo-thar* my age wearing an AC Milan shirt and sat adjacent invited me for a drink. His eyebrows were caterpillars caught in a static chase, his teeth sparkled and his eyes twinkled. Three large Myanmar bottles stood before him and he was suitably chirpy.

Where did he come from?

Myitkyina.

Where was he going?

Yangon.

Did he like Yangon?

No idea: he'd never been!

How long would he be there?

He didn't know that either!

What was he going to do?

Haven't a clue!

Where would he stay?

With his brother.

Well at least he knew something.

"I want to be rich," he told me, hands clenching imaginary bucks. "I feel I *have* to be rich."

He was one of thousands doing the same, and I had met young people just like him in Yangon. They came from all over Myanmar, often with little or no savings, saying only, *"aloke-loke-chin-de"* ('I want to work'). "Yangon" means 'end of strife': perhaps that's what they hoped to find there.

The train was still rocketing along by the time we finished our drinks. To my amazement, we looked set to arrive in Nabar before 8pm. I returned to my carriage – and we ground to an ominous halt. Two policemen embarked and announced that we would have to let a train coming the other way pass, meaning we would be stationary for three hours.

Ugh.

Disgruntled but unsurprised, I wandered outside and found a DIY noodle shop, where two teenagers sat strumming guitars and singing about timeless themes – poverty and wealth, patriotism, family, love – reminding me of how *hla-de* the Myanmar language was: simultaneously melancholic and uplifting, naturally rhythmic and rhyming.

Two hours later, I returned to the train and settled back down in my seat. While 90% of the carriage tried to get some shut-eye, two monks at the front got out their phones and went at it full volume, the one watching music videos and the other playing a football game. So there we sat, slumped and sleepy, listening to Miley Cyrus serenade the venerable *hpone-gyi* as he guided Lewandowski to consecutive hat-tricks.

We arrived in Nabar at 1am; luckily there was a cheap ride to Katha. I did not enjoy being right.

*

The best travel books make the reader eager to visit a country and retrace the writer's own route. This has never been truer for me than of Norman Lewis' *Golden Earth*, my favourite travel memoir on Myanmar. His vignettes of life on the Ayeyarwady – Myanmar's largest river, which runs down the centre of the country like an artery and is the lifeline of countless thousands – had made me impatient to set sail.

And so it was with great anticipation that I boarded a passenger boat for Bhamo the next morning. The vessel was slightly shorter than the Chindwin ferries, but like them had wooden decking and was furnished with raised, hard benches. As usual, the cabins at the front were occupied by monks. I caused a great kerfuffle by trying to adjust the boatside tarpaulin so that I wouldn't get sunburnt but could still see the passing scenery – until an *a-myo-thami* smothered in *thanaka* came over and pulled the whole thing down, casting us in darkness. She grinned.

Problem solved?

Up to a point, but I did want my view, so I switched to the other side of the boat, which was empty and shaded. This sparked further commotion, for it wasn't my designated seat, but eventually special arrangements were made to accommodate the foreigner and its bizarre ways. Then we left, only five minutes late; and as we shlooped along, crocodile logs bobbed with the current and floating beige foam splodges gave the impression that we were giants sailing through a contaminated archipelago. Grass grew in clumps on the sand tracts, like an adolescent's facial hair, and shanty huts with corrugated iron roofs lined the riverside, reflecting the tropical sun. Behind them, the jagged hills rolled on with their usual allure, fading into a realm of indistinct curves before disappearing entirely.

Norman Lewis relates that the Myanmar regularly reported sightings of Ayeyarwady Loch Ness monsters, "undulant creatures with the inoffensive heads of assess or sheep, which appear at times of national crisis, or when comets are seen", and details how the monks at Thihadaw had tamed a resident population of "five-feet dogfish",[32] which they fiercely protected from the British barbarians, who found the river-dwellers quite palatable.

---

[32] N. Lewis (2011), pos. 3183.

Only one specimen of the Ayeyarwady Shark, which allegedly inhabits heavily silt-laden mangrove swamps in the delta, has ever been found, but the river is still home to the endangered Ayeyarwady Dolphin. In a remarkable practice known as "cooperative fishing", a phenomenon found in only two other places in the world, these dolphins drive fish into local fishermen's nets and collect a portion of the catch for themselves. Sadly, the symbiotic relationship is dying out as modern fishing techniques take over, though a portion of the river has been designated as the Ayeyarwady Dolphin Protected Area and conservation efforts are being made.

After an unsuccessful hour of looking for polymorphic river monsters belching smoke, I switched on my Kindle and opened *Ghost Train to the Eastern Star.* A kid behind me leaned on the back of my chair, arms folded, and peered over my shoulder. So when I got my phone out to jot down notes, I decided to play with him:

`Are you enjoying Paul Theroux?` I wrote.

No response.

`Do you like football, friend sitting behind me?`

No response.

နားလည်လား ('Do you understand?')

"Understand!" he shouted, and we returned to reading Paul.

"Is it India?" he barked.

It was: Paul was on the train to Jaipur.

"You can read it?" I asked, only now noticing he was of Indian descent.

"Yes, I understand. Where are you from?"

"England. And you?"

"Shwegu."

We continued reading Paul until the boat stopped at a village of stilted houses overlooking the mighty Ayeyarwady. Beside them sat a neo-colonial brick tower with a teak balcony that encircled the building and presumably once served as a lookout platform. Hawkers and passengers waited on the bank below, perched next to a tree whose dangling roots resembled filthy feather dusters.

Lunchtime was a more civilised affair than on the Chindwin River: the hawkers walked onto the boat, rather than leaping on from a speedboat and hijacking it, and rice-sellers paddled sampans up to the stationary vessel and handed out their grub from there. While young and elderly women flogged prawns, fried chicken legs and mango salad from their circular woven food trays, two mothers sat on the platform occupying the front of the boat's interior fed their toddlers fried locusts. Kupi, my Indian friend, and I watched as the mothers played with their boys, flicking their foreheads, biting their arms affectionately and tickling them into hysterical frenzies. The toddlers laughed with the consuming, life-affirming charm that only young children can produce; it softened our souls. The *kale* in solar system pyjamas then bumped his head on the wall and began wailing, so his mother grabbed a shawl, wrapped it into a ball, blew on it, and pressed it to his head, successfully nursing her child back to health through the aid of superstition or the placebo effect. They only stopped their games when a monk appeared carrying a silver donation bowl containing money, boiled sweets and a speaker playing Pali prayers. The mothers each gave him K1000 and received a handful of blessed lemon drops in return.

When the monk had returned to the stern, Kupi's sister, a pretty eighteen-year-old with dark brown eyes and a face caked in *thanaka*, joined us. She was desperate to Facebook me – which she succeeded in doing after downloading the app, having deleted others to clear space for it.

"I don't like Myanmar," she told me.

"Have you ever been to another country?"

She shook her head.

"I dream of moving to America, but it is very impossible."

My Indian friends left me at Shwegu, then the boat cruised on towards the Ayeyarwady's second defile. The foam islands vanished, the river narrowed and the hills drew into a pass, to which a simmering heat haze lent a mystical air. Colourful pagodas were cut into steep hillsides dotted with skeletal trees protruding from the verdant canopy in a desperate bid for attention. Best of all, the vessel's helm was cast in forgiving shadow, the relentless sun having finally passed its zenith.

We pulled into a hamlet opposite an imposing cliff to deliver sacks of rice and orange oil tanks. Here, my heart was stolen by an *a-myo-thami* wearing a purple *longyi* decorated with blue and red roses, a short-sleeved pink blouse with black trimmings, a hairband that turned her hair into a soft cascade, and two ghastly green bangles. Traces of *thanaka* glistened beneath soft eyes. When I caught her gaze, she gave me a beautiful, bashful smile. I doubted she would ever leave that hamlet.

Recently, I had been falling in love as quickly as the Myanmar and Shwe Ei had begun occupying my thoughts once more. I put these emotions down to sentimentality induced by my imminent departure, but they surprised me nonetheless, for my journey in Myanmar had included several hardships, mainly personal. It seemed, however, that Myanmar had lodged itself even deeper within my being than I had first imagined, and I began questioning whether it would be possible for me to leave a country in which I had experienced so much.

My arrival into Bhamo was spectacular: silhouette speedboats and sampans sliced expanding arcs through the Ayeyarwady, staged before a crimson sun. Towering rain trees lined the riverbank, casting in shadow hawkers and taxi drivers milling around the riverside steps.

The town itself was an amiable web of smooth streets and stylish shops. Smiles were everywhere, as was Chinese script. A Chinese Yunnan monastery stood proudly and a disproportionate number of large, upmarket hotels dotted the centre. By virtue of Bhamo's proximity to the border, China was everywhere.

"What businesses are the Chinese involved in? Teak? Jade? Industry?" I asked my friend Khaing, a smart and gentle native of Bhamo who favoured Western dress. We had met for the evening in a beer station that was showing the Leeds United vs Myanmar football game – a tour the Championship team had been criticised for carrying out in light of the ethnic cleansing campaign in Rakhine State.

Across the room, a handful of Chinese guys were ripping through the lager. A few women of Chinese descent were also drinking.

Khaing nodded. "All those things." She paused. "Also heroin." Khaing then explained that some drug barons came over to buy brown sugar in Myanmar and flog it back in China, where the price had sky-rocketed.

"And do people here like the Chinese?"

A firm shake of the head. I got the same answer wherever I asked this question. Myanmar is in the fascinating and worrying position of loathing the Chinese – an animosity partly born through the superpower's impositions of enormous extractive and industrial projects that have devastated local communities – while being attracted to their wealth. Moreover, Myanmar's increasing disillusionment with the West, precipitated by the West's condemnation of Aung San Suu Kyi over the recent Rohingya crisis, is pushing it towards China. While Western businesses pull out of Myanmar, Chinese firms remain invested; the number of Western tourists visiting Myanmar has dropped radically in the last two years, but the Chinese keep coming. Myanmar's ties to China are tightening, but not entirely by choice.

A straggle of unmade-up, hungover Chinese-Myanmar girls in short shorts turned up to the hotel breakfast the next day – a scene I had not previously witnessed in Myanmar and another indication of Chinese cultural influence in Bhamo. The buffet was enormous, diverse and delicious, ranging from sweet pastries to flavoursome curries, and I felt sorry for the party girls who could only stomach weak coffee and toast.

Sated, I went to stroll around the town, pausing briefly in the hotel lobby to glance at *The Myanmar Times*.

"Where are you from?" asked a tall, bald *a-myo-thar* sitting in a chair, reading.

"England. And you? Are you Kachin?"

"No, I'm Bamar, but I used to live in Bhamo. Now I live in Myitkyina." He folded his newspaper and gazed at me with round, inquisitive eyes. "Where are you going after Bhamo?"

"I was hoping to go to Muse."

He shook his head, eyes closed. "You can't: the KIA have blocked the road because they have laid landmines there."

"Ah."

"And how long will you stay here?"

"Um, I think I'll leave in three days. I want to visit the bamboo bridge and the monastery, and I'd also like to see the logging camps with the working elephants."

He shook his head again. "You could do that two or three years ago, but now it's too dangerous. The KIA are felling teak trees and selling them to China."

Well there were my plans shattered.

"I have friends living near there, but one time I visited, a KIA soldier took down my name and asked what I was doing. The next time I went, a different soldier stopped me. This guy was armed, and I had to write down my address and the names of my family members. Perhaps he thought I was a spy." He shrugged, causing his shiny scalp to reflect the lamplight and create the impression that he had just had a bright idea. "I haven't returned since. Maybe they could come to my home. They know all my family."

"And do you think the KIA are freedom fighters?" I asked, baiting him.

"They want independence and control of the jade mines, but it won't happen. It can't happen."

"But do you think they are doing a good thing by fighting? Have the residents of Bhamo been affected?"

He put his hand to his lips and looked pensive for several seconds. Then he shook his head.

"They are not doing a good thing. They are not fighting for freedom. And they've made life difficult for the people of Bhamo. We can't travel to certain areas, such as Nam Khan just 60 kilometres away, because of conflict."

Once again, I was surprised to hear such criticism of the KIA from a Kachin State resident. Like May Be, this man was not ethnic Kachin, and so for the sake of unbiased review I asked an educated Kachin friend what he thought of the KIA. However, he was uncomfortable speaking about them.

With my day's plans in tatters, I cycled to a celebrated bamboo bridge nearby. The sun was blistering, but the massaging breeze generated by pedalling, coupled with the spectacle of the raised bridge stretching over the mighty river and towards the distant hill line, seduced me into a soporific calm – when suddenly I was thrown head first onto the floor. My thin front wheel had got caught in a small gap between two wooden planks and the momentum had flung me over the handle bars. Another close shave, and yet another scar for the collection: this time on my foot.

Fortunately, the blood was minimal, and I was able to wheel my bike over the thatched bamboo bridge and cycle into the neighbouring village of dusty paths and predominantly wooden houses. Plastic bags of soup were tied onto the wooden fence of someone's home; a thousand sweetcorn cobs were spread out on a rug outside another. The girls were giggly, the kids shy and curious. Everyone smiled as I passed – the story of rural Myanmar, and one I could never tire of. Once again, it dawned on me that in a few weeks I would be returning to England, where nobody bats an eyelid when I pass – let alone smiles. I had become so used to strolling through Myanmar villages and being invited inside for cups of *yay-nway-kyan* that I had hardly dwelt on the peculiarity of this lifestyle and its privilege. Soon I would no longer be trying to "find" Myanmar but rather a job, and these pleasant rural wanderings would become mere memories.

As I dwelt on these thoughts and everything I would miss back in England, I stumbled upon what appeared to be a wedding: colourful hangings were draped over the wooden beams of an unroofed hall, beneath which were assembled several wooden benches and around 30 people. Everyone was wearing conical, primary-coloured hats and casual dress – or perhaps the mass-produced *longyis* and *ingyis* of poor-quality fabric, decorated with garish images of cartoon white girls, were simply more prestigious than their traditional counterparts.

"Htaing-ma-lar?" ('Will you sit down?') asked a plump, jolly lady. *"Hkauq-hswe-sine"* ('It's a noodle shop').

Confused, I took my seat as friendly faces turned my way. I was stealing the show.

But then, was this really a wedding? Where were the bride and groom? If I invited a stranger off the street to my friend's wedding, advertising it as a "wine and cheese tasting", I would get ousted immediately.

The promised bowl of noodles was brought over, as were biscuits and a fizzy drink which contained large chunks of lychee. I began eating my *Shan hkauq-hswe*, then a teenager with flawless skin and a greedy grin came over and introduced himself to me as Ba Hein.

"Is this a wedding?" I asked.

He nodded, smiling.

"Where are the bride and groom?"

"They are changing clothes," he answered.

Shortly after he said this, the married couple returned. The husband, broad-shouldered and sporting soft facial features, wore jeans and a stylish tattered black T-shirt. The bride was not in ceremony garments, either, but had donned a classy cream dress with rose trim. Her hair was arranged into a double bun and her mascara eyelashes contrasted with her large, bright eyes, accentuating their magnificence. Something about her looked unnatural, but I couldn't put my finger on it.

They came over and I congratulated them on getting married. He was 22 and she was 20; both seemed delighted. Up close, I was finally able to tell what hadn't seemed right about the bride's appearance.

Her face was tinged blue.

Chapter 22: Pulling the Strings

Two days before I was planning on travelling to Muse via Mandalay, nineteen people, including fifteen civilians, were killed there in clashes between the Ta'ang National Liberation Army, an ethnic insurgent group active in northern Shan State, and security forces cooperating with two militia groups. It was a crossfire that cast a cold shadow over the Nationwide Ceasefire Agreement (NCA) and its aspirations for peace. In a paradoxical, cruel twist of fate, the fighting in much of Shan State has intensified since the NCA was introduced. Furthermore, armed insurgent groups have been less willing to negotiate with Aung San Suu Kyi's government than with the previous state, led by Thein Sein's Union Solidarity and Development Party, since its semi-democratic structure lacks transparency. Under Thein Sein, the ethnic militias knew they were essentially talking to the *Tatmadaw*, for his cabinet largely consisted of retired military officers. Today, however, it's unclear how much decision-making ability the NLD politicians have, without having to consult the generals.

I had been hoping to visit Muse, northern Shan State, to experience the influence of China on the Myanmar border. It's a sleazy town that caters to Chinese gamblers and gang crime. Corpses are regularly found in ditches, mostly the work of loan-sharks, and recently young Chinese have been lured over with the offer of employment in casinos, forced to gamble, then tortured into begging their parents to pay off their debts.

Another Myanmar border town living under the thumb of China is Mongla. Myanmar Tourex Travel Service

Ltd. provides a description of Mongla on their website (you can insert [sic] where needed):

> *Monlar (Mailar) can be reached from Kyaing Tong by road and on the Chinese border Mong La has been transformed within few years, from a large sleepy village into a booming town. Mong La is a flourishing town where the border trade, especially the tourist industry is booming. Tourist across the border pour in daily to do shopping, see the highly popular elephant circus and crocodile show or just to relax at a pleasant picnic site surrounded by emerald green mountains. Now Mongla has newly erected pagoda a top a high hill with marvelous view of the farms, orchards and rubber plantation of the surrounding country side. This is also alarge Church for the Christian in the areas. There is a freedom of worship in our country even in the remote border town. In the tour itself, are schools and hospitals where once there had been none.*[33]

It's an adorable piece of denial. Mongla, part of Special Region 4, is an autonomous area controlled by the ethnic Shan National Democratic Alliance Army and infamous as Myanmar's "Sin City." Most of its income comes from the illegal wildlife trade, (child) prostitution, gambling, money laundering, and drug trafficking. The lingua franca is Mandarin and the Chinese Yuan the official currency. Although technically part of Myanmar, Mongla relies on China for everything from telecommunications to

---

[33] http://www.myanmartourex.com/travel_myanmar_destinations/travel_info_mong_la.shtml <accessed: 13.05.2018>

electricity. It was granted independence in a peace agreement signed 30 years ago, when rebel fighters agreed to stop their insurgency. Initially funded by revenue from opium production, Mongla has transformed into a "Burmese Las Vegas" catering to Chinese tourists. At the zoo, you can throw live ducks into the jaws of crocodiles; at restaurants, you can eat black bear, pythons and pangolins. Anything goes in lawless Mongla. Myanmar Tourex Travel Service Ltd. do not arrange travel there.

  I had failed to acquire travelling permission for Mongla, and with Muse now off the cards I was forced back to Mandalay. On the overnight coach from Bhamo, as the TV screamed cacophonic *pwe* music, novice monks in the front seats curled up in each other's arms while people lay down in the dirty aisle to sleep – or began chucking up, skilfully missing their sick bags. I picked my way down the aisle, stepping over vomit and hopeful sleepers, and asked for the music to be quieter. The driver apologised and turned it down, only to crank it up again when I reached my seat. Then the road turned unpaved and bumpy, catalysing another onslaught of vomiting.
  Many Myanmar are sick on bus journeys, even when the *lan* is smooth. I believe it's simply because distance travel is new to them: travel was restricted during the junta days and there were hardly any coach companies. The vomit is proof of progress.
  We arrived early in the morning and I checked into a hostel, empty except for two Chinese guys who worked in the jade industry. It was my fourth – and final – time in Mandalay, so I spent most of my time inside, working. My

lack of adventurousness was compounded by the presence of a quality Noddle Shop next door to my hostel. I went for dinner there three days in a row, drinking Tourist Water and watching strutting sylphs whose beauty qualified them to wear hideous two-tone Marlborough dresses and go around flogging cigarettes.

"What will you eat?" asked the waiter on day three.

"Steamed rice, please."

"Yangon or Mandalay?"

I had never eaten the Mandalay *tamin paung*, so I went for that. But it turned out to be as disappointing as Mandalay itself: tasteless fried – not steamed, even though that's what *paung* means – rice with a greasy egg on top. I bought fried vegetables to supplement it, hoping to transform it into the succulent Yangon version, but only succeeded in paying double.

"How was it?" the waiter asked.

I smiled and nodded, Myanmar style. He understood. Then I ordered a Grab motorbike taxi to take me to the marionette theatre for an evening puppet show. Grab caused quite a fuss when it first came to Myanmar in 2017 and in many ways still does, since few Myanmar taxi drivers can read maps. When you order a Grab, the driver calls you immediately and asks where you are. Once he's found you, he asks where you're going. The ability to speak Myanmar is often essential.

My driver arrived in five minutes and handed me a half-head Grab helmet.

"Mandalay Marionette Theatre," I told him.

"Ah yes, I know."

He set off and turned down the smaller, slightly less filthy side streets. The moon was up, but the stars were yet to appear and the humidity had not relented.

"Where are you from?" asked the driver.

Bored of answering "UK" or "England" to this question, which all Western travellers in Southeast Asia are asked at least five times a day, I said, "America."

"How many days in Myanmar?" he asked.

"Hmm, about 500. I live here."

"Aww, I understand."

He fell silent for a minute as he passed through a set of red lights and turned left onto the main *lan*. Pedestrians were strolling by the Mandalay Palace moat, pausing to watch the reflection of the palace shrink into the water. Cars and motorbikes rushed along, beeping their horns, and Mandalay Hill shone up high.

"Your president is Donald Trump," said the taxi driver, twisting his head round. "He is my favourite."

"Why?"

"He is our favourite because he is businessman."

I sighed and attempted to explain that Trump was not actually a good businessman, that his father had been extremely rich and that many of Trump's projects had failed. But it was all in vain. Trump is loved all over Myanmar, mostly because he is a businessman. It's depressing on so many levels, but I could understand how appealing a businessman-president sounded to someone from a country as poor as Myanmar. The majority of Myanmar's recent progress had been economic, and the economic progress was easily visible.

I stepped into the theatre reception and was greeted by a beaming teenager with betel teeth and cropped hair, dressed in a smart white shirt.

"How may I help you, sir?" he asked in a colonial accent tinged with American intonation.

"Could I buy a ticket for tonight's show, please?"

"I'm afraid it's been cancelled because we need to finish decorating. I'm sorry, sir. "It will be on tomorrow night." He handed me a DVD of a puppet show as compensation. "How long in Myanmar?"

"I live here. I was teaching in Yangon and now I'm travelling."

"English teacher?"

"Yes."

"We have a class tomorrow here at 5-6pm," he said with a keen smile. "Would you come along?"

"Umm, who's the teacher?"

"Daw Ma Ma Naing, the theatre owner. You can talk to her."

Success: a chance to learn about Myanmar puppetry.

"Okay, I'll see you tomorrow."

I returned the next day and stepped into the reception, where the same teenager was chatting with two other smartly dressed workers his age.

"Oh good," he said. "You're here. We can start."

"Wait, where's Daw Ma Ma Naing?"

"She's not here. It's just you."

Oh cock.

I peered round the curtain – and to my horror saw 60 full seats. There were young teenage girls, elderly men, monks, and everyone in between.

My deceiver led me down the aisle, past pairs of staring eyes and astounded expressions, and handed me a temperamental microphone. The pupils were giggling, whispering, smiling, excited and curious to be taught by an Englishman. Could they sense my terror?

"How long did you say the lesson was?"

"One hour," he replied. "But we're ten minutes late. You should start now."

There was no going back. I hadn't come here to teach, but these pupils were expecting a lesson. I was completely unprepared and suspected that my nine months' experience of herding Reception Class children towards the toilet would not be of much use. However, I did have a whiteboard, a pen and two teaching assistants.

"You should introduce yourself, sir," said one of them, a seventeen-year-old Shan with short curly hair. "They can do introductions."

"Umm, okay." I coughed professionally into the microphone and produced a hideous, high ring of feedback, making the pupils giggle.

"Hi, I'm James from England," I spluttered. "I've been living here for a year and a half. First, I worked in Yangon as a teacher and now I'm travelling round, working as a travel journalist. Can anyone tell me what a travel journalist is?"

Blank stares.

"How about a journalist?"

More blank stares.

"You know, sir, we have the shame culture in Myanmar," said my Shan TA. "They will not answer."

"Right."

"You have to motivate them, sir."

"I can try."

"And they are all beginners. But actually some are nearly fluent."

Yay.

"Err, okay... Let's talk about... umm... I know. We'll talk about our homes. That can be our topic."

A room of expressionless stares greeted my decision.

"What could we talk about for the topic 'My Home'?" I asked, writing the words on the whiteboard in my illegible handwriting.

No answer.

"Maybe I should start." I glanced at the TAs, who nodded and smiled as social conduct dictated. "We could ask: 'Where do you live?'" I scribbled the question on the board. "What other questions could we ask about our home?"

More blank stares.

"You could call the seat number, sir."

"Nineteen!"

A *longyi'd* lad stood up and accepted the mic.

"Where do you live?" I asked him.

"Mandalay."

"Do you live in a house or a flat?"

Silence. Excruciating silence.

The TA translated the question.

"A house."

Time for full sentences, methinks.

"Thank you. Now choose a seat number."

The pupil hesitated and looked round.

"Thirty-four."

The TA took the mic from him and walked over to a young teenage girl in a pink skirt and grey sleeveless top.

"Hello. Where do you live?"

"Mandalay."

"Full sentences please: I live in..."

"I live in Mandalay," she mumbled.

"Where in Mandalay?"

"Between 82nd and 81st street."

"I live..."

"I live in Mandalay between 82nd and 81st street." She giggled and bent over to receive a whisper from her friend.

"Good. And do you live in a house or a flat?"

"A house. I live in a house, not a flat."

Progress!

"Excellent," I said. "And what other question could we ask?"

Silence.

I wrote 'Who...', on the whiteboard and cooed, "whooo...."

The girl smiled, ashamed, and hid her face behind a curtain of sleek hair.

'Who do you...', I wrote on the board. "Who do you live...."

"Who do you live with?" she finished, looking relieved.

"Thank you. Now say a seat number."

And so it continued for another quarter of an hour. I can't say I "elicited" information, but gradually we made progress. At long last, we had a list of five questions written on the board.

"Where do you live?" I asked a monk.

"I live in Mandalay, in a monastery."

"Who do you live with?"

"Monks."

"How many rooms are there in your house?"

The monk gesticulated confusion.

"Do you have any pets?"

He shook his head.

"What is your favourite room in your home?"

He laughed and held his hands up, as if to say, "Have you ever been to a monastery?" They were not the best questions for monks.

I tasked the pupils with asking their partners these five questions, thereby buying myself some time to think about what we could do next. Progress was excruciating and there were still over 30 minutes to go. My heart was thumping and my brain was whirring desperately to think of activities suitable for a mixed-ability class of 60...

"Okay, here's what we'll do next," I said, not knowing what we'd do next. "We'll, umm, we'll talk about ... about my home!" I wiped the whiteboard and wrote ENGLAND at the top. "What does 'England' make you think of?"

More silence.

"You have to motivate them, sir."

"Come on! You all know England. Just shout out. Please."

"Manchester United!" said someone. Everybody laughed.

"David Beckham."

"Rooney."

"Johnnie Walker." Even more laughs.

"Whisky."

"Rolls Royce."

"Big Ben."

"Buildings."

"Oxford University."

"Double Decker Bus."

I copied down these defining aspects of English culture and wondered how on earth to proceed.

"Maybe a game, sir," said the receptionist, who was my second TA. "They know Simon Says."

"Bingo! That's it: we'll play Bingo." I turned to the sea of expectant faces. "Okay, does everyone have a pen and paper? Good, now write down five of these words. I'm going to tell a story and if I say a word you have, cross it out. When all of them are crossed out, you have to shout 'bingo!' Does everyone understand?"

No reaction.

"What do you mean, sir?"

I explained Bingo to the Shan TA and he translated it into Myanmar. There were nods and two minutes of scribbling, then everybody looked up.

We were ready.

"So, I went the other day to visit my brother," I began. "Err, he didn't go to Oxford University and now lives in Manchester. Although he isn't a football fan, we went to Old Trafford because we wanted to see David Beckham. Unfortunately, the game was boring and we didn't see him. Then we went for a walk round town because my brother really likes… buildings." Some people looked down at their pieces of paper. "Err, after we had looked at the clock tower, which isn't Big Ben because that's in London, we rented a Rolls Royce and drank some Johnnie Walker – but not at the same time, because that's illegal in England."

Nobel Prize for Literature, here I come.

"And after that, we decided to go to London so that we could look at more... buildings and ride a double decker bus while drinking whisky... Has nobody got bingo yet?!"

A dozen people put their hands up.

"Ah, you're meant to shout "bingo!" Okay, never mind," I said. "Well done anyway."

What a flaccid end to a riveting story.

"Maybe for the last ten minutes we could do questions, sir?" said a TA.

"Great idea. For the last ten minutes you can ask me questions," I announced.

Several hands shot up.

"Err, yes. You," I said, pointing at a boy in a baseball cap.

"What do you think of life in England?" he asked.

"Good question. I think it's nice. I have a comfortable life at home. The food isn't great, and people don't smile as much as in Myanmar. Also, the weather is awful. But I like my family and friends. Next question?"

"Do you like living in Myanmar?" asked a young girl at the front.

"I do. I especially like how welcoming the people are. And street food culture, and I see something new every day."

Then the proficient English speakers – who had so cruelly refused to contribute earlier, preferring to watch me suffer through awkward silences – finally decided to speak up and persecute me with dastardly questions.

"What is democracy and do we have it?" asked my Shan TA.

He was supposed to be helping me!

"Christ. Umm, well, democracy means the people have power. Does Myanmar have power? Partly, but the *Tatmadaw* still has seats reserved for them in the *Hluttaw*, so it isn't a true democracy. Who's next?"

The mic was passed to an elderly gentleman in the back row.

"What do you think of the new government?"

Oh, come on.

"I think they have a difficult task and have only been in power for a few years," I said cautiously. "The country's problems will not be solved immediately. Also, the new government still consists of people from the old government, so it isn't all that new. And one of the main problems they have is that the NLD formed because it was opposed to the military dictatorship; that doesn't mean its members have the same political views. However, I must also say that I think they have tried too hard to push economic reform and not focused enough on political change, though I know that's difficult. Anyone else?"

"What do you think of the civil war?"

I could see where this was going and was getting nervous.

"There are lots of civil wars in Myanmar," I began. "I don't believe federalism is the driving force for all of them anymore. Drugs, jade, teak, oil: business plays a key part. We shouldn't forget China's hand. I also think the

Tatmadaw needs to permit insurgent groups who haven't signed the Nationwide Ceasefire Agreement to take part in peace talks. Err, yes, you," I said, pointing towards a smart *a-myo-thar* in the middle row.

The Shan TA took the mic from my last tormentor and began walking over to the next.

Please not Rakhine State. Please not Rakhine State.

"What do you think about Rakhine State?"

Oh no.

I raised the mic to my lips.

"Well, I have been doing some research on this for my book. Umm, it's an old conflict – that's important to remember – and very complex."

I paused. To say Rohingya, or not to say Rohingya?

"There is lots of evidence to show that the... that the Rohingya have been in Myanmar for centuries, and we can trace the exact point in time that they became "illegal immigrants." Everyone was silent. All eyes were on me. "However, I don't think where they came from is important anymore. The Myanmar government can contest where the Rohingya came from, brand them terrorists and declare foreign journalism "fake news", but that won't change the fact that Myanmar is suffering because of this crisis: business is failing, tourism has dropped, fighting has flared anew all over the country, and Myanmar is being pushed closer to China because of their power of veto at the UN."

Everybody was watching with bated breath. I was shaking yet oddly confident – passionate and gradually finding my voice.

"I believe that if Myanmar wants to continue developing, it needs to be respected by the international community. For this to happen, the refugees must be granted citizenship and repatriated. Otherwise, Myanmar will falter. Aung San Suu Kyi has talked about "unity in diversity". Myanmar must now embrace that idea. The ethnic and religious animosities must be cast aside, so the country can be peaceful and prosper. Myanmar can call the Rohingya "Bengalis" and persecute them, or it can look at the bigger picture and see that the country cannot function like this."

Perhaps all of five people had understood me – and it terrified me to think they had. But I was also honoured to have been asked such questions, and at the end of the lesson a couple of students even asked about my book. The views of foreigners on such topics are usually derided and dismissed, so I was humbled that these people wanted to know my opinion. It gave me hope that many Myanmar were curious to know what the international community thought of their country, and that not everyone had been indoctrinated by state media, which had been disparaging foreign news outlets for months. It also made me optimistic that open dialogue on these situations was a genuine possibility.

Whatever the case, I was just glad not to have been quizzed on the intricacies of puppet theatre.

Chapter 23: A Snapshot of Myanmar

Although the accidental English lesson had been terrifying at the time, I realised later that I would miss such quirky surprises when I returned home. With only three destinations remaining – the verdant Shan town of Kalaw, Taunggyi (the Shan State capital) and Loikaw (the Kayah State capital) – I was feeling sentimental both about my experiences in Myanmar and the country itself. After the episode in the Mandalay marionette theatre, I began dwelling on the many challenges facing the peace process. From what I had learned, especially on this fourth leg of my journey, a myriad of factors was driving civil war – not only entrenched ethnic animosities but also drug trafficking, the precious stones business, extractive industry projects, the *Tatmadaw's* desire to forge a Bamar-Buddhist nation, and the looming hand of China. The more I had travelled, the more I had come to appreciate the fragility and complexity of Myanmar's political situation. Yet it troubled me to think that such a long and turbulent journey lay ahead of this country, which had been my home for almost two years.

Following a smooth minibus ride replete with Myanmar translations of Western songs, including a catchy rendition of *Eye of the Tiger*, I arrived into Kalaw the next afternoon. The final part of the journey felt somewhat like a homecoming, since I was going to meet up with a friend and the Shan hills have the quality of making every traveller feel at ease. It was also my third visit to the colonial hilltop station, though my first in the dry season. It didn't disappoint: Kalaw dozed in a sunlit bowl, encircled by winding hills, a world away from Mandalay, the heat and the mosquitoes. Prim hedgerows and twisting trees turned the town into an idyll and profound shades of green induced cathartic ambulation. Blooming azaleas and purple orchids lined peaceful roads cast in cool shadow by proud pines. Mellifluous birdsong emanated from tranquil copses, wafted on the gentle Shan breeze. Renovated colonial houses of historic splendour crowned curving hillsides while derelict ones evoked fancies of a bygone age. Teenagers wearing pin-striped Shan trousers and traditional bags lounged around in floral front gardens, watching *Tatmadaw* jeeps chug through town.

At sunset, I went to the roof of Golden Kalaw Inn with Els, my amiable Dutch roommate, who was planning to trek from Kalaw to Inle Lake. There we met a stout, balding Finn named Mikael.

"It's a great sunset," said Els. "Did you see the sunset in Bagan?"

"Yes," replied Mikael in a low tone. "I have a great photo."

He pulled out his phone and showed us a picture of the sun setting over a sublime Bagan pagoda, the sky glowing a dusky amber.

"Wow, that is a good photo."

"Yes, it cost me 300 euros."

Els and I stared.

"Some Burmese men offered to show me a nice sunset spot and said I could buy souvenirs from them. And they had lots of souvenirs. I bought them all, without haggling." He sighed. "I'm too nice. I cannot say no."

He reached into his pocket and pulled out a set of jade earrings, followed by two jade necklaces. He was wearing a T-shirt of the Myanmar alphabet.

"I looked up the scams online," said Mikael, nodding. "I did all of them. In Mandalay, too. They even took me to their friends' stalls, so I could buy more souvenirs. I have almost 10kg of souvenirs."

Els and I exchanged glances and tried not to giggle. Mikael's delivery was perfect: slow and serious, with a self-aware smirk.

"Are you going trekking?" I asked.

"Yes, with my souvenirs. I want a challenge."

The adhan sounded at the local mosque, encouraging us to pause and look out over the colonial buildings, the rising hills, and the *paya-gyi* glittering in the twilight.

"What do you do for work?" asked Els.

"I was not working for the last two years," said Mikael. "In Finland, you get money from the government. It is only enough to stay alive – the last week of every month was a struggle – but then I thought I could make more money by growing... herbs."

Silence.

"You mean weed?"

"Yes. My parents were very confused how I got the money to travel. I told them I had savings."

"And do you still grow... herbs?" asked Els.

"No, now I work for an underwater cable company. It is perfect. I work ten days straight, lots of night shifts, but then get six days off."

"What do you do there?"

"I'm a newbie, so I sit and watch 20 kilometres of cable curl into a container. That is all. It takes one month. All the beginners do this job." He took a photo of the sun setting over the houses on a nearby hillock. "My boss told me I could move onto another job soon – but no, I don't want to: I like sitting and watching the cable," he said, his piercing eyes locked onto an imaginary cable.

"Err, I'm glad you enjoy it," said Els, grinning. "Are you sharing a room here?"

Mikael snorted, not in derision but astonishment.

"No, in Finland we have a five-metre rule."

"As in, no people within five metres of you?"

"Exactly. I had to have my own room."

Naturally, Els and I took an immediate liking to our gentle Finnish giant and invited him for dinner. Then I went to meet Thet Htoo, a friend who also goes by "TJ". He was my trekking guide the first time I came to Kalaw and it was he who named me Ko Kyaw Thu.

I won't forget how we met: I was waiting outside Eversmile Trekking, watching the organisers sort out the groups and make final preparations. Everyone had been waiting a while and was beginning to get edgy.

"Will these sandals be okay?" asked a German tourist.

"No," replied the owner. "You need proper shoes."

"But they are trekking sandals."

"No," she said again. "They won't be good enough."

"But is it a difficult trek?" he asked, his accent getting stronger with every sentence. "These sandals are very strong."

"You cannot go without proper shoes, sorry."

The tourist turned red and began complaining to his partner in rapid *Deutsch*. And while he ranted and searched through his backpack for proper shoes, up turned TJ wearing ragged sneakers and in jeans so baggy his bum hung out. A chain trailed from his belt and his rucksack was barely more than a few pieces of cloth stitched together haphazardly. The German looked at him in disgust; I looked on in admiration, knowing we would soon be friends.

There's only one place you spend your evenings in Kalaw: Hi Bar, perhaps Myanmar's sole dive bar. Cast in hazy orange light and dominated by tattooed locals smoking cheroots and slurping straight whisky, it's as atmospheric as you get. Round an elongated oval bar stand a dozen wooden stalls; the bare brick walls have been tagged in white ink and foreign notes dangle from the bar top. Everyone loses their status in Hi Bar and becomes the same as any other human. A guitar is kept above the bar, which guys pull down to play plaintive Myanmar tunes; everyone sings along, animated and entranced. Occasionally, tourists want to play a song – fine, so long as it fits the vibe: maybe Cohen or Waits, but backpacker crap is a no-go. The day *Wonderwall* is played in Hi bar is the day Myanmar has lost its charm.

TJ was waiting for me at the bar, clutching a Mandalay Rum. He's a short, handsome Shan with a round face, a slim build and an infectious laugh. His jeans never come off and he usually wears a cane bowler hat.

Today, however, TJ wasn't quite his upbeat self. The other night he had crashed into a stray dog and fallen off his motorbike. The Kalaw council regularly poisons strays to control their numbers. If TJ wasn't pro-poisoning before, I'm sure he is now.

We caught up on the usual – life, travel, girls: still with your girl? No, I left her, for better or worse. And you? I had something with a Korean girl last month, but she had to go home – while listening to guys strum songs. One player in particular displayed such passion when he sung, raising his head to the ceiling and closing his eyes, living in the moment.

"And how's work?" I asked.

TJ shrugged.

"Not many tourists anymore, only enough during the high season. I have to look for other jobs."

"Why are there no tourists?"

TJ drained his rum.

"Too much fighting, especially in Rakhine. The Asian tourists still come, but they don't like trekking. My work comes from Western trekkers."

In the 2016-2017 high season (roughly November-March), TJ earned nearly K900,000 (£472); in the 2017-2018 high season, he earned half that. He has taken on a painting job on the side and had recently applied for a passport, hoping to move to Bangkok or Korea. Of course, he first has to save the money to do so.

"Have you been to Bangkok?" I asked.

"No," said TJ. "But I think anywhere is better for work than Myanmar."

*

As with Myitkyina, I couldn't be tempted to linger in Kalaw – TJ's depressing news had marred its charm – so I jumped on a minibus to Taunggyi, the Shan State capital. Having recently visited several destinations whose beauty had been overshadowed by their troubles, most notably Indawgyi Lake, Bhamo and Kalaw, I was particularly sombre on this countryside journey. In fact, everything looked forlorn, barren: the clumsy bamboo fencing ringing thatched huts; the sparsely vegetated, undulating hills; the fields of red soil that resembled southern Spain; the pagodas glimmering atop scrappy summits; the cowherds shepherding their skinny livestock along the roads, directing them with taps of a bamboo staff. All seemed hopeless and unchanging, yet perhaps my perception was simply being shaped by my concerns for TJ's future as well as Myanmar's.

As we drew into Taunggyi, the *lan* improved and became lined by countless *Tatmadaw* bases. It was a trend I had noticed all over Myanmar: the roads were better near the military bases. An arch loomed, wishing us a "Warm and cordial welcome to Taunggyi, the city of Shan State", then we began ascending the hill, upon which Taunggyi perched. More *Tatmadaw* bases, more signs:

NEVER HESITATING ALWAYS READY TO SACRIFICE
BLOOD AND SWEAT IS THE TATMADAW

They could have at least inserted a comma.

Taunggyi appeared wealthier than I had expected. Although the city was essentially a single main road with branching side streets, there were lots of shiny new shops, including a Chiang Mai clothes shop which offered the "latest foreign wears", and over the road hung a banner advertising the Education Malaysia Exposition, an event about gaining scholarships for studying in Malaysia. The food *zay* was bustling and the clothes *zay*, which sold Western dress, Shan bags, Shan shirts, Akha jackets, and other garments, was a hit. Ethnic Pa-O, distinguished by their black or dark navy tunics and colourful turbans, made up a considerable proportion of the population. Taunggyi felt like a gateway city to eastern Shan State, China and Thailand. It also seemed to be the city of the independent monk: everywhere he drove motorbikes, hatchbacks and even jeeps, zipping past the laydrivers.

I rented a motorbike and set off for Kakku, the foremost Pa-O pilgrimage site, passing by pick-ups of ethnic Pa-O and golden Buddha statues. The women crouched beneath umbrellas, clutching books and reciting Buddhist prayers; in the vehicles behind them, guys beat cymbals and drums in a tuneful and rhythmic manner, undeterred by the rain.

Numbering roughly 2.6 million, the Pa-O are the second largest ethnicity in Shan State. They settled in Myanmar around 3,000 years ago and are thought to be of Tibeto-Burman stock, related to the Karen. Like many Myanmar ethnicities, the Pa-O claim descent from a dragon. Most are Buddhist, though some are Christian or Animist. In Taunggyi live the Highland Pa-O; in Thaton, Mon State, dwell their Lowland cousins.

According to a local nursery rhyme, the Pa-O wore multicoloured clothing until King Anawratha conquered their king and forced them to wear indigo-dyed dress to signify their "inferior" status. Their turbans are usually chequered and majestic orange, though in Taunggyi I saw the whole range: blue, green, blue and white, green and white, purple and red, blue with gold stars, multicoloured, and more.

My journey to Kakku was dogged by rain and I was forced to seek shelter three times. The road was flanked by hillsides, but they bore no resemblance to the verdant Kalaw slopes. Instead, they were rugged, like the Sussex Downs gripped in the tightening claw of winter. I bought a cagoule large enough to cover my rucksack and rode on, through the fields, beneath a grey sky, praying for the storms to keep away. Just as I arrived into Kakku, a glimmer of sunshine broke through the clouds, softly illuminating some 2500 stone stupas. Most were a faded rose, orange or cream, decorated with fabulous stucco reliefs and sculptures. These clung to corners in the form of mythical creatures, watched over the pathways as goddesses with omniscient eyes, or perched on ledges as humans swathed in elaborate dress and locked in evocative poses. The closely packed stupas created a maze of elegant piety; *hti* bells tinkled in the breeze, euphonious and mystical.

According to local legend, Kakku was founded in the 3rd century BC by Buddhist missionaries of the Indian Emperor Ashok. One day, many pagodas sank into the earth. Worshippers searched the ground for them unsuccessfully until a wild boar came from the woods and began digging a different patch of earth. The people focused their efforts here and uncovered the sunken stupas. To this day, people honour a golden boar enshrined in glass and "feed" it by placing money in round openings; these donations go towards restoring the site.

Everyone takes the same photo of Kakku, utilising a small pond to capture the reflection of the sublime stupa series. I did likewise, only mine included what most travel photographers omit: the mark of warfare. Kakku is patrolled by Pa-O National Liberation Army (PNLA) soldiers wearing digital khaki and supply belts, M16s slung over their shoulders. The PNLA are the armed wing of the separatist Pa-O National Liberation Organisation, who control three townships in Shan State and are one of the ten Nationwide Ceasefire Agreement signatories.

"Are you fighting the *Tatmadaw*?" I asked a *sit-thar*.

He nodded and smiled.

"How old are you?"

"Twenty-three."

He was just a year younger than me. I could have been him.

My Kakku photo isn't as pretty as the ones you'll see online, but I prefer it because it reveals the fuller picture. In it, the rebel fighter stands beside the pond and gazes into the water, smiling. His reflection spills out the frame and spoils the row of beautiful stupas. He's the single element of the image which doesn't fit, yet his presence combines much of what I had come to associate with Myanmar: beauty, religious fervour, charming smiles, civil war and ethnic division. It was a snapshot of Myanmar.

Chapter 24: A New Destination?

This was it. My last stop: Loikaw. In just a few hours, I would have travelled to every official state in Myanmar, which – although I don't measure travel by the number of destinations reached – nevertheless felt like an achievement.

I wasn't, however, going to Kayah State to tick boxes. Travel restrictions on the area had recently been loosened, meaning travellers could visit the local tribal villages independently. Also, a fellow travel journalist had given me a few tips for the city – one of which was to find Victoria, a philanthropic local who would be able to answer my many questions.

The bus left Taunggyi early in the morning and wound up the hill, granting its passengers a superb view of the shallow green basin below: sunrays fell onto a hilltop temple, lending it a divine glean, and *shwe* pagodas exuded Buddhist zeal. Verdant fields and swathes of uncropped soil spread across the flatland, transforming the basin into a hide of ochre-green bands. In the distance sparkled Inle Lake, numinous and inviting.

We paused at a *zay* in Pinlaung, one of the Pa-O Self-Administered Zones, allowing me to enjoy travel voyeurism to the extreme. Concealed by the blacked-out minibus window, I observed an elderly Pa-O lady squatting beneath her parasol and haggling with customers over her lumpy pumpkins (not a euphemism). Beside her sat a paddling pool-sized basket of circular tofu crackers skewered into stacks. It was a wonderful five minutes. At home, the idea of watching someone going about their daily business would be unappealing, yet it's the traveller's primary activity – and a rewarding one at that. The scene looked as though it had not changed in decades.

Back on the road, as we passed the southern part of Inle Lake, I gazed over the twinkling water, watching farmers waist-deep in the shallows cast their bamboo rods, framed against a sunlit hill range contoured like a crumpled piece of paper. Soon Christian churches appeared by the roadside, as did red-blue flags flapping in the wind. A checkpoint loomed: the Shan-Kayah boundary. My "search" was almost at an end.

Loikaw was the perfect final destination for me. Enough tourists came to the town for the residents not to be suspicious, but not so many as to diminish their curiosity and friendliness. The town was quiet and clean and was home to both teak buildings and modern ones. Young nuns, certainly younger than seven, strolled along newly asphalted roads, bamboo baskets strapped to their backs. The gentle Balu Chaung River meandered through town, providing dinner for local boys, teenagers and men fishing with makeshift bamboo rods that had tin cans for reels. Couples sat on colourful benches beside the water, snuggled beneath their umbrellas in intimacy. After sunrise and before sunset, families stood on wooden platforms or in open metal huts on the riverside and washed. Youths freestyled home-taught strokes from bank to bank and the magnificent Taung Kwe Paya, spread across towering limestone rocks and connected by fairy tale stairways, overlooked the centre.

To my surprise, I was not the only tourist in Loikaw: two sightly South Americans, Martina and Manuel from Argentina, had come from Nyaung Shwe. Like me, they planned to visit the long-necked lady village and had been advised to meet Victoria. In fact, they already had.

Victoria was a bubbly, hamster-cheeked ethnic Intha who ran a Kayin clothes shop. She always wore a colourful Kayin *ingyi*, usually purple, with glistening *thanaka* leaves on her cheeks. She was entrepreneurial, owned a 4x4 and had family in Australia. Whenever she didn't understand something in English, which wasn't often, she giggled and cast her eyes away in playful embarrassment.

"People in the villages cannot drive well," said Victoria as she whizzed along the road and we stared at the speedometer. "So many accidents in Myanmar."

My original plan had been to visit Pan Pet village by motorbike, but I had been more than happy to accept a lift from Victoria when rain clouds loomed.

"This is the market in Demoso," she said, slowing down and pulling into a dirt car park. We got out and wandered past the stands, which, bar a few local alcoholic beverages, sold nothing that interested us.

"Much better on Saturday," said Victoria, smiling as always. "More people, also villagers." She picked up a bag of curious snacks. "Maybe you should buy presents for the long-neck ladies."

"What sort of presents?" asked Martina.

"Sweets. Energy drinks. I always bring them sweets," said Victoria.

"Are you sure?"

"Yes, yes. They like the sweets very much."

The idea seemed positively medieval to us, but we bought bottles of Speed energy drink and a selection of sweets nonetheless.

We drove on, passing through a government checkpoint and into Karenni National Progressive Party (KNPP) territory. Then we reached Pan Pet, an ethnic Kayan village and a cousin tribe of the Padaung. Like their counterparts in Shan State, the Kayan women elongate their necks using brass coils and are regularly referred to as "giraffe-necked ladies" – a term, I believe, that encourages tourists to consider them circus acts. In *From the Land of Green Ghosts*, ethnic Padaung Pascal Khoo Thwe records how a white man came to his village in 1936 and asked to take two Padaung ladies to England and exhibit them as freaks in the Bertram Mills circus show. Since the concept of a "freak" did not exist among their tribe, Pascal's grandmother gladly went. She found shoes and the cold of England torturous, but she liked London's moving stairs. She couldn't understand what spirits the English appeased by drinking tea every day at a set time but adored the cakes that went with this ceremony.

> *"The English are a very strange tribe," said Grandma Mu Tha. "They paid money just to look at us – they paid us for not working. They are very rich, but they cannot afford to drink rice wine. Their trees are unable to grow leaves in the rainy season. They say "Hello," "How are you?" and "Goodbye" all the time to one another. They never ask, "Have you eaten your meal?" or "When will you take your bath?" when they see you.*[34]

---

[34] P. K. Thwe (2003), *From the Land of Green Ghosts*, Flamingo, p. 28.

As Pascal noted, had his tribe had the notion of "freaks", his grandma would likely "have put the whole English race into that category."

In the hope of appearing modern to the developed world, the junta discouraged the wearing of neck coils – compelling many Kayan to flee for Thailand, where they could practise their tradition in peace. Recently, the KNPP have invited these refugees to return to Myanmar.

No one is quite sure why the Kayan and Padaung women wear heavy brass coils on their necks. As with the facial tattooing in Chin State, one theory considers the coils beautiful while another deems them a deliberate deformation to deter rival tribesmen from committing kidnap. Some anthropologists have hypothesised that the coils were supposed to make the women look like dragons, which are important in Kayan folklore, or to increase attractiveness by exaggerating sexual dimorphism.

The brass coils were originally believed to affect the vertebrae; however, according to an information sheet titled "The secret of the giraffewomen [sic] finally revealed", this would have brought on "creeping paralysis." The author, who spent six months in Pan Pet village and "clear[ed] the way to perfect understanding" by disregarding all previous research of "doubtful" origin, discovered that the effect of neck elongation was achieved by compressing the rib cage.

Despite the dubious English, the information sheet was essentially correct: the coils do not lengthen the neck itself but deform the clavicle, making the neck appear stretched. Kayan girls begin wearing the brass coils at around the age of five; as the girl gets older, her guardians replace the coil with a longer one and add more turns. Removing the coils is a lengthy procedure and rarely undertaken.

Mu Shant, a 56-year-old mother of ten from Pan Pet, boasted 21 coils when we visited. She wore a simple white *ingyi* with pink trim, four gold bracelets, a pink and green headscarf, and colourful tassels that dangled beneath her chin. The coils made her head look smaller and rounder, as if perched on a post, but I found nothing unnatural about her appearance. Deep-set wrinkles lined her chestnut eyes and the sides of her mouth. She played a homemade guitar and a violin and seemed pleased to see us.

To our relief, a community-based tourism project had been set up in Pan Pet village, meaning sweets and energy drinks would not have to be our only contributions. I bought a couple of Mu Shant's thin scarves; Martina favoured her bracelets. We also tried on sample brass coils, which were absurdly heavy.

Suddenly Victoria appeared from the car with an armful of army camo umbrella hats. Did Mu Shant and her daughter-in-law (who wasn't wearing her coils because she had recently given birth) desire these curious Western products? The Kayan ladies were certainly intrigued and muttered in excited tones as they turned the hats over in their hands and tried them on. But eventually they decided the goods were too pricey, or that they were senseless crap.

We ventured on and encountered scruffy kids tramping along the dirt road. A toddler was bawling, so Manuel strode over and casually picked him up. The mother, swaddled in dirty rags and carrying a basket containing a baby on her back, rightfully found his behaviour odd.

"Time for sweets," said Victoria.

We duly began handing out crunchy syrup rolls to the kids, who accepted the artificiality with glee. I also tried one, hoping to make our donations not look like charity, but it was unpalatably sweet.

"Here," said Victoria, watching Manuel cradle the toddler. "Kayan pepper."

She handed me a tiny green sphere, which I instantly gobbed. Then I experienced a culinary sensation as never before: it was distinctly peppery – and made the lips buzz far more so than a chili – yet wasn't spicy. The effect was bizarre and oddly pleasing, as if all the best qualities of black pepper, chillies and wasabi had been combined into a single foodstuff.

"We can go here," said Victoria, wandering into someone's front garden of compact red mud. The house was made of wood and sported a quaint sheltered balcony; buckets and various tools lay strewn about the floor. The property belonged to a 70-year old couple, though the husband wasn't at home. As soon as we arrived, his wife disappeared inside to get her traditional spindle, then bade us sit down on the wooden benches. Her name was Mu Dan, "Mu" being a prefix shared by every Kayan lady. She wore traditional garments and multiple brass coils. Like most of the elderly Pan Pet villagers, Mu Dan could not speak Myanmar, so a younger lady translated for Victoria and Victoria translated into English.

"I'm always embarrassed when foreigners come," mumbled Mu Dan, "for I can never get the benches clean. You wouldn't believe how difficult it is."

I smiled, imagining my mother would have said a similar thing if she were in Mu Dan's position. Mu Dan was chirpy, grandmotherly, and keen to show Martina how to use the spindle. Meanwhile, Manuel gambolled round the property, reappearing at random intervals clutching an object and asking what it was. Once again, I found his conduct questionable, but no one else seemed bothered, so I put my being offended down to my Britishness.

"I love having visitors," said Mu Dan, nodding in agreement with her own thoughts. "It's such a shame I cannot speak English, for there are so many things I would like to tell you." She paused and looked towards the village entrance. "I've been to Loikaw twice, you know. I want to go again, but don't have the money."

"What's this?" asked Manuel, emerging from behind Mu Dan.

Thirty seconds of uncertain mumbling in three languages followed.

"A bucket."

Manuel looked at the tyre bucket and nodded his approval, before vanishing once more.

"Victoria, could you ask Mu Dan whether her life has changed much over the past decade?"

The question took time to translate, but Mu Dan answered immediately.

"Ten years ago, I was working on the fields to earn money. I was always tired. But now that tourists can visit our village, I can make enough money by selling my bracelets and scarves." She grinned. "Only my husband still has to work on the fields."

I asked if she had experienced any conflict in the area. When she was young, she said, the Kayan and Padaung had fought each other for eighteen months. Otherwise life had been mostly peaceful. On one occasion, the Myanmar Police Force had come to Pan Pet and taken away the men to use them as assistants in fighting Karenni rebels. However, her husband had escaped and returned home.

"Ahah!" said Manuel, materialising from around the wall, pot in hand. "This is like what we use for *maté* tea. What's in this?"

The answer was millet wine. We all took a sip. Then the grey clouds finally gave in: rain pattered onto the earth, dreary and persistent, signalling that the monsoon season was nigh.

"I have something for you," said Victoria, passing Mu Dan a pack of biscuits.

"Ooh, good," she said, smiling. "I never normally get any, because my grandchildren eat them all."

Five minutes later, we said goodbye and returned to the car, exhausted.

"You know," said Victoria, "some of the women here have never been to Loikaw."

She set off. As we drove out of the village, I watched women weaving on their porches and children eating sweets in the street.

"Oh no."

"What is it?" asked Martina.

"We forgot about the energy drinks."

Victoria stopped beside the small *zay* of traditional handicrafts near the village entrance, allowing me to jump out and charge through the rain, desperately handing out bottles of Speed to the long-necked women, who accepted the gifts with pleasure. Then, sodden but empty-handed, I climbed back in. And off we went, back to Loikaw.

"Look, look. You see this?" asked Victoria, smiling.

She reversed slowly and come to a halt after ten metres.

"There, in the field on the right."

It was a scarecrow.

Martina and I exchanged grins. Victoria accelerated.

"What do people in Loikaw think of the KNPP?" I asked Victoria. "Is there much fighting here?"

"Not much fighting," she said, eyes ahead. "But people found a landmine outside a village near here."

"And do people like the KNPP?"

She shrugged. "Some people do, but there was a big demonstration last week. Look," she said, handing me her phone.

She played a video of thousands of people demonstrating in the streets of Loikaw.

"They were demanding that the KNPP to sign the NCA."

"Did they?"

No, but the KNPP had promised to continue working towards peace with the government. Considering the *Tatmadaw* had unlawfully killed three of their captive soldiers just six months earlier, this was a promising development.

Victoria pulled out and began accelerating past two trundling lorries. A big truck in front of us was doing the same, blocking our sight. Before we had overtaken the second lorry, the truck ahead began pulling over.

"No! No! Victoria, stop!"

She didn't, forcing a motorbiker heading straight for her to swerve off the *lan* at the last second. Victoria smiled. The rest of us let out a huge sigh of relief.

"And what do you think of Aung San Suu Kyi?" asked Martina.

"She cannot do much," said Victoria. "The military is powerful in Myanmar."

"But the government can make some decisions," I said. "What do you think of the Aung San statue?"

"Oh, that is so stupid," spat Victoria. "It is such a waste of money."

On 1st February 2018, Napyidaw announced plans to build a K150 million (£78,687) equestrian statue of independence hero General Aung San in Loikaw. Previous military governments had downplayed the importance of Aung San, presumably because he was father to Aung San Suu Kyi, but the cult of the *Bogyoke* had experienced a revival under the NLD-led government. While Aung San statues are ubiquitous across almost all of Myanmar, attempts to erect those of ethnic minority heroes were blocked on several occasions by the junta. The planned *Bogyoke* Aung San *yo-to* for Loikaw was to be the biggest in Myanmar and the first in Kayah State. Critics argued that it compromised his promise of "equality without discrimination."

"Forcefully erecting the statue, without respect and recognition for what *Bogyoke* said, can only be viewed as trying to show this is a Bamar area," Ko Ba Nya, director of the Karenni Human Rights Group, told *Frontier*.[35]

*

On my final evening in Loikaw, I enjoyed a spectacular sunset all to myself – one so *hla-de* I'll never forget it. Having scaled a hilltop pagoda, I watched the crimson sun sink between a gap in the clouds directly above a mountain pass, listening to the birds tweeting and the monastery sounding its wooden gong. The sky set a hazy rose, insubstantial and ethereal, before finally turning indigo. Then the *paya-gyi*, sprawled across its craggy crown, lit up: a beacon of shimmering *shwe* in the dusky cityscape.

And the next afternoon I was off, bound for Yangon. I remained glued to the window for as long as there was daylight, watching children splashing in rivers, motorbikers transporting bamboo cages of live chickens, guys playing *chinlone*, and toddlers pressing their faces up against the railings of white pick-ups – everyday scenes, but the everyday especially acquires a nostalgic edge when you won't see it again for a long time.

So had I "found" Myanmar? Had I achieved my travelling aim?

When I first set out, I had hoped to "find" Myanmar by travelling to its four corners, imagining that would

---

[35] https://frontiermyanmar.net/en/nlds-gilded-bogyoke-building-spree-prompts-ethnic-backlash <Accessed: 11.01.2019>

provide me with a comprehensive understanding of the country as a whole. But it had later become clear that it was the actual process of "looking for" Myanmar which had really mattered. Rather than asking whether I had "found" some authentic, true appreciation of the place, I realised that the really enduring legacy of my travels would be the daunting, profound, and often baffling experiences I had collected, the memories with which I'd be left – travelling to conflict areas, speaking to locals about drug trafficking, being questioned by immigration officers, and so much more.

While "searching" for Myanmar, I had come to learn that a country so diverse and undergoing such monumental change cannot be defined by the simple terms that Western media often gives it – that, for example, labelling the Rohingya genocide a solely "religious conflict" is damagingly inaccurate. And although I had been partly disappointed to discover how complex and fragmented Myanmar was – for it made me realise that I would be returning home, having barely scratched the country's surface – its very multiplicity made me appreciate that I could not try to understand Myanmar simply by applying Western ideas and terminology, such as "right-" and "left-wing." For we cannot compare countries with such distinct ethnic groups, and fractured by civil war, ongoing cronyism and state-funded drug trafficking, with those that share hardly any comparable traits, no matter how prone we are to do so.

Above all, my trip had taught me that Myanmar was a vibrant, quirky land of tradition, beauty and hope. Although it appeared to be developing quickly, its religious and ethnic tensions, as well as its toxic military influence, appeared firmly rooted. Once crippled by foreign powers and repressive regimes, Myanmar was now in recovery – a shattered mosaic trying to restore itself, only its pieces numbered a million and did not all fit together easily. It had the potential for a colourful future, but its burdensome past was shortening its forward steps.

I had also found that the Myanmar harboured the desire and the will for change and that most of their lives had improved over the past decade. Their selflessness and hospitality had stunned me, and nowhere in the world have I seen so many magical smiles.

Yet it was the smiles that had also disturbed me. How could such benevolent people support genocide? How could they be so selfless to me but so heartless towards the Rohingya? It was a dichotomy that had dogged my entire trip. Although I would like to say that the sheer number of honest and philanthropic characters I had met in Myanmar assured me this animosity would soon dissolve, I can't – it would be untruthful and naive. History has proven that mindsets moulded over generations – and which are still being shaped by populist rhetoric – do not simply reform when brought under criticism; nor is this dynamic unique to Myanmar. And yet I am optimistic that the more democratic structure of modern Myanmar will allow different ideas and viewpoints to permeate into the country's psyche, and that this in turn may catalyse a change of perception.

And what about me? Had I changed during my trip, as travellers so often claim to have done?

Well, I may not have found myself in the traditional sense (of taking acid in Goa and getting a tattoo of a religious symbol on my upper arm), but I certainly wasn't altogether the same person. I had learned that, for me, travel was all of the best and all of the worst – sickness, loneliness, pain, euphoria, charm – and that people would always interest me more than places. My various travelling experiences had taught me how to deal with unpredictability, that I had the willpower to follow an ambition all the way through, and that sometimes the most meaningful and enriching relationships can be those you form with people fundamentally different to yourself. Perhaps most importantly of all, I had also learned that imperfection was enchanting and that not every love story was romantic.

Eighteen hours later, I was back in Yangon – among the countless taxis, the cramped buses, the lepers, the rats, the smiles, my friends, Shwe Ei. I had missed her, and she had missed me. Although our meeting was still warm and loving, we had been apart so long that we now had our own, separate ambitions, desires and responsibilities. However, I believe they will entwine again as I shall certainly return to Myanmar one day – for you cannot form such an emotional attachment to a country, without it becoming a meaningful part of your future.

By now I had been broken by travel: cuts, burns and scars littered my legs; staples, cable ties and superglue held my clothes together; I had a throat infection and Shigella bacteria had found their way inside me, meaning I would spend the next two weeks propitiating the toilet. I had begun and ended my travels with dysentery, thereby finding the closure we all long for.

    Dosed up on Imodium, I took a cab to the airport and checked in. Then I made my way to immigration – passing *longyi'd* parents squatting round traditional lunch boxes, admiring the escalator with that first-time air I had so often seen in Yangon shopping malls, and watching their children leave Myanmar to begin journeys of their own.

Epilogue

The world, particularly the West, imagined Myanmar would swiftly resolve its issues when Aung San Suu Kyi came into power. The transition to democracy was portrayed as the fairy tale ending of *The Lady and the Generals*, which is why the world was disillusioned to discover that Myanmar was still facing tough times.

Countries do not instantly recover from colonialism and fascist governments. It should come as no surprise that Myanmar is neither yet peaceful nor entirely democratic, and I personally see much of the West's condemnation of Suu Kyi as a scapegoat reaction against its own reductive, unfulfilled narrative.

Although I can understand the West's viewpoint – and agree that Aung San Suu Kyi deserves heavy criticism for her poor handling of the Rohingya genocide and for propounding the decline in free press – I consider calls for her resignation short-sighted. After all, who would replace her? Anti-Rohingya sentiment irrigates almost the entirety of Myanmar politics; and while Aung San Suu Kyi remains de facto leader of the country, Myanmar will continue to make international headlines. Would the Rohingya crisis really receive so much global attention if another Myanmar politician were in power?

Federalism has historically been depicted as the answer to Myanmar's fractured political landscape, but this comes with its own problems. Each state has its own agenda, prejudices and income sources: if Rakhine State were autonomous, the situation for the Rohingya would almost certainly be even more severe; similarly, the drug trafficking in Shan State could easily increase. Mongla is a good example of autonomy being abused.

There is no single answer to Myanmar politics, and all possible solutions are much easier said than done. Ultimately, the country must embrace its diverse ethnic make-up, but this will only happen, I believe, if the *Tatmadaw* can be ousted from the *Hluttaw*. While the *Tatmadaw* are the dominant force in Myanmar politics, peace will remain a distant prospect. The government cannot wait for the ethnic insurgent groups to cooperate but must itself alter the playing field. Myanmar needs a new Ko Ni, an inspired, capable lawyer committed to attaining true democracy. Once the country's legislation has been reformed to make the *Tatmadaw* politically powerless, progress will be catalysed. I hope to see this happen in my lifetime and believe it will.

James Fable
09.09.2018, London

Glossary of Myanmar terms

Most Myanmar words used in this book are either explained or translated when first mentioned or can be understood in context. Nonetheless, for ease of reference – and for those wishing to use the vocabulary themselves – here is a glossary of key, useful or regularly employed terms:

- *A-myo-thami* = Myanmar for 'lady'
- *A-myo-thar* = 'man'
- *Ah-nar-de* = a Myanmar code of conduct governing consideration of others
- *Bamar-hsan-chin* = 'Burmeseness', the value of being quintessentially "Myanmar"
- *Belauk-le?* = 'how much?'
- *Chinlone* = a traditional sport played using a ball made from woven rattan
- *Chit-de* = to love/'I love you'
- *Chit-thu* = 'lover'
- *Hkauk-hswe* = 'noodles'
- *Hla-de* = to be beautiful
- *Hluttaw* = name of the Myanmar parliament
- *Hpone-gyi* = 'monk'
- *Ingaleik saya* = 'English teacher'
- *Ingyi* = a traditional short-sleeved blouse worn by Myanmar women
- *Kadaw* = the act of kneeling down and touching the palms and forehead to the ground three times. It is performed before monks and Buddha images to denote respect

- *Kalar* = a derogatory term mostly used for 'Muslim'
- *Kale* = 'child'
- *Kyat* = the local currency
- *Kyay-zu-din-par-de* = 'thank you'
- *Lan* = 'road' or 'path'
- *Lay-deh* = to be heavy
- *Lepet thoke* = 'tealeaf salad'
- *Longyi* = a traditional looped sarong worn by Myanmar men and women
- *Mingalabar* = 'hello' or 'welcome'
- *Mu-de* = to be drunk
- *Myan-myan* = 'quickly'
- *Myin-kwar-ywet-thoke* = 'pennywort salad'
- *Nat* = a spirit-being generally ambivalent towards humans; *nat* worship predates Buddhism in Myanmar and remains popular today
- *Paya* = 'pagoda'
- *Paya-gyi* = a village, town or city's main pagoda
- *Pa-ye-thi* = 'watermelon'
- *Pwe* = a religious festival
- *Po-myan-myan* = 'more quickly'
- *Pyay-pyay* = 'carefully' or 'slowly'
- *Saya* = 'teacher'
- *Sar-pi-pi-la?* = the traditional Myanmar greeting, which literally means 'have you already eaten?' The affirmative response is *sar-pi-pi* ('I have already eaten')
- *Shi-me* = 'I'd like to pay', literally 'I will clean up'
- *Shwe* = 'gold'

- *Thet-that-lut* (pronounced "tar-tar-lut") = 'vegetarian', though the Myanmar conceptualisation of vegetarianism excludes egg and includes fish
- *Tatmadaw* = the name of the Myanmar military
- *Taung-paya* = 'hilltop pagoda'
- *Thanaka* = the traditional Myanmar sunscreen made from ground bark mixed with water
- *Thi-chin* = 'song'
- *Thingyan* = the Myanmar new year, which falls in mid-April and is celebrated with a water festival lasting four-five days
- *Yadanar* = 'gem'
- *Ye-nway-kyan* = the gratis green tea offered at teahouses
- *Yoma* = 'hill range'
- *Zay* = 'market'
- *Zay-gyi-deh* = 'expensive', literally 'big market'

List of abbreviations

Abbreviations are explained in full when first encountered or when no recent reference has been made to the organisation in discussion. Nevertheless, for ease of reference, here is a list of important abbreviations used in this book:

AA = Arakan Army
ARSA = Arakan Rohingya Salvation Army
BSPP = Burmese Socialist Programme Party
KIA = Kachin Independence Army
KIO = Kachin Independence Organisation
KMT = Kuomintang
KNPP = Karenni National Progressive Party
MSF = *Médecins Sans Frontières*
NCA = Nationwide Ceasefire Agreement
NGO = Non-Governmental Organisation
NSCN-K = National Socialist Council of Nagaland-Khaplang
NLD = National League for Democracy
OBOR = One Belt, One Road
PNLA = Pa'O National Liberation Army
SEZ = Special Economic Zone
SPDC = State Peace and Development Council

Acknowledgements

There are numerous people who have helped to make *In Search of Myanmar* a reality. First, I would like to thank Chuu Wai Nyein for her exquisite maps and illustrations. Without her patience, persistence and skill, this book simply would not have been the same.

For their expertise on cultural and linguistic aspects of the text, I am indebted to Shwe Ei, Ko Ko and Thida.

On the literary side, I am enormously grateful for the inputs of Alex, Diane, Dominic, Emily, Jessica, Rory, Peter, Kirsty and my parents.

I also extend a special thank-you to Benedict, Thea, Sam and, most of all, Lorcan for their help with my journalistic articles.

Heartfelt thanks also go to Alex, Dominic, Charlie, Cherrie and Benedict, who have all shaped my writing over time.

I would also like to thank Alice for encouraging me to move to Myanmar in the first place, Shwe Ei for all her support, Jennifer for her advice on self-publishing, Charlotte for enriching my year of teaching in Yangon, and Mario for his travel tips.

Last, but certainly not least, I would like to extend my sincerest thanks to the people of Myanmar, especially those who put themselves at risk for my sake. After all, it was only because of their benevolence and selflessness that I had such an incredible time there.

Select Bibliography

Books:

Aung San Suu Kyi (1997), *Letters from Burma*, Penguin.

R. Cockett (2015), *Blood, Dreams and Gold: The Changing Face of Burma* (Kindle Edition), Yale University Press.

D. Eimer (2019), *A Savage Dreamland: Journeys in Burma* (Kindle Edition), Bloomsbury.

N. Kynaston (ed., 1998), *The Guinness 1999 Book of Records*. Guinness Publishing.

Ma Thanegi (2011), *Defiled on the Ayeyarwaddy: One Woman's Mid-Life Travel Adventures on Myanmar's Great River*, ThingsAsian Press.

R. Maclean (2013), *Under the Dragon: A Journey through Burma* (Kindle Edition), Wander2wander Press.

F. McLynn (2011), *The Burma Campaign: Disaster into Triumph, 1942–45*, Yale University Press.

N. Lewis (2011), *Golden Earth: Travels in Burma* (Kindle Edition), Eland Publishing.

B. Linter (1999), *Burma in Revolt: Opium and Insurgency since 1948*, Silkworm Books.

B. Rogers (2012), *Burma: A Nation at the Crossroads*, Ebury Publishing.

E. W. C. Sandes (1951), *From Pyramid to Pagoda: The Story of the West Yorkshire Regiment (The Prince of Wales's Own) in the War, 1939-1945 and Afterwards,* Parsons.

I. Sargent (1994), *Twilight over Burma: My Life as a Shan Princess* (Kindle Edition), University of Hawaii Press.

Saw Myat Yin (1994), *Culture Shock! Burma*, Graphic Arts Centre Publishing.

B. Schiller (2011), *Gute Geister im Land der goldenen Pagoden* (Kindle Edition), Picus Verlag.

M. Symes (1800), *An Account of an Embassy to the Kingdom of Ava: Sent by the Governor-General of India in the Year 1795,* W. Bulmer and Co.

P. Theroux (2012), *Ghost Train to the Eastern Star: On the Tracks of* The Great Railway Bazaar (Kindle Edition), Penguin.

P. K. Thwe (2003), *From the Land of Green Ghosts*, Flamingo.

F. Wade (2017), *Myanmar's Enemy Within: Buddhist Violence and the Creating of a Muslim Other* (Kindle Edition), Zed Books.

Articles:

D. Bernstein and L. Kean (1996), 'People of the Opiate: Myanmar's dictatorship of drugs', *The Nation*, 263 (20): 11-15.

General Tuan Shi-wen (1967), *Weekend Telegraph*.

B. Lintner (1994), 'Foreword' to *Twilight over Burma: My Life as a Shan Princess* (Kindle Edition), University of Hawaii Press.

United Nations Office on Drugs and Crime (2013), *Southeast Asia Opium Survey, Lao PDR, Myanmar*.

D. Preecharushh (2010), 'Naypidaw: The New Capital of Burma', *Engineering Earth*.

Online resources and articles accessed online:

https://www.theguardian.com/world/2016/dec/30/myanmar-Myanmar-royal-family-monarchy-king-thibaw-comeback <Accessed: 22.01.2018>

http://www.myanmartourex.com/travel_myanmar_destinations/travel_info_mong_la.shtml <accessed: 13.05.2018>

http://www.globalnewlightofmyanmar.com/good-friends-really-needed/ <Accessed: 09.08.2018>

http://investvine.com/myanmar-revamps-education-system-ditches-rote-learning/ <Accessed: 09.08.2018>

https://frontiermyanmar.net/en/as-preaching-ban-on-u-wirathu-ends-split-in-the-sangha-widens <Accessed: 13.09.2018>

https://www.mmtimes.com/lifestyle/11469-going-fair-at-any-price.html <Accessed: 14.09.2018>

http://svaradarajan.blogspot.com/2007/02/dictatorship-by-cartography-geometry.html <Accessed: 03.01.2019>

https://www.bbc.co.uk/news/resources/idt-sh/who_stole_burmas_royal_ruby <Accessed: 07.01.2019>

https://frontiermyanmar.net/en/nlds-gilded-bogyoke-building-spree-prompts-ethnic-backlash <Accessed: 11.01.2019>

https://www.reuters.com/article/china-silkroad-myanmar-port/china-to-take-70-percent-stake-in-strategic-port-in-myanmar-official-idUSL4N1MS3UB <Accessed: 25.02.2019.

http://www.mizzima.com/news-opinion/geopolitics-rakhine <Accessed 25.02.2019>

https://frontiermyanmar.net/en/kyaukphyus-kaman-community-confined-against-their-will <Accessed: 4.03.2019>

https://frontiermyanmar.net/en/myanmar-pardons-8500-prisoners-in-thingyan-amnesty <Accessed: 17.03.2019>

https://www.irrawaddy.com/news/murky-waters-burmas-law-on-pornography.html <Accessed: 20.03.2019>

https://frontiermyanmar.net/en/myanmar-to-buy-russian-fighter-jets-in-deal-worth-more-than-200m <Accessed: 25.03.2019>

https://frontiermyanmar.net/en/war-and-misery-a-fact-of-life-for-civilians-in-myanmars-northeast <Accessed: 02.04.2019>

https://www.aljazeera.com/indepth/features/2016/12/drugs-bullets-myanmar-161220064632150.html <Accessed: 11.04.2019>

https://www.thehindu.com/news/international/Beijing-calls-for-restoration-of-Stillwell-Road-connecting-India-China-Myanmar/article14425879.ece <Accessed: 20.04.2019>

https://www2.irrawaddy.com/article.php?art_id=971 <Accessed: 21.04.2019>

https://www.irrawaddy.com/news/burma/kokang-warlady-olive-yang-dies-91.html <Accessed: 21.04.2019>

https://www.nytimes.com/2017/07/21/world/asia/burmese-warlord-olive-yang.html <Accessed: 22.04.2019>

https://www.irrawaddy.com/news/burma/three-bombs-rock-myanmars-northwestern-city-sittwe-policeman-injured.html <Accessed: 24.04.2019>

https://www.irrawaddy.com/news/myanmar-says-verified-fewer-400-rohingya-repatriation.html <Accessed: 24.04.2019>

https://frontiermyanmar.net/en/myanmar-ready-to-begin-repatriation-process-despite-disagreements <Accessed: 25.04.2019>

https://www.bbc.com/news/world-asia-41224643 <Accessed: 01.05.2019>

https://www.irrawaddy.com/opinion/guest-column/peace-nagaland-myanmar-india-role-play.html <Accessed: 01.05.2019>

https://kite-tales.org/en/article/widow-and-dragon-king <Accessed: 07.05.2019>

https://www.mmtimes.com/lifestyle/travel/15777-sin-city.html <Accessed: 07.05.2019>

https://www.mmtimes.com/opinion/19435-visiting-mong-la-this-is-why-you-shouldn-t.html <Accessed: 07.05.2019>

https://frontiermyanmar.net/en/chinese-casino-scam-victims-held-captive-tortured-in-myanmar-says-beijing-daily <Accessed: 09.05.2019>

https://frontiermyanmar.net/en/innocent-victims-indiscriminate-carnage-the-legacy-of-myanmars-landmine-menace <Accessed: 25.06.2019>

https://www.theguardian.com/environment/earth-insight/2013/apr/26/fossil-fuel-secret-burma-democratic-fairytale <Accessed: 25.06.2019>

Printed in Poland
by Amazon Fulfillment
Poland Sp. z o.o., Wrocław